FIGHT

THE

IRS

AND

WIN

A Self-Defense Guide for Taxpayers

No. 30021
$24.95

FIGHT
THE
IRS
AND
WIN

A Self-Defense Guide for Taxpayers

Cliff Roberson
author of THE PERSONAL TAX ADVISOR

LIBERTY HOUSE®

LIBERTY HOUSE books are published by LIBERTY HOUSE, a division of TAB BOOKS Inc. Its trademark, consisting of the words ''LIBERTY HOUSE'' and the portrayal of Benjamin Franklin, is registered in the United States Patent and Copyright Office.

FIRST EDITION
SECOND PRINTING

Library of Congress Cataloging in Publication Data

Roberson, Cliff, 1937-
Fight the IRS and win! : a self-defense guide for taxpayers / by
Cliff Roberson.
p.   cm.
Includes index.
ISBN 0-8306-0521-5 ISBN 0-8306-3021-X (pbk.)
1. Tax protests and appeals—United States—Popular works. 2. Tax
auditing—United States—Popular works. 3. United States. Internal
Revenue Service. I. Title.
KF6324.Z9R63 1988
343.7304'0269—dc19
[347.30340269]
88-632
CIP

TAB BOOKS Inc. offers software for
sale. For information and a catalog,
please contact TAB Software Department,
Blue Ridge Summit, PA 17294-0850.

Questions regarding the content of this book
should be addressed to:

Reader Inquiry Branch
TAB BOOKS Inc.
Blue Ridge Summit, PA 17294-0214

Table of Contents

INTRODUCTION

An old saying has it that the art of taxation consists in so plucking the goose as to get the most feathers with the least hissing.

(from USLIFE v. Harbison, 784 F2. 1238)

Will Rogers once remarked that only two things were certain, "death and taxes." If Rogers were alive today, he probably would add to his short list of things certain, "trouble with the IRS." The purpose of this book is to provide advice and guidance to taxpayers involved in tax controversies and collection problems with the Internal Revenue Service.

Justice Oliver Wendell Holmes once said: "I like to pay taxes. With them I buy civilization." Probably few taxpayers today actually enjoy paying taxes. Most of us more likely agreed with Judge Learned Hand when he stated: "[N]obody owes any public duty to pay more than the law demands: taxes are enforced exactions, not voluntary contributions." This book is not designed as a manual for tax evasion, nor for use as a tax protest guide, but to assist the honest taxpayer in ensuring that his/her rights and property are protected to the full extent allowed by the law when dealing with the IRS.

Care has been taken to discuss the issues in common everyday English without resorting to legalese or technical terms. This manual is not designed for attorneys or certified public accountants, but for persons who are interested in exercising and defending their individual rights when dealing with the IRS. Each chapter is discussed as a separate subject to permit the readers to quickly locate information needed when dealing with the IRS.

Chapter 1 contains a discussion of how the IRS works. This chapter provides the foundation to assist you in understanding in later chapters the various functions of different IRS divisions and sections. Chapter 2 provides guidance to those taxpayers who owe taxes. Chapter 3 discusses how the IRS selects returns for audits. Chapter 4 is concerned with reducing your chances of an audit. Audit defenses and negotiating tactics are covered in Chapter 5.

Getting professional help is discussed in Chapter 6. Chapter 7 contains a discussion on appealing IRS decisions, and Chapter 8 discusses when and how to take the IRS to court. In Chapter 9, how the IRS gets information about you and how to stop them is discussed. Chapter 10 contains a discussion on tax fraud and other criminal problems. Researching tax issues is covered in Chapter 11, and Chapter 12 contains the procedures for appealing and winning your case in Tax Court. In Chapter 13, the key provisions of the Internal Revenue Code regarding tax administration and collection are discussed. Record-keeping requirements are contained in Chapter 14.

Appendix A is a list of toll-free numbers for Offices. Appendix B is a copy of IRS Form 433-A (Collection Information Statement for Individuals). Appendix C is the form used for refund claims (Form 843). The IRS Audit Manual is included as Appendix D. Appendix E is a copy of the standard IRS Form 2848 (Power of Attorney), and Appendix F contains a list of the cities where the Tax Court regularly holds trial sessions. Appendix G provides copies of the Tax Court forms. Appendix H is a copy of IRS Publication 908, which discusses the effects of bankruptcy on tax liability.

PostScript: During the time that this manuscript was being developed, a typical case on taxpayer frustration with the IRS was decided by the Tax Court. This case, *Mahon v. Commissioner*, involved Mr. Mahon, a retired Air Force Colonel and his wife, Mary Sunny. In 1977, Mary dropped her husband's name claiming that it was a form of slavery and used her own last name of Sunny. For several years, she and her husband attempted to get the IRS to accept her last name as Sunny. This being unsuccessful, she and her husband filed separate returns, each in their own name. They divided his retired pension and income equally and filed separate returns. Each claimed one-half of the pension and income with a statement attached to each return noting that fact. The IRS issued a tax deficiency to Mr. Mahon stating that he had understated his income by 50 percent. The IRS also billed him for a negligence penalty. The Tax Court rejected the tax penalty based on the taxpayer's "frustration and confusion" in dealing with the IRS.

CHAPTER 1

How the IRS Works

Above all remember that when you are dealing with the IRS you are dealing with a large bureaucratic organization that behaves like a bureaucratic organization.

The Internal Revenue Service is the world's largest collection agency, and in order to successfully deal with them, it is necessary to understand how they work. Some key concepts are listed below.

☐ The IRS strategy of tax collection is to scare most taxpayers into voluntarily paying their taxes.

☐ The mission of the IRS is to assess and collect federal taxes and thereby increase voluntary taxpayer compliance with the taxes requirements.

☐ The basic and primary operating offices of the IRS are the District Offices.

☐ The primary contact point between taxpayers and the IRS is the Regional Service Center.

☐ Revenue agents assigned to the Examination Division are responsible for taxpayer compliance and examination of tax returns.

☐ Revenue officers assigned to the Collections Division have the responsibility of monitoring delinquent tax returns, enforcing collection of taxes, penalties, and interests due the government, and referring cases to the Criminal Investigations Division.

☐ Special agents assigned to the Criminal Investigations Division are the police force of the IRS.

☐ The primary responsibility of the Examination Division is to encourage voluntary taxpayer compliance with the tax requirements by examining and auditing selected tax returns.

☐ The primary responsibility of the Collections Division is to collect taxes, penalties, and interest. Normally the Collections Division does not assess taxes.

☐ Revenue officers have a great deal of power and discretion in dealing with taxpayers.

☐ A constant problem for the IRS is the inconsistencies throughout the tax assessment and collection process.

In this chapter, a brief discussion of how the IRS works is presented. This chapter should provide the taxpayer with an understanding of the functioning of IRS and provide insight on how better to handle contested tax issues. The Internal Revenue Service is a component part of the U. S. Treasury Department. The Commissioner of Internal Revenue is the senior official within the IRS. The IRS operates at two levels, the national office and field organizations.

NATIONAL OFFICE

The national office is located in Washington, D.C. Included with the national office is the National Computer Center in Martinsburg, West Virginia, and the National Data Center in Detroit, Michigan. Both of these centers are under the direct operational control of the Assistant Commissioner (Data Services). Because the centers are involved in the audit selection process, their functions are discussed in Chapter 3. The Office of General Counsel is also part of the national office.

The Chief Counsel acts as the legal advisor to the IRS Commissioner. If the Commissioner and Chief Counsel disagree on any legal question, the matter is referred to the Under Secretary of the Treasury for resolution. Within the Office of Chief Counsel, there is a Deputy Chief Counsel (Litigation) and Deputy Chief Counsel (Technical). The latter deputy is responsible for issuing IRS regulations.

FIELD ORGANIZATIONS

The field organization has 7 regions, 63 districts, and 10 service centers. Each region has a Regional Director who reports directly to the Deputy Commissioner of IRS. The Regional Directors are responsible for tax collection, taxpayer service and returns processing, examination, criminal investigations, and appeals within their regions.

The four functional divisions of the field organizations that are of most concern to the taxpayer are the *examination, collection, appeals,* and *criminal investigations* divisions. Each of these are discussed below.

Within each region is a *Regional Counsel* who reports directly to the Chief Counsel. In addition, there are *Deputy Regional Counsel* for Criminal Tax, Tax Litigation, and General Litigation in each region. All Tax Court litigation is handled by the branch offices and supervised by a *District Counsel.*

The 10 service centers are headed by a director, who is under the regional director. The service center director is also responsible to the national office for implementing programs assigned to that center.

There is a district director for each of the 63 districts. Within each district there is a collection division that is responsible for the receipt and transmittal of returns and other documents received in the office. These collection divisions are also responsible for the collection of delinquent accounts and seizing of property for failure to pay federal taxes.

EXAMINATION DIVISION

It is the *Examination Division* of the IRS that selects taxpayers' returns for further examination (audit) and conducts the examinations. The Internal Revenue Code gives the IRS broad powers to examine taxpayers' books, records, and documents. As discussed in Chapters 3 and 4, however, only a relatively small percentage of taxpayer returns are examined in depth. In most cases, the selections and examinations are conducted by the examination division of service centers.

COLLECTIONS DIVISION

The *Collections Division* is responsible for the collection of taxes, penalties, and interests resulting from the assessment of liability. In most cases, the division is not concerned with the actual assessment, which is usually accomplished by the Examination Division.

The Collections Division also is responsible for investigating those taxpayers who did not file tax returns. The division is charged with the responsibility of referring possible criminal tax violations to the Criminal Investigations Division for investigation.

The collections functions are accomplished at the district level. In each of the district offices, there is a Collections Division. The Collections Division acts similar to a normal commercial collection agency in that it screens and processes assessments.

Under the direct supervision of the district Collections Divisions are the field collection branches. The revenue officers assigned to the collection branches are those who deal directly with the taxpayers. They have the responsibility for the investigation and enforced collection of past due accounts. The role and discretionary powers of the revenue officers regarding tax liabilities are discussed in Chapter 2.

Warning: the collections branch is responsible for the referral of more cases to the Criminal Investigations Division than any other division of the IRS. Accordingly, be on guard when discussing anything with a revenue officer from the Collections Division.

Within the Collections Division is a Special Procedures Section to handle other than routine collection problems. This section also handles the processing of offers to compromise. In addition, federal tax liens are processed by this section.

When you have been contacted by an officer of the Collections Division, the worst possible thing to do is to ignore him or her. It is very important to maintain the correspondence link to prevent or delay the Collections Division's collection procedures. Remember, their job is to collect money. As long as it appears that progress is being made, the Collections Division will normally try to work with the taxpayer.

APPEALS DIVISION

Within the national office is an Appeals Division whose purpose is to resolve tax controversies in those cases where the taxpayer appeals decisions of the district director, service center director, or certain cases pending in Tax Court. In the field organization, there is also a Regional Director of Appeals for each of the seven IRS regions. Settlements made at the regional level are made with Chiefs of the Appeals Office, who are under the direct supervision of the Regional Director of Appeals.

CRIMINAL INVESTIGATIVE DIVISION

The *Criminal Investigative Division* is the police force of the IRS. The special agents who work in this division are armed like regular police and can arrest taxpayers for criminal violations of the Revenue Code. In addition, *special agents* can obtain search warrants and conduct searches pursuant to the warrant.

Special agents normally conduct the tax audits in those cases where criminal fraud is suspected. Sometimes special agents will work with revenue agents in those cases where the revenue agents feel the need to use search warrants to discover taxpayers' assets.

Always ask to see identification when contacted by any IRS employee. If you are contacted by a special agent, do not provide any information. Consult with an attorney. This is not the time to cooperate with the IRS, because special agents are only involved in cases where fraud or other criminal violations are suspected. As will be discussed in Chapter 6, do not consult with your accountant until after you have talked to your attorney. There is no accountant/client privilege to ensure the confidentiality of your discussions.

CHAPTER 2

If You Owe Taxes

In the summer of 1987, an employee of the Internal Revenue Service slapped a tax lien on the President of the United States and his wife.

The above-noted lien entered against the President was a mistake and should not have been placed against him. It's scary to think that even the President is not immune from the mistakes of the IRS. The IRS quickly filed a correction to the lien filed with the Travis County Courthouse in Austin, Texas. In this case, the wrong buttons were pushed on the electronic lien system, and the lien was recorded automatically. Had this been a taxpayer other than the President of the United States, it probably would have taken months to correct the mistake.

KEY CONCEPTS TO REMEMBER

☐ The Collections Division is the least known-about division of the IRS and the one that can do the most damage.

☐ There are few checks and balances to the power of the Collections Division.

☐ Postal zip codes are used to assign collection cases to collection groups within the Collections Division.

☐ If you owe taxes and cannot pay, time payments can be a successful tactic to use with the revenue officers.

☐ Prior to the assessment of an additional tax liability, the IRS will issue a Notice of Tax Deficiency (90-day letter).

☐ The IRS has six years after the assessment to collect the taxes or institute judicial proceedings.

5

☐ The *tax lien* is the primary weapon to enforce tax collection.
☐ Revenue officers have considerable power, which can disrupt a taxpayer's business and life.
☐ A Petition to Tax Court will stay the collection of a tax assessment.
☐ The frontline collection activity of the IRS is accomplished at the Field Collection Branch by revenue officers.

THE COLLECTION PROCESS

As noted in Chapter 1, in most cases the Collection Division has no authority to make assessments of tax liabilities. (Note: unless otherwise noted, the term *tax liabilities* includes not only tax liabilities but also liabilities for penalties and interests.) In most cases, the Collections Division cannot take any action against a taxpayer until there is an assessment of liability by the Examination Division, and the case is formally forwarded to the Collection Division.

In cases where the taxpayer reports a tax due on his/her return but fails to pay the tax, or where additional tax is due because of mathematical and clerical errors, the IRS can immediately assess a liability and refer the case to the Collections Division. In other cases, there are certain procedures that the IRS must follow before an additional assessment of tax liability can be made.

In most cases, before the IRS can assess additional tax liability, the taxpayer must be issued a statutory 90-day notice and provided with an opportunity to petition to the Tax Court. If the taxpayer petitions to the Tax Court within 90 days of the statutory notice, the assessment must be stayed until the Tax Court makes a decision regarding the correctness of the proposed assessment. Exceptions to this procedure are those cases where the IRS can establish that there is a likelihood that the taxpayer will dispose of or waste his/her assets within the 90-day period (*jeopardy cases*).

The IRS has six years after the assessment of a tax liability to collect the assessment or to initiate judicial proceedings. This six-year limitation period may be waived by the taxpayer. Within 60 days after the assessment of additional tax liability, the service center will serve the taxpayer with a written notice of the amount due and demand payment. Failure to pay within 10 days may result in additional penalties against the taxpayer.

The standard IRS practice is to send the taxpayer several final notice(s) which warn the taxpayer that enforced collection action will be taken if the deficiency is not paid within ten days. If there is no response by the taxpayer, or the taxpayer does not pay the deficiency, then the case is forwarded by the service center to the Collections Division. The center uses a Taxpayer Deliquent Account (TDA) form to forward the case to the Collections Division.

DEALING WITH A REVENUE OFFICER

As noted in Chapter 1, the frontline collection activity of the IRS is accomplished at the field collection branch by revenue officers. Factors that should be considered when dealing with a revenue officer are:

☐ The revenue officer's job is to collect the liability either by persuasion or forced collection.

☐ Most revenue officers have large case loads and are under pressure to collect their assigned accounts. Accordingly, the officer can spend only limited time on each case.

☐ Many revenue officers, because of the above noted pressures, tend to operate by ultimatum.

☐ The revenue officers have considerable power to disrupt the business or life of a taxpayer, ruin his/her credit rating, and attach or place a lien on taxpayer's property.

☐ The revenue officers have considerable discretion.

☐ In some cases, it will be impossible to defeat the collection process because of the tools available to the revenue officer.

TAX LIENS

A *tax lien* is a claim placed on the taxpayer's property to satisfy a tax liability. It is the basic weapon used by the IRS to enforce collections of tax debts. Under the Internal Revenue Code, Section 6321, a statutory tax lien is created automatically with the assessment of a tax deficiency. The lien may be formally filed with a Notice of Federal Tax Lien (Form 668). This filing of notice acts as a public notice that a federal tax lien had been filed against a taxpayer. Until the lien is filed, it has no effect on persons dealing in good faith with the taxpayer. It is to the taxpayer's advantage to prevent the filing of the notice of the lien. As noted below, there is considerable discretion by IRS personnel regarding the decision to file the lien.

Before a tax lien is recorded three requirements must be met:

1. An assessment of a tax deficiency must be made pursuant to section 6203 of the Internal Revenue Code.
2. The taxpayer is given notice and a demand for payment is made. The requirement for assessment, notice, and demand may be waived by the taxpayer.
3. The taxpayer has failed to pay the assessment.

(Note: even if all of the above conditions exists, the IRS may still decide not to file the notice of a lien. This aspect will be discussed below.)

In most cases, the taxpayer must receive notice within 60 days of the assessment. In addition, demand on the taxpayer for payment must be made at least 10 days before collection action is taken.

Notice is usually given by mailing it to the taxpayer's residence, place of business, or last known address. It can also be served by personally giving a copy of the notice to the taxpayer or leaving the formal notice at taxpayer's dwelling or usual place of business.

An assessment is accomplished by an IRS assessment officer at an IRS service center completing a Form 23-C (Assessment Certificate). The date on the Form 23-C is the date used when determining priority of tax liens. This date is also considered as the date of commencement of collection activity by the IRS.

IRS Policy on Filing Liens

Listed above are the requirements that must be met before a lien may be filed. As noted earlier, while a tax lien results automatically with the assessment of a tax liability, until the lien is recorded, it has no practical effects on persons dealing with the taxpayer without knowledge of the tax lien. The Internal Revenue Code and IRS regulations do not provide any guidance regarding when a formal filing of the tax lien should be made. The Internal Revenue Manual indicates that in cases of doubt, the revenue officer should file the lien. Accordingly, the officer has wide discretion in making this decision.

Factors that the IRS has considered in the past prior to filing a tax lien include:

☐ Filing a tax lien restricts the ability of the taxpayer to borrow funds to pay the tax liability.

☐ If the officer has made attempts to contact the taxpayer by telephone, or if the taxpayer has failed to respond to IRS correspondence. Normally the revenue officer will attempt to contact the taxpayer and try to resolve the problem without filing of the lien. If, however, the revenue officer is unable to contact the taxpayer, a lien will normally be filed. (This is another good reason to promptly return all IRS telephone calls and answer IRS correspondence without delay.)

☐ Does it appear that the taxpayer is attempting to dispose of his/her property and disappear? If there is any question in this regard, the IRS will file notice.

☐ If the balance owed is more than $2,000, and the present financial ability of the taxpayer indicates that the amount cannot currently be collected from the taxpayer, the IRS will normally suspend collection proceedings, file a tax lien, and take no further action until the taxpayer's financial condition improves. When the taxpayer owns real property, and the tax is currently considered as uncollectable, the IRS will file a tax lien if the unpaid balance is more than $500.

☐ If the taxpayer indicates that he/she intends to file for bankruptcy, then IRS will attempt to file a lien before the bankruptcy petition is filed. Filing of a bankruptcy petition acts as an automatic stay on court actions. Accordingly, if the taxpayer intends to file bankruptcy, it may be best not to mention this fact to the tax examiner. A detailed discussion of the effects of bankruptcy on a tax liability is contained in the IRS Publication 908, Bankruptcy. This publication is attached as Appendix H.

☐ If the IRS officer has indications that the taxpayer is attempting to sell some property or has property in escrow pending a sale, a lien will be filed.

☐ On installment payments where the balance is $5,000 or more, or the payment period exceeds one year, normally the lien will be filed.

☐ When installment payment arrangements are made and the taxpayer defaults on a payment, IRS will file the notice of lien.

☐ If the case is covered by the Automated Collection System discussed below, a lien is automatically recorded against the taxpayer.

☐ If there is some doubt as to the correctness of the assessment, a question as to whether the tax debt has been paid, or an adjustment is pending, normally the IRS will not issue the notice of the tax lien.

Effects of a Tax Lien

When Notice of Federal Tax Lien is filed, it will be listed on the taxpayer's credit record at the credit reporting agencies. Accordingly, the notice of a federal tax lien will make it practically impossible for the taxpayer to obtain credit. It also restricts the transfer of property which has paper titles, such as real estate and personal property where the title to the property is recorded (automobiles, boats, airplanes, etc.).

Property Subject to Lien

Any property owned by the taxpayer is subject to the lien. In addition, until the lien is removed, it attaches to any new property which the taxpayer acquires. Once a Notice of Federal Tax Lien is filed, anyone buying or otherwise obtaining the taxpayer's property normally takes the property subject to the lien. This means that anyone who purchases any property from the taxpayer may be required to pay the tax lien to get a good title. (Note: there are several exceptions to this general rule which will be discussed later.)

Place of Filing

Where the notice of a tax lien is filed depends to some extent on state law. If the state has a designated office or location for the filing of a notice of tax lien, then notice is filed in that office or place. If there is no state law on the subject, then it is filed in the U.S. District Court in which the taxpayer lives and/or owns property. If the taxpayer lives in one state or district and has property in a different state or district, normally the notice must be filed in both locations.

Notice Period

Once the notice lien is filed, the lien is valid for a six-year period unless otherwise extended. If, however, the taxpayer agrees to waive the six-year period by signing a Form 900, Tax Collection Waiver, then the lien is extended for the agreed period of time. (Note: this waiver must be signed prior to the expiration of the six-year period. If the period is extended, then the notice of a tax lien must be refiled within 30 days of the expiration of the original notice.)

Court-Ordered Judgment Lien

The above rules and limitations do not apply to those cases where the lien is the result of a court-ordered judgment. In these cases, the court judgment need not be filed to act as a lien. In addition, the six-year limitation period does not apply.

TAX LEVY

A *tax levy* is defined under the Internal Revenue Code as the power to collect taxes by *distraint* or *seizure*. The major difference between a tax lien and a tax levy is that when a lien is filed, IRS does not take possession of the property as they do when a levy is executed.

The IRS can use the levy to attach a taxpayer's property that is in the hands of a third party. For example, a notice of a levy can be used to attach funds in a bank account that belongs to the taxpayer. This is the method used to attach a taxpayer's checking or saving accounts. Normally it is less burdensome and time consuming to levy on property in the hands of a third party.

The levy may also be on property in possession of the taxpayer followed by a seizure and public sale of the property. All property, except that exempt from attachment, may be attached and sold. A levy allows a continuous attachment of the nonexempt portion of the wages or salary of a taxpayer.

Before levying on any property of the taxpayer, the IRS must notify the taxpayer in writing of its intention to levy. No court judgment or court order is required. Prior to entering the taxpayer's property to seize any of his/her property however, the IRS must either have consent of the taxpayer or a court order permitting the entry. In addition, IRS agents may not enter on the taxpayer's property to search for property to be seized without a search warrant.

Jeopardy Situations

The IRS policy is that the taxpayer should be first given an opportunity to voluntarily comply with the revenue laws. Accordingly, unless a jeopardy situation is present, the taxpayer will be informed and provided a reasonable opportunity to voluntarily pay the taxes. A jeopardy situation is defined as those cases where the IRS has reasonable cause to believe that the taxpayer will dispose of his/her property and disappear.

Except in jeopardy situations, at least one final notice must be issued before the IRS will serve the levy. Once the taxpayer has been advised and fails to make satisfactory arrangements within a period of not less than 10 days, then IRS may serve the levy.

Fishing Expeditions

A notice of levy will be served on a third party only when there is reasonable cause to believe that the third party has property or rights to property belonging to the taxpayer. The IRS is not allowed to use the notice of levy to go on a "fishing expedition" for taxpayer's property.

Property Subject to Levy

With certain exceptions, any property belonging to a taxpayer may be levied. It does not matter who has possession of the property, only that it belongs to the taxpayer. "Property" includes rights to property, stocks, bonds, currency, patents, etc. As a matter of policy, the IRS does not presently levy on social security or veterans benefits. The term "tax" as used regarding levy authority of the IRS includes taxes, interest on taxes, penalties, and costs involved with the levy.

As a general rule, the IRS can levy only on property that belongs to the taxpayer. The levy can, in the case of wages or salary payments, attach as the taxpayer earns them.

The authority to levy permits the IRS to select which property it intends to levy. There is no requirement that the IRS first levy on any particular property.

Search for Taxpayer's Property

Before the IRS can levy on the taxpayer's particular property, the property must be discovered or located. One method used by the IRS is to have the revenue officer interview the taxpayer. At this time, the taxpayer will be requested to complete a Form 433 Collection Information Statement (Appendix B). If the taxpayer refuses to voluntarily complete the form, then he/she can be ordered to complete it by use of the IRS summons authority. (Note: when the taxpayer completes the form, he/she is required to sign it under penalty of perjury.)

During the levy process, the IRS has the authority to compel third parties, such as banks, to provide information regarding what property they have that belongs to the taxpayer. In the case of banks, the IRS can require that the taxpayer's account records be provided for examination.

Sale of Taxpayer's Property

After the IRS seizes the taxpayer's property, before it can be sold, the taxpayer must be provided with notice of the seizure and an accounting of the property seized. Unless the property is perishable, the IRS may sell the property at a public auction at least ten days after notice and not more than 40 days after the notice.

AUTOMATED TELEPHONE COLLECTION SYSTEM

The *Automated Telephone Collection System (ACS)* is an automatic telephone system that places telephone calls to a delinquent taxpayer's residence. If someone answers the call, then a trained collector takes the call and attempts to collect the past due taxes. ACS is also programmed to issue automatic wage garnishments and to attach the taxpayer's bank accounts. In certain cases, the ACS will automatically issue a formal Notice of Federal Tax Lien. These liens are discussed in Chapter 2. The earlier discussed tax lien on the President was triggered by the ACS when incorrect computer data was entered into the system.

The biggest problem in dealing with this system is the inability to communicate with an actual person. Telephone calls to ACS are normally conducted through tape recorded messages. If the taxpayer's case is being handled by the ACS, steps should be taken to have it transferred to a revenue agent.

OBTAINING A COMPROMISE

There are two types of compromise that the IRS and a taxpayer can make. In one type, the compromise is based on doubt as to the tax liability in issue. The other type is where the tax liability is established, but the taxpayer is unable to pay the entire amount due.

Compromises Based on Validity of Assessment

The Collections Division has the authority to compromise any assessed tax deficiency if there is a legitimate dispute as to the validity of the assessment. (Note: the ability of the taxpayer to pay the assessment is not a factor in this type of compromise. An offer of compromise can raise issues previously submitted to the Examination Division and any new issues available. An offer of this type cannot be made concerning the same issues involved in a Tax Court decision or in an earlier agreed settlement with the taxpayer.)

Any offers for compromise should be in writing, addressed to the revenue officer. A detailed statement concerning the validity of the assessment should be included. The written offer should also include any facts and authorities that support the taxpayer's position. The taxpayer may submit a deposit in the amount of the offer with the offer. The taxpayer may indicate that if the compromise offer is not accepted, the deposit is to be returned.

If the revenue officer rejects the offer to compromise, the taxpayer may appeal within 15 days of notice of the rejection to the appeals office. The officer reviewing the appeal may overrule the revenue officer and accept the offer. In addition, the review officer can submit a counteroffer to the taxpayer.

Compromises Based on Inability to Pay

The Collections Division also has the ability to accept partial payment as payment-in-full based on the inability of the taxpayer to pay the entire sum. The IRS collections policy manual indicates that in evaluating an offer based on inability to pay, the amount agreed to should reflect all that can be reasonably collected from the taxpayer. There is an Attorney General's opinion which states that the IRS is not authorized to accept a compromise based solely on hardship, sympathy, or equity. It is IRS's policy to reject otherwise acceptable offers if the taxpayer is "notorious," involved in criminal activity, or on "public policy" grounds.

The revenue officer will estimate what proceeds can be expected from a forced sale of the taxpayer's business. The estimated amount will be used as the guide in accepting a compromise offer. Because a taxpayer may be able to raise additional money by borrowing, etc., often this method provides the small business person with a method to continue in business, especially because many aspects of a small business, such as goodwill, have no value in a forced sale.

In most cases, the taxpayer should attempt to reach an informal agreement with the revenue officer on the forced sale value of the taxpayer's assets. An agreement would greatly improve the taxpayer's chances of getting a formal compromise agreement approved.

In most cases, the IRS will require that the compromise include an agreement to pay an additional amount equal to excess of the taxpayer's projected profit minus reasonable living expenses for the next three to five years, or a *future income agreement*, which requires the taxpayer to pay a percentage of his/her after-tax income for the next three to five years.

The taxpayer submits a formal request for a compromise. This offer is reviewed by the IRS's *Special Procedures Office*. This office has the authority to approve or deny the offer. In most cases, the office will follow the recommendations of the revenue officer. If the office considers the offer acceptable before approving it, an officer will hold an offer conference with the taxpayer. At this conference, any needed additional information will be requested. Amendments to the offer can be suggested by the IRS officer. In addition, normally the IRS will require the taxpayer to execute a waiver of the statute of limitations and waiver of future tax refunds up to the amount that will not be collected.

Once the compromise offer is formally accepted by the IRS, it is a binding contract on both the taxpayer and the government. If the taxpayer fails to keep his/her part of the agreement, the IRS can attempt to collect the entire tax liability.

FIGHTING THE COLLECTION PROCESS

The taxpayer's best chances of stopping the collection process is by court action to establish that the tax liability should not be assessed against him/her or by a compromise agreement with the IRS. Getting a court to stop the collection process of a valid tax assessment is almost impossible. In many cases, if the taxpayer can establish a valid attempt to meet his/her obligations, the revenue officer may forego the coercive collection procedures.

The revenue officer can grant a taxpayer an extension of not more than 45 days, based on an oral promise to pay the tax liability in full. For longer delays, the revenue officer will require the taxpayer to follow certain procedural requirements.

Negotiation Installment Payments

In most situations, negotiating installment payments for payment of the liability in full will be the easiest agreement to obtain from the IRS. The IRS can permit the payment of delinquent taxes in installments if a taxpayer is unable to currently pay the full amount due. The IRS guidelines used in approving installment agreements are:

- ☐ Taxpayer must provide assurance that future tax returns and taxes due will be timely filed and paid.
- ☐ Equal monthly payments should be required. Payment agreements may, however, be increased or decreased as necessary.
- ☐ The installment agreement will be monitored through routine provisions unless the installment payments are less than $10.
- ☐ The taxpayer should be allowed to select the payment due date. If the taxpayer indicates no preference, then a date will be selected that enhances payment.

- ☐ If the taxpayer and the interviewer cannot agree on amount of installments, the taxpayer should be advised of his/her right to appeal to the next supervisor.
- ☐ If the installment agreement lasts more than two years, it must provide for review at least every two years.
- ☐ In determining the required installment payments, the revenue officer will consider the apparent financial ability of the taxpayer.
- ☐ In some cases, if the taxpayer has excess cash, the IRS may require the taxpayer to pay an initial payment.
- ☐ Installment agreements are subject to review if the taxpayer's financial conditions change.

Anti-Injunction Act

The Anti-Injunction Act prohibits suits by a taxpayer to restrain the assessment or collection of any tax owed to the IRS. In a 1962 U.S. Supreme Court case, the Court held that a District Court could grant a taxpayer relief from the IRS collection process only if the taxpayer could establish:

- ☐ Failure to stop the collection action would cause irreparable damage to the taxpayer.
- ☐ There is no other adequate remedy available to the taxpayer.
- ☐ The taxpayer can establish that his/her chances of ultimately winning are very good.

Transfers of Property

The IRS can set aside or void a transfer of property by the taxpayer to another person even before the formal notice of a lien is filed if IRS can establish the below conditions:

- ☐ The tax claim existed at the time of the transfer.
- ☐ The taxpayer received less than fair market value for the property.
- ☐ At the time the taxpayer transferred the property, he/she lacked sufficient funds to pay his/her debts at the time of the transfer or because of the transfer.
- ☐ The IRS has been unable to collect the deficiency from the taxpayer.

FIGHTING TAX PENALTIES

In 1987, the Assistant Treasury Secretary of Tax Policy stated that he regretted that Congress had been unable to "stem the bulging flow of tax penalties." He also stated that "The problem with compliance right now is that we have too many penalties in a sort of crazy-quilt fashion. The idea of a penalty should be to induce compliance, not to raise revenue."

In all penalty issues, the best tactic to take is that the taxpayer's conduct was reasonable under the circumstances and that the assessment of the penalty would not increase tax compliance. The original purpose of penalties was to increase tax compliance. This purpose is still the official stated policy reason.

The types of penalties that the IRS has the authority to impose include:

- ☐ Failure to file.
- ☐ Late filing penalty.
- ☐ Failure to pay penalty.
- ☐ Failure to deposit funds collected for taxes (employers).
- ☐ Penalty for negligence.
- ☐ Bad-check penalty.
- ☐ Civil fraud penalty.

In determining the amount of the penalty, four factors are considered. They are:

- ☐ The rate of the penalty. Normally expressed in percentages of tax liability.
- ☐ The period of time for which the penalty is due.
- ☐ The principal of tax liability to which the penalty rate will apply.
- ☐ Penalties are not imposed on penalty amounts in most cases. Interest, however, may be charged on past due penalties.

If the IRS imposes a tax penalty on the taxpayer, there are four steps that the taxpayer may use to eliminate or reduce the penalty. First, the taxpayer should request a reconsideration by the officer who imposed the penalty. This step is discussed later in this chapter. If this request is not successful, next, the taxpayer may file an administrative appeal with the IRS as discussed in Chapter 7. If this second step is not successful, then the taxpayer may either file an offer to compromise based on the question of correctness of the penalty. If this is not successful, then the taxpayer may pay the penalty and file a claim for refund on Form 843 (Copy attached as Appendix C).

If the IRS denies the request for refund or takes no action on the request within six months after the request is submitted, then the taxpayer may file a refund claim in U.S. District Court or the U.S. Court of Claims as discussed in Chapter 8.

Failure to File Penalty

If the taxpayer can establish a reasonable cause for filing late without getting a valid penalty, the IRS will excuse the penalty for late filing. Reasons that the IRS have accepted for excusing the late filing penalty fee include:

☐ Delay was caused by erroneous information provided by the IRS to the taxpayer.
☐ The taxpayer visited an IRS office before filing date and requested to see an IRS representative, but was not allowed to.
☐ The IRS failed to answer a timely request for required forms.
☐ First time taxpayer was mistaken regarding filing requirements.
☐ The taxpayer was absent for unavoidable reasons.
☐ Return filed on time, but to the wrong district.
☐ Fire destroyed taxpayer's place of business.
☐ Death of a close member of the family.

(Note: The same reasons may not be accepted by all offices.)

Civil Fraud Penalty

The *civil fraud* penalty can be as high as 75 percent of the amount by which the tax liability is understated. In order to constitute civil fraud, the IRS Policy Statement requires clear and convincing evidence that some part of the understatement of tax liability is due to tax fraud. To establish fraud, there must be evidence of a willful attempt to evade taxes that are legally due. Negligence or carelessness is not sufficient. In litigation regarding tax fraud, the burden is on the IRS to establish that the taxpayer willfully failed to pay taxes due.

Bad Check Penalty

It is amazing how many bad checks that the IRS receives each year. Section 6657 of the code provides that if the check amount is less than $500, then the penalty shall be $5 or the amount of the check, which ever is less. If the amount of the check is over $500, then the penalty shall be one percent of the amount. The section also provides that the penalty shall not apply if the person writing and forwarding the check to the IRS believed in good faith that the check would be paid when presented to the bank, and the person had reasonable cause to believe that it would be paid.

Negligent Understatement of Tax Liability

The penalty for the *substantial negligent understatement* of tax liability is an amount equal to 25 percent of the amount understated. For the purposes of this penalty, a substantial understatement of tax liability is 10 percent of the total tax liability for that tax year or $5,000.

Abatement or Reconsideration of Penalty Assessments

One taxpayer, John Gore, was unsuccessful in his attempt to be relieved of a late-return penalty just because his tax advisor recommended that he file his taxes late to avoid an audit. The IRS has the authority to relieve a taxpayer of most tax penalties. In most cases, the taxpayer must establish that the penalty was not due to willful actions on the part of the taxpayer.

The Collections Division has the authority to review certain penalties and may waive or reduce them on a showing of "reasonable cause." Although the revenue officer can not waive or abate those penalties assessed by the Examination Division, he/she can request that the Examination Division reconsider their assessment. The penalties that may be reviewed by the Collections Division (revenue officer) include late filing penalties, valuation overstatement, failure to deposit taxes, failure to file information returns, and substantial underpayment.

Any requests for abatement or waiver should be made in writing and forwarded to the revenue officer. The requests should establish the probable cause necessary to set aside or abate the penalty. The probable cause is normally set forth in a sworn statement of facts presented by the taxpayer.

Some of the reasons that taxpayers have used to avoid or abate penalties include records not available, mistakes as to requirements, reliance on advice of counsel, confusion regarding new tax law changes, and confusion regarding filing dates.

If the revenue officer refuses the requested relief, then the taxpayer may file an appeal to the Appeals Office within 15 days of the notice of the revenue officer's decision. Except in those cases involving jeopardy assessments, the IRS must suspend collection action during the appeal period.

The revenue officer can also refer the case back to the Examinations Division for reconsideration of the original assessment of taxes or penalties. A taxpayer's request for reassessment should be in writing and addressed to the revenue officer. It should contain a statement establishing that the present assessment is in error. The policy requirements for reconsideration are:

☐ The taxpayer has new information or substantiation that will support the taxpayer's position or migitate the circumstances.
☐ The taxpayer has an excusable reason for not obtaining and presenting this information to the examinations branch prior to the first determination of penalties.

CHAPTER 3

Why Your Return Is Selected for Audit

Some of the key concepts regarding selection of returns for audit are listed below:

- ☐ Most returns are selected for audit because of audit triggers.
- ☐ IRS's audit strategy is to maximize voluntary compliance with the Internal Revenue Codes.
- ☐ Most returns selected for audit are computer selected.
- ☐ The most important selection process is the DIF program.
- ☐ Returns with high DIF scores are then manually screened for audit potential.
- ☐ The information matching program allows the IRS to match various information sources to the taxpayer's return to detect unreported income.
- ☐ Returns audited under the Taxpayer's Compliance Program are selected at random.
- ☐ Under the Taxpayer's Compliance Program, the taxpayer is required to establish the correctness of each line of his/her return.
- ☐ IRS uses a questionable W-4 Program to detect returns with improperly claimed exemptions.
- ☐ The Delinquent Returns Program is designed to discover those persons who fail to file tax returns as required.

HOW IRS TARGETS RETURNS FOR AUDIT

The word "audit" strikes terror in the heart of most taxpayers. When a taxpayer is notified of a pending audit, the feeling is always, "Why me?" In this chapter, the manner in which the IRS selects returns for audit will be discussed. In Chapter 4, reducing audit risks are discussed.

The overall selection rate for returns is less than 2 percent. There is no procedure to completely eliminate the possibility of an audit. Tax returns, however, are not selected randomly for audit. It depends on the nature of the return as to your possibility of being selected for an audit. The highest percentage risks for audits are major corporations. Most major corporations are audited annually. The lowest percentage risks for audits are the single taxpayers with no dependents who file a short form 1040A. They rarely get audited.

Tax professionals use the term *audit triggers* to refer to those items or combinations of items that cause a taxpayer return being selected for audit.

The returns are normally selected for audit on one of four bases:

1. Taxpayer's Compliance Program (TCP).
2. Based on type of return: individual and joint Form 1040s, partnership Form 1065, or corporate Form 1120.
3. Special audit issues, i.e., office in home, tax shelters, tax protesters, etc.
4. Size or amount of certain line items on the return.

The Form 1040 class of returns and the Form 1120S (subchapter S corporations) are audited only at a rate of about 1.75 percent. The rate of audit for corporations is in excess of 5 percent, with major corporations rating almost 100 percent.

According to Rabkin and Johnson, *Federal Income, Gift, and Estate Taxation*, IRS's audit strategy is to maximize voluntary compliance with tax requirements over all tax classes and to maximize revenue collection where appropriate. With this in mind, it is noted that the Forms 1040 (individual) class average audit assessment is only about $1,000 whereas with corporate returns the average is about $60,000.

THE AUDIT PROCESS

Taxpayers mail their returns to one of 10 regional service centers. At the center, the returns are opened and screened for completeness. Mathematical errors, missing signatures, etc. are noted and action is taken to correct the error. In cases of mathematical errors or use of wrong tax tables, a corrective letter with a statement as to the new computation of taxes is forwarded to the taxpayer.

Next, information from the returns is entered into the computer data banks. Next, the computer data is transferred to the National Computer Center at Martinsburg, W.Va. At Martinsburg, the returns are screened for possible audit under the DIF program.

AUDIT SELECTION PROGRAMS

The actual selection process is accomplished by various programs. The most important of these programs are discussed below.

DIF Program

The IRS has developed a computer screening program that selects out those returns which have the highest potential for a significant change in tax liability. The program, *Discriminant Function Program (DIF)* presently allows the screening of Forms 1040, 1041, and 1120. DIF establishes a score for each return. The higher the return, the greater the potential for significant change in tax liability from an audit. As of this date, the IRS has been successful in resisting court attempts to require publication of the formula used in the DIF. The IRS has taken extreme precautions to ensure the secrecy of the DIF program. IRS employees are given only select information regarding it and only on a "need to know" basis.

About 90 percent of the Form 1040 returns are excluded from additional screening under the DIF at this point because of their low score. Data on the remaining 10 percent of the returns are stored in inventory files, and these returns are subject to further inspection in the audit selection process. The information in the inventory files is sorted by several categories and then by service centers. Each service center receives computer data identifying the returns submitted to the center that have been assigned high DIF scores.

Those returns receiving high DIF scores are then screened at the service center for audit potential. The screening is accomplished by experienced auditors. Some of those selected for audit will be referred to a *revenue agent* and the rest to tax auditors. Revenue agents will audit most field audits and those involving suspected criminal fraud. Tax auditors will handle IRS office audits and mail audits. Normally, tax auditors are directed to those items to focus on, where as revenue agents are not.

Some of the factors used in selecting which of those returns with high DIF scores will be audited include:

☐ The potential for significant change in tax liability.

☐ The comparative size of questionable items in relationship to the return as a whole. For example, under this factor, a casualty loss of $4,000 when the gross income is $80,000 is more significant than a casualty loss of $40,000 when the gross income is $1,200,000.

☐ Character of the items being questioned. A deduction of $1,200 for professional books by a retail store clerk is an example.

☐ Evidence of fraud.

☐ Overall effect of questionable item on the return.

If, after using the above factors, the return is not selected as audit-worthy under the DIF Program, and it is not selected for audit on one of the below discussed target programs, no further action is taken on it.

The majority of returns audited each year by the IRS are selected for audit under this program. Prior to 1981, the DIF program was based on the taxpayer's adjusted gross income. The emphasis was changed in 1981 to *total positive income (TPI)*. Total positive income includes all income received by a taxpayer before any deductions or adjustments. TPI is discussed in detail in Chapter 5. As noted earlier, the DIF program is a highly guarded secret within the IRS. It is noted that after the change to total positive income, the DIF program has increased the audit rate for high income taxpayers and reduced the rate for low income taxpayers.

Targeted Items Program

A second manner in which a return is selected for audit is under the Targeted Items Program. Under this program, certain items are selected by the IRS for audit. Approximately 20 percent of the returns selected for audit each year are selected under this program. Each year, the Commissioner directs that returns with certain items be targeted as high audit potential returns for that year. In the past, these items have included tax shelters, office in the home, and casualty losses.

The purpose of the Targeted Items Program is to encourage voluntary compliance with the tax laws by applying a concentrated effort to selected items on the returns. Publicity regarding these items is expected to encourage taxpayer compliance.

Information Matching Program

Under the Information Matching Program, information received by the IRS from sources other than the taxpayer is matched with the information on the taxpayer's return. For example, a Form 1099 submitted by a bank, which indicates that the taxpayer has received interest income, will be matched against the taxpayer's return to determine if the taxpayer reported the interest income.

Each year, the IRS receives over 6 billion information documents from multiple sources. Recently, the ability of the IRS to match these documents with taxpayer returns has improved significantly. IRS has a goal of matching the information documents to taxpayer returns in excess of 90 percent.

This program is designed to identify those taxpayers who underreport their income and who fail to file returns.

Taxpayer Compliance Measurement Program (TCMP)

The *Taxpayer Compliance Measurement Program (TCMP),* unlike other programs, is not designed to identify those returns with a potential for significant change in tax liability. Its purpose is to measure the level of voluntary compliance with the tax laws. (Note: our federal tax system is based on the concept that the majority of taxpayers will voluntarily comply with the federal tax requirements.)

Approximately 50,000 returns are selected nationwide to be audited under this program. Each item on the return is checked and verified by the examiner. One taxpayer who was audited under this program stated that his examination by the auditor went substantially as follows:

> Your name?
> (taxpayer provided name)
> Prove it.
> Your address?
> (taxpayer provided address)
> Prove it.
> Social Security Number?
> (taxpayer provided SSN)
> Prove it.
> Age?
> (taxpayer stated age)
> Prove it.

The taxpayer stated that the examination continued in this manner for each item of information in the return. The taxpayer was required to produce his marriage certificate and birth certificates for each of his children.

The IRS' purpose in requiring the taxpayer to establish the correctness of each item is to determine taxpayer "norms" for validity of each item of information. By using the 50,000 return samples, the IRS can make estimations of taxpayer norms for honesty on each item of information on the return.

It appears that the IRS uses the estimations obtained to modify or further develop the DIF program formula discussed earlier in this chapter. Former IRS employees have stated that the norms developed under this program are used to compare items on the taxpayers' returns in the secret DIF computer program. The norms allow the IRS to determine the composite taxpayer: what he/she earns, spends, deducts, etc. This program also helps the IRS identify those items on the tax returns that taxpayers are more likely to answer incorrectly.

Questionable Refund Program

The Questionable Refund Program is designed to detect those fraudulent tax returns that are filed to obtain refunds. Each service center has a Questionable Refund Detection Team whose purpose is to detect phony returns prior to a refund check being issued. Computer selected returns with a high potential for fraud are hand reviewed before return checks are issued. If the manual screening detects the possibility of fraud, additional investigation will be made prior to issuing a refund check. This program is used to detect phony Form W-2 and other common fraud schemes.

Questionable W-4 Program

The Questionable W-4 Program is designed to detect those returns with improperly claimed exemptions. Prior to the Tax Reform Act of 1986, if a taxpayer claimed 14 exemptions or a sufficient number that no taxes would be withheld on an income of more than $200 per week, Form W-4, Exemptions was examined. After tax reform, the number claimed was reduced to 10. Now if a taxpayer indicates to his/her employee on the W-4 that the employee has 10 or more exemptions, the W-4 is referred to this program.

Questionable Preparer Program

Under the Questionable Preparer Program, the IRS selects out those income tax returns that were prepared by certain preparers. The IRS now has the ability to conduct a computerized sort of all returns prepared by certain preparers. The IRS contends that certain preparers use questionable practices in preparing income tax returns. Accordingly, taxpayers whose returns were completed by one of the IRS-identified questionable preparers are more likely to have their returns audited.

Delinquent Returns Program

The Delinquent Returns Program is designed to discover those persons who fail to file required tax returns. Information received by the IRS from multiple sources such as banks, employers, etc. are matched with taxpayer returns to ensure that the taxpayer filed a return and included the income item on the return. When the IRS has information that a person has received income and cannot locate the return, the person is contacted and requested to submit proof that a return was filed. If the taxpayer does not produce the evidence, the case is forwarded to a District IRS Office for appropriate action.

Special Returns

Certain returns are manually selected for audit for various reasons. Examples of these are returns filed by suspected drug dealers, returns that have been identified by informants as false, angry spouses, and delinquent returns. This group, however, accounts for only a small portion of the returns audited each year.

AUDIT ASSIGNMENT PROCEDURES

Returns selected for audit will be assigned to either a revenue agent or a tax auditor. Most returns will be assigned to tax auditors. Revenue agents conduct most of the field audits and audits which require a high degree of accounting knowledge and understanding. Tax auditors are restricted in the scope of their audit, whereas revenue agents have free rein regarding the scope of the audit.

Returns that are selected for audit will have check sheets attached to their face. The group managers will indicate on the face sheets of those returns assigned to tax auditors items to be considered for audit, location of examination, and clerical information regarding the contact letter used to notify the taxpayer of the audit.

The check sheets are also used to assign the returns to the various auditors. (Note: In most cases, the IRS do not indicate over three items to be examined by tax auditors.)

CHAPTER 4

Reducing the Risk
of an Audit

Some of the key concepts in reducing the risk of an audit are listed below and further explained in this chapter.

☐ No return is audit proof.

☐ Only a small percentage of tax returns is audited.

☐ Certain items on a return greatly increase a taxpayer's chances of being selected for audit.

☐ High total positive income and high gross receipts are the most important audit triggers.

☐ An office-in-home deduction is frequently the subject of target audit programs.

☐ Tax shelters increase a taxpayer's chances of being audited.

☐ Large deductions that are not normal for a taxpayer's possession are an audit trigger.

☐ Care should be taken to present items in such a manner that removes any questions regarding the possibility of abusive tax shelters.

☐ One method that the IRS uses to identify tax shelters is by noting substantial losses claimed on Schedule C.

☐ Any indication of unreported income is almost certain to trigger additional examinations of the return by the IRS.

☐ Many taxpayers wrongly believe that as long as they pay a small amount of tax when they file their return, the IRS will be less likely to audit them.

CHANCES OF AN AUDIT

In this chapter, the methods that a taxpayer may use to reduce his/her chances of a tax audit are discussed. An important thing to keep in mind is that any person who submits a tax return is subject to being audited. Tax returns, however, are not randomly selected for audit. As discussed in Chapter 3, the IRS uses certain procedures and programs to select the small number of returns that will be audited each year. The IRS has only about 2,500 persons to audit 2.5 million returns per year.

As will be discussed later, in some cases, it is recommended that the taxpayer attach statements explaining certain items on his/her return. This statement will have no effect on the DIF score of the return. Those returns with high DIF scores are manually screened before being selected for audit. During the manual screening process, the statement could make a difference. (Note: the statement should explain the item. This is not the time to attach receipts verifying the expense.)

RETURN PREPARATION

One step that a taxpayer can take to reduce his/her chances of being selected for an audit is to complete the tax return as required by IRS regulations. Incomplete forms, missing forms, or forms that are incorrectly completed greatly increase the taxpayer's chances of being audited. Returns should be double checked to ensure they are correctly completed, have the necessary supporting forms, and are signed.

The return should be neat and have a professional appearance. This is not the time to take shortcuts in filling out the forms. The taxpayer should attempt to have a return that gives the impression that the taxpayer is a very precise and careful person. This impression could make a difference if the return is manually screened.

AUDIT TRIGGERS

Certain items on a tax return increase a taxpayer's chances of having his/her return selected for audit. These items are commonly referred to as *audit triggers*. Audit triggers also produce higher scores on the DIF Program. As discussed in Chapter 3, a high DIF score increases the chances of being audited. It appears that the most popular audit triggers currently being used by the IRS are:

☐ Business returns with total adjusted gross receipts in excess of $100,000.
☐ Nonbusiness returns with total positive income of more than $50,000.
☐ Tax shelters.
☐ Using a tax preparer who is listed as a problem tax preparer.

☐ Large travel and entertainment expense deductions or adjustments.
☐ Substantial business automobile expense deductions or adjustments.
☐ Casualty loss deductions.
☐ Hobby losses (Schedule C with losses that reflect a hobby rather than a business).
☐ Home office deductions.
☐ Unreported income.

In the following sections of this chapter, all but the first two triggers (which involve high income) are discussed. If the taxpayer is in the high income bracket, he/she should accept the fact that his/her return is more likely to be audited. High total positive income and high gross receipts are probably the most important audit triggers used by the IRS. Steps, however, to reduce total positive income can create problems with the IRS and may in the long run cost more than accepting the high possibility of an audit.

TOTAL POSITIVE INCOME

For years, the IRS used a taxpayer's *adjusted gross income (AGI)* as a factor in selecting returns for audit. Now the IRS uses the total positive income (TIP) and nonbusiness total positive income (NBTIP) as an audit factor in lieu of AGI. Total positive income is defined as the sum of the below items. (Note: losses are treated as zero):

1. Total Positive Income (TIP)
    a. Wages
    b. Interest
    c. Dividends
    d. Other Income
       State Tax Refunds
       Alimony
       Schedule D profits
       Capital Gains Distributions
       Form 4797
       Fully Taxable Pensions
       Rents and Royalties
       Miscellaneous Income
    e. Distributions
       Partnership
       Small Business Corporations
       Estate and Trust

   f. Schedule C- Net Profits
   g. Schedule F- Net Profits
2. Nonbusiness Total Positive Income (NBTPI) includes all TPI items less:
   a. Schedule C- Net Profits
   b. Schedule F- Net Profits

BUSINESS OR NONBUSINESS RETURN

Whether or not the return is treated as a business return or nonbusiness return will have a factor on audit selection. (Note: the selection rate for business returns is higher than for nonbusiness returns.)

Nonbusiness returns have one of the following conditions:

☐ No Schedule C or F.
☐ *Total Gross Receipts (TGR)* under $25,000 and TPI exceeds TGR.
☐ TGR is over $25,000 but less than $100,000 and non-business TPI (NBTPI) is under $50,000.

HIGH RISK ITEMS

In this section, those audit triggers that are considered as high risk items are discussed. The presence of these items greatly increases a taxpayer's chances of an audit.

Office in the Home Deductions

An *office-in-the-home deduction* increases the taxpayer's chances of being audited. Although no exact figures are available on this, former IRS employees indicate that home office deductions are quite frequently subjects of IRS target programs and that it will increase the DIF score of a taxpayer. If the amount of the home office deduction is small compared to the taxpayer's total positive income, consideration should be given to foregoing this deduction to reduce the chances of an audit.

Unreported Income

Any indication of *unreported income* is almost certain to trigger additional examinations by the IRS. The taxpayer should explain any situation that indicates unreported income. Failure to report interest or dividends, high bank deposits without supporting reported income, and the taxpayer's living style can suggest unreported income.

One taxpayer in a community property State was required by a State divorce court to divide his military pension with his ex-wife. This taxpayer was apparently audited two years in a row because he failed to explain the difference between the amount of military pension that he reported and the amount reported by the government.

Unreported income may be from the one-time sale of a taxpayer's residence. Failure to report the sale of a residence is likely to cause an audit of the taxpayer's return. The IRS computers can also identify senior taxpayers who attempt to use the one-time exclusion for the sale of a personal residence more than once.

Travel and Entertainment Expenses

If the computer selects the taxpayer's return as one with high audit potential, any travel and entertainment expenses will be examined by the screener. Accordingly, careful attention should be paid to the manner in which the expenses are claimed. Do not leave any questions unanswered on the forms. A statement justifying the expenses may help prevent the return from being selected for audit during the manual screening process. Unexplained high travel and entertainment expenses, when compared to a taxpayer's total positive income, are clear invitations for audit.

The claiming of travel or entertainment expenses without attaching a Form 2106 or a Schedule C increases greatly a taxpayer's chances of being audited.

Automobile Expenses

Claiming automobile expenses can be a red flag. Accordingly, if the taxpayer has automobile expenses, ensure that they are correctly claimed and that complete justification is explained on a statement attached to the claim.

Casualty Losses

Casualty and theft losses have traditionally been high audit triggers. A taxpayer increases his/her chances of audit with this deduction. This is based on the past history of abuse of this deduction. One of the changes in the Tax Reform Act of 1986 was to reduce the tax advantages of casualty losses. One reason for this change is its past history of abuse. If claiming a casualty or theft losses, include a statement regarding the loss, a police report of the loss (if applicable), why the loss was not covered by insurance, and the methods used to arrive at the monetary value of the items destroyed or stolen.

The IRS has indicated that the below questions should be checked by an auditor when dealing with claimed casualty losses:

☐ If a loss actually occurred?
☐ When the loss occurred?

☐ The amount of the loss?
☐ Has the taxpayer made any deductions for depreciation of the item?
☐ Was the item insured?

Hobby Losses

The Internal Revenue Code requires that for the deduction of business expenses, the activity be engaged in for profit. The IRS has traditionally examined those returns where it appears that the taxpayer is not engaged in a good faith attempt to make a profit and is claiming a deduction for hobby expenses. Care should be taken when preparing the return to substantiate that the activity was engaged in for profit.

OTHER ITEMS THAT AFFECT AUDIT SELECTION

Although the following items are not considered as audit triggers, it appears that they can be factors in the selection process.

Mailing Labels

For years, the rumor has persisted that mailing labels printed by the IRS to be used by the taxpayers on their returns contain secret coded information. The IRS has insisted that the labels do not contain any secret information and that the chances of a taxpayer being selected for audit are not affected by the use of the labels. Former IRS employees have indicated that the IRS is being honest about this fact. Because using the labels helps the IRS to process the forms, it would appear that the IRS would not do anything to discourage taxpayers from using the labels.

Filing Status

With few exceptions, filing status appears to play no major role in audit selection. One exception is for those taxpayers who file as head of household. The IRS has demonstrated a tendency to require taxpayers to verify head of household status. In some cases, the IRS attempts to determine if single taxpayers are actually married and filing separately to avoid the marriage penalty tax.

Exemptions

On Form 1040A, the listing of multiple exemptions increases the chances of a taxpayer being audited. A similar situation exists when the taxpayer files as a single taxpayer but lists dependent children. In either of these situations, the taxpayer should attach a statement to the return explaining the situation.

Refund

Many taxpayers wrongly feel that as long as they pay a small amount the IRS will be less likely to audit their returns. In addition, there is the common opinion that a large return will trigger an audit. A large refund, normally, will not trigger an audit unless it appears to be an unusual situation. For example, a refund of several thousands of dollars on a return with a gross income of ten thousand dollars would be unusual. Any time the refund exceeds approximately 10 percent of the tax withheld, the taxpayer should submit a justification statement. Note: large refunds may be subject to screening under the fraudulent returns program discussed in Chapter 3.

Alimony

Alimony is frequently checked to ensure that the taxpayer has reported the entire amount. Now that taxpayers are required to provide the social security numbers of persons to whom alimony is paid, the IRS can use the Information Matching Program to identify persons receiving alimony who do not include it on their returns. In addition, sometimes large deductions for alimony and a head of household filing status trigger an audit to determine if the taxpayer is including child support payments under the alimony deduction.

Interest and Dividends

Failure to report interest and dividends received can be detected by the IRS matching program and thus trigger an audit. The IRS has the ability to match interest and dividends reported by financial institutions with taxpayer returns. Failure to claim interest and dividends earned can cause the taxpayer's return to be selected for audit. (Note: social security numbers are required for saving bond purchases and when establishing most interest bearing banking accounts in order to facilitate the matching program.)

Rental Income

Normally, rental income will not affect the taxpayer's chances of being selected for an audit. If there are unusual deductions, huge losses, or the appearance of a tax shelter, the taxpayer should provide an explanatory statement regarding the questionable items.

Gambling Losses

Because gambling losses are not deductible unless the taxpayer also has winnings, any large gambling loss is apt to be questioned by the IRS. This is an area in which the IRS has determined that a high possibility of fraud exists.

TAX SHELTERS

The Tax Shelter Program has been a targeted program of the IRS since the early 1970s. Any items on a return that give the appearance of a tax shelter will most likely trigger an audit. Care should be taken to present items in a manner that removes any questions regarding the possibility of abusive tax shelters.

Certain industries have traditionally been considered by the IRS as tax shelters. These industries are hobby farming, movies, oil and gas, leasing investments, and commodities.

One method that the IRS uses to identify tax shelters is by noting substantial losses claimed on Schedule C. In addition, audits based on items contained on Schedule C are more likely to be selected for a field audit. Care should be taken to explain any activities that have the appearance of a tax shelter.

Some taxpayers have failed to answer questions on Schedules C and F because the answers would raise the issue of a tax shelter. Failure to answer one of the questions on those schedules is a clear invitation for an audit.

OCCUPATIONS

The IRS has demonstrated a definite tendency to audit taxpayers with certain occupations, especially doctors and lawyers. In addition, the IRS will frequently select an occupational group for audit under target programs. Sometimes the occupation of the taxpayer is considered when examining the taxpayer's deductions or adjustments. For example, it would appear that a school teacher would have a difficult time justifying a deduction for the business use of a private airplane.

Taxpayers should consider how their occupation interrelates with their claimed deductions and expenses. If the deduction or expense is unusual for that occupation, a statement justifying the item should be attached to the return.

PROBLEM TAX PREPARER LIST

If the taxpayer is unlucky and uses a tax preparer that is listed with the IRS as a *problem tax preparer*, the return will at least be screened manually for audit selection. A problem in this area is determining if the preparer is one of those targeted by the IRS. There is no published list, and it is difficult for the average taxpayer to discover this fact. The best method of avoiding a targeted preparer is to use a local preparer with a good reputation and one whose clients are not normally audited. If the preparer has multiple clients being audited by the IRS, this may be an indication that the IRS has targeted that preparer.

AMENDED RETURNS

There seems to be a difference of opinion as to the risks of audit for *amended returns*. In 1987, the IRS announced that a closer look at amended returns would be made. Several key IRS officials believe that some taxpayers attempt to by-pass computerized audit selection by waiting until shortly before the three year statute of limitations expires and then filing an amended return with higher than normal deductions. By doing this, it appears that while the returns may be screened manually, they are not subject to audit selection based on the secret computerized DIF formula. It is expected that the IRS will, in the future, take a closer look at amended returns where the taxpayer receives a large refund.

CHAPTER 5

Defending Yourself
at the Audit

The key concepts in defending yourself at the audit and negotiation tactics are:

- ☐ Keep the objective of reducing the adverse impact of the audit foremost in your mind.
- ☐ Audit defense goals should be:
    - a. no referral to criminal action,
    - b. no penalties,
    - c. no additional taxes,
    - d. prevent re-audit, and
    - e. obtain a no-change audit.
- ☐ Be friendly and courteous, but not necessarily cooperative.
- ☐ Wear normal dress. Dressing down or up creates suspicion.
- ☐ Be on time for any audits. Auditors are working under pressure. Accordingly, do not make them angry or impatient.
- ☐ Provide only the information requested—do not volunteer unsolicited information.
- ☐ Let the auditor do the talking.
- ☐ Do not underestimate the abilities of the auditor.
- ☐ Try to act natural during the audit.
- ☐ Be serious—this is no time to crack jokes.
- ☐ Do not rush the auditor. To the auditor, this may indicate that you have something to hide.
- ☐ Bring only the specific records, documents, or materials requested to any hearing.

☐ In any appearance before an auditor, have records in order.

☐ The IRS can insist that the taxpayer be present at the audit.

☐ In most cases, the IRS does not insist that the taxpayer be present at the first or initial conference. There are definite advantages for the taxpayer if she/he is not present.

☐ Answer promptly any IRS correspondence requesting additional information or clarification of a portion of your return.

☐ Not only is the return being examined, but the taxpayer is also being examined.

☐ Normally, the less information the examiner learns about the taxpayer the better.

☐ There are special IRS audit guidelines for certain professions such as doctors, farmers, and lawyers.

☐ The taxpayer should use his/her psychological and negotiating skills when dealing with an IRS examiner.

☐ When dealing with the IRS, always request that the person identify themselves.

☐ If you are unhappy with the auditor, complain to his/her boss and continue up the chain of command if your complaint is valid.

☐ The IRS is sensitive to taxpayer complaints to Congress.

In this chapter, it is assumed that your return has been selected for audit. Accordingly, reducing the adverse impact of the audit is discussed. The specific tactics to use vary with the type of audit and the circumstances of each case. In some cases, the primary objective should be to prevent referral for criminal action. In other cases, it may be simply to prevent additional assessment of taxes or penalties. Although the IRS policy manual states that the selection of a tax return for audit does not suggest any wrongdoing, the taxpayer should approach the examination in a very cautious manner. The IRS Audit Manual is included in Appendix D.

TYPES OF AUDIT

In this section, a discussion of the types of audit that are conducted by the IRS will be presented to acquaint the taxpayer with the different approaches and what to expect from each. The IRS defines an audit as "an impartial review of the taxpayer's return to determine its completeness and accuracy." A 1976 General Accounting Office study indicated that the IRS is biased toward auditing for underpayment of taxes and not the overpayment. Audited taxpayers define it as "sheer torture." There are three basic types of audits currently being used by the IRS. They are: *mail audits*, *IRS office audits*, and *field audits*.

Mail audits normally involves noncomplex issues that can be settled without face-to-face discussions. Items such as justification for certain deductions, verification of deductions, etc. qualify. *IRS office audits* normally involve issues more complex than those handled by mail audits. If the issues involve individual judgments, then face-to-face discussion is considered necessary. The *field audits* are normally reserved for those audits that contain complex issues or involve in-depth examinations. Corporate audits are usually conducted as field audits.

The more experienced auditors (revenue agents) are normally assigned to field audits. This does not mean, however, that the individual conducting an IRS office audit is not experienced. In many cases, these individuals are experienced and very competent. The IRS office auditors are, however, controlled by their appointment calendars. The number of appointments per day per auditor is determined by IRS standards and group managers. Accordingly, the office auditors are working under a tight time schedule, which can be to the taxpayer's benefit.

The Audit Letter

Normally a taxpayer is notified of the pending audit by mail. This letter (audit letter) will direct the taxpayer to either: (1) mail in his/her receipts or other verification of certain items, (2) call the local IRS examination office and set up an appointment, or (3) request the taxpayer to appear for an examination at the time and place set forth in the letter.

If you receive an appointment to appear at an IRS branch office, the notification will also indicate what records you are required to bring. If you filed a business return, it is not unusual for the IRS to request the taxpayer to bring all journals and ledgers of the business. If the taxpayer is unclear as to which records to bring, or the time and date is inconvenient, there is a telephone number in the letter that the taxpayer may call for additional information.

In most cases, the IRS will allow the taxpayer to reschedule the appointment one time. Do not expect a last minute change however. The taxpayer should provide the IRS with as much notice as possible when requesting a change in appointment time and date. Most IRS offices consider the appointment confirmed if they do not hear from the taxpayer at least seven days prior to the appointment.

It is almost impossible to obtain substantial delays in the audit. If the taxpayer can establish a substantial hardship, the IRS will allow the delay of the audit until a better date. Delays in excess of 60 days must be approved by the IRS audit group manager. If it is a hardship for the taxpayer to come to the IRS office, the IRS can, at the request of the taxpayer, change the place of audit to the taxpayer's home. (Note: the problems with in-home audits discussed later in this chapter should be considered before requesting a home examination.)

Mail Audits

Mail audits or correspondence audits are used to examine questionable issues that are susceptible to direct verification from records or receipts. Inspection of previous returns normally are not conducted for mail audits. Issues that may be the subject of mail audits include simple itemized deductions, payments to an Individual Retirement Account, (IRA), child care credit, credit for elderly, residential energy credit, and self-employment tax.

The following items are not considered as normally suitable for mail audits: exemptions; income from pensions, tips, rents, etc.; deductions for travel and entertainment; deductions for bad debts; and determinations of basis of property.

(Note: IRS policy is that mail audits will generally include more than one issue. This is based on the concept that single issue audits rarely result in significant tax changes.)

In cases involving mail audits, the audit letter will inform the taxpayer which items are being examined. This may be by means of red checks in certain boxes on a form letter. The letter will also inform the taxpayer what records are needed to conduct the audit. In many cases, there will be blue information notices attached to the letter which describe types of records needed to substantiate various items on your return. These information notices are general in nature and may not fit your particular situation. If this is the case, call or write the IRS and ask for an explanation as to which records to submit.

In some cases where the taxpayer receives notice of an IRS office audit, and it appears that the matter can be handled by correspondence, the taxpayer can submit the documentation and request that the IRS accept the documents in lieu of an office visit. If the IRS does, then the taxpayer has eliminated the requirements for an office visit and removed the risk of the examiner asking additional questions regarding other items.

Office Audits

The IRS policy manual provides that returns selected for office interview audit should be those returns that require an analytical approach and individual judgment. In addition, office audits include those returns in which office interviews are considered necessary to protect the rights of taxpayers. (Note: recent testimony before Congressional sub-committees seem to indicate that the IRS is not overly concerned with protecting the rights of individual taxpayers.)

PRECONTACT ANALYSIS

Certain returns are subject to examination planning and analysis by an auditor before the taxpayer is contacted. Audits selected for precontact analysis include returns with complex issues, returns with possible unreported income, and returns which indicate a need for a visual inspection of the taxpayer's place of business or residence.

Often the precontact analysis includes a visit to the taxpayer's place of business. Such visits are usually reserved for those cases where the IRS has evidence that the taxpayer is committing criminal fraud.

AUTHORITY TO EXAMINE RECORDS

During a tax audit, IRS has the authority to examine the books and records of the taxpayer and those of any third party pertaining to the taxpayer. Refusal to permit the examination normally results in an agent's summons which, if not complied with, may be made a court order. The court order is enforceable by contempt proceedings. When the IRS examines records in possession of a third party which pertains to the taxpayer, the IRS is required to notify the taxpayer of the examination.

When an IRS agent issues a summons for the taxpayer to appear and produce certain records, at least 10 days notice is required. Chapter 9 contains a more detailed discussion on IRS summons.

The IRS is limited in examining the books of a taxpayer to once per taxyear unless others are permitted by the taxpayer or the IRS requests in writing and establishes the need for additional examination. This limitation, however, does not apply to public records or records belonging to others, such as records pertaining to your bank account kept by your bank.

In one case, where the IRS agent had violated the above rule regarding a second examination of the taxpayer's books, the Court of Claims allowed the IRS to establish a tax deficiency based on information obtained as a result of the second examination. The Court stated that not every infraction of a notice requirement requires nullification of an otherwise valid tax deficiency.

TAXPAYER'S PRESENCE AT AUDIT

In some cases, it is to the taxpayer's advantage not be personally present at the audit. The taxpayer may authorize an attorney or tax accountant to handle the IRS audit. The IRS audit manual was recently amended to indicate those situations where the auditor should insist on the presence of the taxpayer. The policy manual indicates that normally the IRS will not demand the taxpayer's presence at the first or initial conference. If the taxpayer is represented by a tax professional, in most cases it is to the advantage of the taxpayer not to be present at the audit. Some of the situations where the IRS will demand the taxpayer's presence include:

☐ Where the auditor suspects fraud.

- ☐ When the taxpayer's expenses exceed his or her income.
- ☐ When the audit concerns the gross receipts on Schedules C or F.
- ☐ Audits involving the possibility of unreported income.

If the audit involves a joint return and the IRS demands the presence of the taxpayer, normally only the taxpayer who either conducted the business or maintained the records will be required to appear at the initial audit meeting.

In those cases where the IRS has demanded the presence of the taxpayer, the IRS manual indicates that the auditor should not bypass the accountant or attorney and direct questions to the taxpayer without first asking permission from the authorized representative.

In most cases where the taxpayer is represented by an attorney or other tax professional, it may not be a good idea for the taxpayer to be present at the audit for the following reasons:

- ☐ Taxpayer may talk too much and thus provide the auditor with additional issues to audit.
- ☐ Taxpayers sometimes become angry and lose control.
- ☐ False statements given by a taxpayer at an audit may lead to criminal charges.
- ☐ Taxpayer may by his/her conduct cause the auditor to become suspicious.
- ☐ It is normally to the taxpayer's advantage for the auditor to know as little as possible about the taxpayer.
- ☐ Additional information that the taxpayer would know without referring to his/her books may be asked for by the auditor. If the taxpayer is not present, it would be more difficult to obtain that information, and the auditor may not wish to expend the additional effort.

YOUR REPRESENTATIVE

If the taxpayer is not going to be present at the examination, the representative must have a power of attorney to represent the taxpayer. (Note: only attorneys, Certified Public Accountants (CPA), and enrolled agents can represent a taxpayer at an audit.) The appointment should be made on IRS *Form 2848* (Appendix E). See discussion in Chapter 6 regarding getting professional help.

CORRESPONDENCE WITH IRS

As noted earlier, the taxpayer should promptly answer any correspondence received from the IRS. Failure to answer permits the IRS to assume that the answer will be unfavorable to the taxpayer. Often when dealing with the IRS, the taxpayer will receive computer-generated notices. Never ignore them. If they are incorrect, and you have previously pointed this out to the IRS, answer the new notice with a short letter enclosing with the letter a copy of your previous correspondence.

When answering the correspondence, answer only the questions asked. Do not volunteer any additional information except on advice of a tax professional. Always keep a copy of any correspondence with IRS. Always send your letters to IRS by *certified mail*. In answering IRS correspondence, always include the *taxpayer identification number (TIN)* and the *document locator number (DLN)* of the correspondence that you are answering.

The taxpayer identification number (TIN) is the nine-digit number which identifies the taxpayer. In cases of individual taxpayers, the TIN is the taxpayer's social security number. The IRS *document locator number (DLN)* is a 14-digit number which indicates the origin of the document, the date it was prepared, and the person who prepared it. For example, the DLN 3414133300134 is interpreted as follows:

34 = IRS District Office Locate Code

1 = tax class code (1 = Employment Tax Returns; 2 = Form 1040 Individual Tax Return and 3 = Form 1120 Corporate Return)

41 = document code (type of document)

333 = control date (denotes numeric day of the year—333th day or November 29th)

001 = block number of documents issued that day (first document)

34 = serial number or code number of preparer.

CONVERSATIONS WITH IRS

When discussing anything with an IRS agent, it is a good practice to follow the conversation with a written letter confirming your understanding of the conversation. If for example, you called the IRS office and had your appointment reset, write a letter to the IRS office confirming the change in appointment date. It is also important to make a log of each person at the IRS to which you have talked. Include in the log the name of the person, telephone number, (including the extension number), and a short summary of the conversation with the IRS person.

PLACE OF EXAMINATION

Except for mail audits, the only statutory rule concerning the place where a tax audit will be held is that the time and place of audit must be reasonable under the circumstances. If possible, a place should be selected that is to the taxpayer's advantage. When the IRS requests that the examination take place at an IRS branch office, it will normally be to the taxpayer's advantage to have the examination conducted there. This aspect is discussed more in detail later.

If the audit involves a business, normally the IRS will want to conduct the audit at the place of business because supporting documents are normally available there. For reasons stated below, it may not be to the taxpayer's advantage to have the audit at his or her business.

The IRS regulations provide the taxpayer with the right to transfer the examination to another district or to another office within the district for good reason. Generally, any request will be honored if the taxpayer has a valid reason, such as a change of address before or during the resolution of the examination.

Audits at Taxpayer's Place of Business

If possible, shift the audit to an IRS branch office or other location. By keeping the auditor out of the business locale, you lessen the chance of the auditor discovering additional information that could reflect adversely on your audit. Unhappy employees can talk to the auditors and posted office notices, may raise additional questions. In some cases, the business surroundings may cause additional questions.

If the audit is conducted in your business, instruct your employees to avoid conversations with the IRS auditor. If the auditor requests any information from your employees, have them channel all requests through one contact point. This allows the taxpayer to control the channels of information available to the auditor and also keeps the taxpayer informed of what records are being examined.

During the time that the auditor is present, do not schedule any sensitive business meetings. Limit the auditor's opportunity to observe the business routine. If at all possible, provide a quiet place away from the mainstream of the business for the auditor to work. Do not give the auditor a tour of the business unless absolutely necessary.

If the IRS requests the audit be conducted at the business site, and the taxpayer decides that it would be to his advantage not to have the audit at that location, the taxpayer should request a change in location. Acceptable reasons for the change include:

- ☐ The facilities are not adequate to provide a reasonable place to hold the audit.
- ☐ An audit at the business will unduly disrupt the business of the taxpayer.
- ☐ Noise or activity levels at the place of business would hinder the examination.
- ☐ Records are available at another location.
- ☐ Business location is inconvenient for the taxpayer's professional representative and therefore unnecessarily increases the taxpayer's expenses.

Audits at Taxpayer's Residence

If the audit is conducted at the taxpayer's residence, his or her standard of living will be under observation. Auditors are trained to observe the standard of living to determine if it is out of line with the level of reported income of the taxpayer. Therefore, if possible, shift the audit to a neutral site. If you have an attorney or accountant present at the audit, using their office as the location of the audit should be considered. This not only prevents an observation of the taxpayer's standard of living, but also may reduce the amount of time (and save money in the process) that the attorney or accountant will be utilized, because there will be no travel time on their part.

An IRS training manual states: "The auditor should observe the neighborhood, furnishings, automobiles, and the quality of clothes worn by the taxpayer and the family." Other items that the auditor is instructed to observe include the types of schools that the children attend; the shopping places and methods; their travel, entertainment, and recreation styles; and other signs of the taxpayer's standard of living.

PRIOR TO FIRST MEETING WITH AUDITOR

Before the first meeting, it is essential that the taxpayer or taxpayer's representative be familiar with the return. Remember the burden is on the taxpayer to convince the auditor that the return is proper. Accordingly, a better presentation can be made if the taxpayer has completely reviewed his or her return shortly before the first meeting.

It is also essential to have records in a logical order. The ploy of bringing a shoebox of receipts will not work. If your deductions are being questioned, take time to put your receipts in order so that they can be presented to your best advantage. Although it is a crime to "manufacture" false receipts prior to an audit, there is nothing wrong in rearranging your records in a logical order and using summary sheets that are backed up with receipts. As will be discussed later, it is permissible to reconstruct records.

DEMEANOR WITH AUDITOR

The taxpayer should be courteous and friendly to the auditor. Do not complain about high taxes—remember auditors also pay taxes. In addition, this is not the time to demonstrate any resistance to the present tax law structure. You do not want the auditor to use your case as an example or to provide him or her with any special reasons to thoroughly examine your tax returns.

Being friendly and courteous, however, does not mean that the taxpayer should be too cooperative. If the audit is conducted at your residence or business, you may offer the auditor coffee, tea, etc., but do not offer lunch or other favors. It may appear that you are trying to influence him or her. A taxpayer who is too friendly may cause the auditor to be suspicious. To prevent prolonging the audit, you do not want the auditor to be too comfortable during the audit.

Do not mistake a friendly, courteous attitude on the part of the examiner as an indication that he/she will be forgiving of the taxpayer and overlook problems. They can be very friendly while at the same time assessing the taxpayer huge additional tax liability. (Note: IRS examiners are trained to be adaptable, flexible, and yet protective of the government's revenue.)

Do not provide the examiner with unlimited access to a copy machine. By requiring the examiner to request of a contact person copies of each document allows you to keep track of each document copied by the examiner. In this regard, the taxpayer should keep a log of all documents that were examined or copied by the auditor. When an examiner has completed examination of requested records, they should be removed and not left in his/her presence.

During the course of the examination, let the auditor set the pace. Answer his or her questions, but do not volunteer any information. Many auditors are very good at piecing together bits of information; therefore, unrelated bits of information may trigger additional inquiry.

Do not argue that you should be allowed to take the deduction because you have always taken it. In this situation, the auditor may decide to audit other years. It is inappropriate to remark that other people are doing the same. This does not make the deduction legal.

If there is a disagreement with the auditor during the conduct of the examination, request that the issue be delayed until the conclusion of the audit. This prevents the agent from becoming stubborn and attempting to teach the taxpayer a lesson.

If the auditor asks questions for which you do not have the answer, inform the agent that you will need to obtain that information and that you will get back to him or her. If the issue is a major one, and you feel that you are right, do not concede the issue. Request that any decision on it be deferred until you have the supporting documents. If, however, you do not have the necessary receipts and will be unable to obtain verification of your contentions, do not promise to submit the nonexisting evidence at a later time. In this situation, it may be better to admit that the records to support your contentions do not exist.

When the Examiner Disappears

If, during the conduct of the audit, the examiner disappears without closing the audit, this may mean that the auditor is referring the case to the criminal division. The IRS manual instructs the examiner to suspend his/her examination and refer the case to the criminal division when criminal conduct is suspected.

If this happens, consult an attorney. Stop any cooperation with the IRS and do not make any statements or provide any additional information without an attorney's approval. Because there is no privileged communications rule for accountant/taxpayer communications, do not discuss the matter with your accountant.

If a new examiner takes over during the course of the audit, ask for identification. Check the identification card that the individual has to determine if she/he is a special agent. If so, stop all communications with the IRS and consult an attorney immediately. If the individual refuses to show his/her identification card or has an excuse for not showing it, call the police.

TO COOPERATE OR NOT

When the taxpayer is being audited, he/she is faced with the difficult decision of whether to cooperate or not to cooperate. By cooperating, the taxpayer may provide the IRS with sufficient information to increase the tax liability and/or establish fraud on the taxpayer's part. To fail to cooperate, however, may cause the examiner to question whether or not fraud is present.

Factors to be considered when making the decision as to whether or not to cooperate with the examiner are given below.

Who is conducting the examination and asking the questions? Is this a routine audit or is it being conducted by a revenue agent assigned to the fraud division? The taxpayer should seek the identity of the examiner and his/her position in the IRS.

Will cooperating with the examiner keep the him/her from reaching faulty conclusions?

Cooperating may, in a close case, prevent the examiner from referring the case for criminal prosecution. (Note: be very careful if possibility of criminal prosecution is present.)

Cooperation can be limited or selected. It should normally not be an all or nothing situation.

What will the taxpayer lose by cooperating? If the information will be obtained by the IRS anyway, such as bank accounts in the taxpayer's name, the taxpayer is only saving the government time in cooperating.

LIMITATIONS ON THE EXAMINER

There are some definite limitations placed on an examiner by IRS regulations and manuals. These limitations include:

☐ The examiner cannot assure the taxpayer that the records provided will not be used for criminal prosecution purposes.

☐ The examiner cannot accept taxpayer records for "restricted" purposes.

☐ The examiner may not disclose information regarding the tax status or the tax returns of a taxpayer unless authorized by regulation, statute, or court order to do so.

CONDUCT OF EXAMINATION

The examiner is instructed that the initial interview is the most important part of the examination. The examiner is trained to spend the first few minutes making the taxpayer comfortable and explaining the examination process to him/her. The taxpayer is asked if he/she has any questions at this point.

Goals of the examiner during the interviews, as set forth in the Audit Guidelines, are to develop sufficient information to make informal judgments regarding:

☐ The financial history and standard of living of the taxpayer.

☐ The nature of employment to determine relationship with other entities and the existence of expense allowances, etc.

☐ Any exchanges or bartering being done by the taxpayer.

☐ Any money or property received which was determined to be tax exempt and/or nontaxable.

☐ The potential for moonlighting income.

☐ Any real property, personal property, and bank accounts etc.

☐ Any recent purchases, sales, or exchange of property.

☐ The correctness of exemptions and dependents claimed.

The IRS guidelines remind the examiner that "the taxpayer is being examined and not just the return. Therefore develop all information to the fullest extent possible."

CLOSING AUDIT MEETING

If, at the end of the audit meeting, the taxpayer or authorized representative indicates that additional evidence is available to support the taxpayer's position, the auditor should either provide the taxpayer with an opportunity to obtain the additional information or issue a report pending additional information. If the auditor takes the latter action, then the taxpayer must submit the additional information within 15 days from the conclusion of the audit meeting. If the additional information is not received within the time alloted, then the report will be issued based on previously submitted information.

RESULTS OF EXAMINATION

The examination is normally concluded by the examiner proposing one of four possible adjustments. They are:

1. A "no change" in tax liability. This is the preferred outcome for the taxpayer. It means that the IRS has accepted his or her return "as filed" and the case is closed.
2. Adjustments are made in the tax liability of the taxpayer by the examiner, and the taxpayer accepts the adjustments.
3. Adjustments are proposed to the tax liability of the taxpayer, and there is only partial agreement by the taxpayer as to the correctness of these adjustments.
4. Adjustments are proposed to the tax liability of the taxpayer, and no agreement is reached between the taxpayer and the examiner.

If the proposed adjustments increase the taxpayer's tax liability, he or she will need to make a decision as to the next steps to take. The choices available to the taxpayer are:

☐ Agree to the new assessments and pay the additional taxes.
☐ Seek review by IRS Appeals Division (discussed in Chapter 7).
☐ To seek review by the judicial route as discussed in Chapter 8.

NEGOTIATIONS

Auditors are under pressure to process a high number of audits in the shortest time possible. Accordingly, the auditor is normally willing to accept a reasonable compromise. The higher the level of IRS involved, the more receptive they may be to negotiate regarding questionable issues.

The Internal Revenue Code does not permit compromise of a tax liability unless there is doubt as to liability, doubt as to collectability, or doubt as to both liability and collectability. If it is clear that the taxpayer owes the unpaid taxes and has the ability to pay them, then the IRS cannot compromise tax, interest, or penalty. Accordingly, equity or individual hardship not amounting to an inability to pay cannot be used to compromise a tax, interest, or penalty liability.

Comprise

Do not be pressured into accepting a settlement offered by the IRS auditor unless it is to your advantage. If you agree, then you may be precluded from litigating this issue later or appealing via the administrative route. In some cases, it may be to the taxpayer's advantage to compromise on an issue. If one is offered, the taxpayer should consider all aspects of the offer, including the time and effort saved in concluding the audit quickly.

Waivers

In most cases, prior to the assessment of additional tax liability, the IRS must issue the Notice of Deficiency (90-day letter). The 90-day letter is discussed in Chapters 7, 8, and 12. One purpose of the notice is to permit the taxpayer to petition to the Tax Court. Unless it is a jeopardy case, the IRS cannot start collective action until the 90-day period has expired.

In those cases where the taxpayer agrees with the additional assessment, the taxpayer is requested to sign a Waiver of Restrictions on Assessment and Collection of Deficiency. Form 870 is used for this purpose. If the waiver is for the entire amount deemed deficient by the examiner, it permits the IRS to immediately make an assessment of additional taxes and start collection activity. By signing the waiver, the taxpayer waives his/her appeal rights and allows the IRS to start immediate collection activity.

The waiver does not prevent the IRS from assessing additional taxes within the authorized period. It appears that the taxpayer may withdraw a waiver before an assessment of additional taxes is made by the IRS. If the taxpayer signs the waiver, no formal notice of deficiency is required. The waiver only binds the taxpayer, not the IRS.

If the taxpayer signs a Form 870, the examiner will normally prepare a report and forward it and the Form 870 to a review group of the Examination Division. Both the report and the form are reviewed. If the reviewer agrees with the examiner, normally the audit is concluded. If the reviewer does not agree, additional examinations or assessments may be made.

Legal Effects of the Waiver

In one case, a waiver was binding against a taxpayer even though the taxpayer signed the waiver by mistake. The taxpayer thought that he was signing a form that allowed for extending the time period of assessment. Note that in this case, there was no evidence that the taxpayer was misled by the auditor.

In another case, the waiver was upheld when the taxpayer signed a blank waiver form. The court stated that by signing a blank form, the taxpayer was authorizing the IRS to complete the form. In either of these two cases, if the taxpayer had been misled by the IRS, the waivers probably would not have been upheld.

If the return discloses an overpayment of taxes by the taxpayer and the taxpayer signs the waiver Form 870 as an acceptance of overpayment, the taxpayer is not required to file an amended return. The form is considered as a formal request for refund.

INADEQUATE RECORDS

Good record keeping is the best proof to substantiate your tax return. The use of running records (kept up daily) are most acceptable to the IRS, and in many cases, can be the difference between a successful and unsuccessful audit. In addition, often keeping good records helps prevent the taxpayer from overlooking deductions or adjustments.

The Internal Revenue Code requires every person to keep such records as the Secretary of Treasury may require. IRS regulations require taxpayers to maintain such accounting records as will enable him/her to file a correct return. The tax code also requires the taxpayer to maintain records sufficient to clearly reflect income. In addition, the taxpayer is required to maintain sufficient records to establish his/her right to deductions and adjustments to gross income. Chapter 14 contains a detailed discussion on keeping records for tax purposes.

If the IRS determines that a taxpayer's records are "inadequate," then they can use certain methods to arrive at the taxable income of a taxpayer. Methods used include *net worth* and *bank deposits*. The IRS's methods of arriving at the taxable income of a taxpayer are discussed later in this chapter.

The IRS has defined "inadequate records" as the lack of records, or records so incomplete that correctness of taxable income cannot be determined. If the IRS determines that the lack of adequate records was intentional, then civil or criminal fraud may be pursued.

If the taxpayer's records are inadequate, there is nothing illegal in reconstructing them. (Note: this is different from back-dating records, which may be a crime.) If the taxpayer claims that the records have been stolen or destroyed, then the examiner will expect a police or fire report to back up the claim. If the fire or police report is dated after notice of audit is received by the taxpayer, the examiner may be suspicious. In most cases, it will be better for the taxpayer to admit the inadequacy of the records rather than attempt to falsify receipts, etc.

ESTABLISHING NET INCOME AT AUDIT

The government often uses indirect methods to establish the net income of a taxpayer. In this regard, it is not necessary for the government to establish the exact amount of the taxpayer's income. All that is required is to establish that the taxpayer has substantially under-reported his/her income. The three most common indirect methods used by the government are increases in the net worth of a taxpayer, cash expenditures, and bank deposits.

Recent court cases have allowed the government to use circumstantial evidence to establish the taxable income of a taxpayer. The IRS may choose to proceed under any of the above methods or a combination of them.

Net Worth Method

The net worth method of establishing a taxpayer's income was approved by the U.S. Supreme Court in a 1943 case. In that case, involving a big-time Chicago gambler, the Court stated that the government could prove the annual taxable income of a taxpayer, when the taxpayers records are inadequate or false, by establishing the net change in worth of the taxpayer during that year.

The steps normally used in establishing taxable income by increase in net worth are:

☐ Taxpayer's net worth at the beginning of the tax year is estimated.
☐ Next, the taxpayer's net worth at the end of the tax year is estimated.
☐ The difference between the above two is then added to the nondeductible expenditures of the taxpayer including the taxpayer's living expenses.
☐ Finally, the government must either establish a likely source of income or negate the possible sources of nontaxable income.

The total is considered as the taxpayer's taxable income for the year. The burden is then on the taxpayer to establish that the increase in net worth is not due to taxable income.

Bank Deposit Method

The bank deposit method is usually used by the government in combination with other methods. The bank deposit method requires:

☐ The government establishes that the taxpayer had a profitable business during the tax year.
☐ That the taxpayer made deposits in bank accounts over which he/she exercised control.
☐ The allowable deductions, adjustments, and exemptions are subtracted from the total of all bank deposits for the year. (Note: deductions and exemptions reflecting cash payments are not allowable adjustments under this method.)
☐ The balance from the above is considered as the taxable income unless the taxpayer can establish otherwise.

In one case, where the government attempted to use the bank deposits method, the court allowed the taxpayer to exclude those deposits which were transfers from another bank whose receipts were already included. In this case, the taxpayer (a blind lawyer) was writing checks on one account and covering those checks with checks from another account (check kiting). He was allowed to exclude from his gross income those deposits that were merely transfers from one account to another.

One taxpayer deposited $30,000 into his bank account, claiming that it was a gift from his parents. The IRS considered this amount as unreported income. The Court stated that the burden to establish that the money was a gift and not income was on the taxpayer and that once the IRS has established that the taxpayer receives money, the IRS is not required to establish a possible income-producing activity.

Cash Expenditures Methods

Using the cash expenditures methods, the government must:

☐ Establish the taxpayer's net worth at the beginning of the taxyear.
☐ Establish that his/her expenditures exceed the initial net worth of the taxpayer.
☐ The amount by which the expenditures exceed the initial net worth is considered as the reconstructed income of the taxpayer. This is determined by adding total cash payments for goods and services and checks drawn to cash which cannot be traced to identifiable purchases.
☐ The government must prove, when using this method, that the defendant has a known source of income. It does not matter if the source of income is legal or illegal.

The cash expenditures method is often used when the government cannot establish the final net worth of the taxpayer.

CRIMINAL PROBLEMS

Chapter 10 contains a discussion regarding the question of criminal investigations and criminal prosecutions. In this chapter, only those criminal issues that effect the conduct of the audit are discussed.

The IRS Audit Guidelines state that the first indications of criminal conduct will be the attitudes and conduct of the taxpayer. The guidelines state that the examiner should be alert for the following actions:

☐ Repeated procrastination on the part of the taxpayer in making and keeping appointments for the examination.

☐ Uncooperative attitude displayed by not complying with requests for records, and not furnishing adequate explanations for discrepancies or questionable items.

☐ Failing to keep proper books and records, especially if previously advised to do so.

☐ A disregard for books and records.

☐ Destroying books and records without a plausible explanation.

☐ Making false, misleading, and inconsistent statements.

☐ Altering records.

☐ Paying in cash rather than using checks.

☐ Failing to deposit all receipts.

☐ A quick agreement to adjustments and undue concern about the immediate closing of the case may indicate a more thorough examination.

AGREEMENT REVIEW

Any agreement reached with the IRS District Offices must be reviewed by the regional office. The stated purpose of the IRS review is to assure unformity. The IRS policy manual states that a case may be reopened if there is evidence of fraud, collusion, etc. In addition, substantial error can be used as a reason for reopening the case. It is unusual for the regional office to set aside a settlement. Regional Directors are instructed not to reopen a case ''unless the ground for such action is a substantial one and the potential effect upon the tax liability is material.''

CHAPTER 6

Getting Professional Help

A taxpayer has the right to the assistance of a tax professional at any IRS audit or examination. Key concepts on arriving at the decision to seek help are listed below:

☐ When to get professional help is a critical decision that the taxpayer must decide.

☐ If a tax return involves complicated accounting issues, consideration should be given to obtaining the assistance of tax accountant.

☐ If a tax return involves possible criminal or civil fraud problems, a tax attorney is needed.

☐ If the audit is being done by an IRS special agent, an attorney is needed.

☐ Not all accountants and attorneys are equally qualified to present a taxpayer before the IRS or court.

☐ It is very difficult to evaluate a tax professional.

☐ Prior to hiring the tax professional, interview him/her to ascertain if he/she is the correct person for you.

☐ Always, before hiring a tax professional, ensure that you have a clear understanding of the costs involved and how the costs will be computed.

For a tax professional to practice before the IRS he/she must be an attorney, certified public accountant, or an enrolled agent. At one time, attorneys and accountants were required to be admitted to practice before the Treasury Department before they could represent a taxpayer before the IRS or any subdivision thereof. Now, attorneys and accountants who are certified public accountants (CPAs) may represent taxpayers by filing a written declaration of their qualifications in their States. In addition, persons other than attorneys or CPAs may take a qualifying examination to practice before the IRS.

In all cases, the professional will need written authorization from the taxpayer to represent him/her in any tax dispute. The authorization is accomplished by the taxpayer signing a Form 2848, *Power of Attorney and Declaration of Representative* (Appendix E). In the case of a joint return, both parties should sign. (Note: anyone familiar with the taxpayer's tax transactions may testify or explain taxpayer's records, but may not present arguments or legal theories unless authorized to practice before the IRS.)

WHEN TO GET PROFESSIONAL HELP

When to get professional help is not an easy question. If the examination is an in-depth one and/or the return is very complex, professional help may be a necessity. Even in those cases where the taxpayer chooses not to have a tax professional represent him/her at the audit, prior consultation with one before the audit is recommended. Factors that the taxpayer should consider in making the decision of whether to obtain professional help include:

- ☐ Type of audit involved. In the case of a mail audit, professional help is normally not needed. If the audit is a field audit, however, careful consideration should be given to obtaining professional help.
- ☐ Type of IRS examiner doing the audit. If the individual doing the audit is a special agent, then an attorney is needed. Special agents are normally involved only in those cases where fraud is suspected.
- ☐ Complexity of the issues involved. If the audit is limited to issues of receipts or verification, professional help may not be needed.
- ☐ If a tax professional will be used, the earlier that the professional is involved in the audit, the better for the taxpayer.
- ☐ Professional help is not cheap. Failure, however, to get expert help when needed is costly.
- ☐ Finally, the ability of the taxpayer to speak for him/herself should be considered, along with the taxpayer's depth of knowledge regarding the tax issues involved.

WHERE TO FIND HELP

If professional help is needed, the taxpayer must decide on whether he/she needs an attorney, accountant (CPA), or enrolled agent. *Enrolled agents* are specialists who have passed a test to qualify them for practice before the IRS. As a general rule, if the issues involve complex accounting problems, bookkeeping questions, etc., the CPA or enrolled agent is recommended. If the issues involve civil or criminal fraud, issues of law, etc., then normally a criminal tax attorney is needed.

SELECTING A TAX PROFESSIONAL

One problem in selecting a tax professional is the inability of the average taxpayer to rate the ability of the professional. In addition, some tax attorneys are good in tax planning, but not in audit problems. The same concepts are true for tax accountants. In selecting a tax professional, the below listed factors should be considered:

☐ Does the professional answer your questions with ease and with apparent technical competence?

☐ Is the professional current on recent changes to tax laws, recent IRS regulatory changes, and court decisions?

☐ Does the professional provide you with a comprehensive analysis of your tax situation in clear and understandable language?

☐ Does the professional spend time discussing legitimate methods to reduce tax liabilities? (This factor may not be important in audit situations.)

☐ Does the professional provide you with practical audit planning suggestions?

☐ Does he/she keep appointments (on time)? Is he/she accessible and prompt in returning telephone calls?

☐ Does he/she provide you with a clear understanding of his/her fees and costs up front? Is his/her price reasonable?

☐ Will he/she represent you at any audits, and if so, at what cost?

☐ Are the two of you compatible?

In selecting an attorney or accountant, remember that many are unfamiliar with IRS procedures and practices. In some cases, an attorney or accountant who does not understand tax law and procedures can be a detriment to your case. Introductory questions that should be asked of them should include:

☐ Have you ever worked for the IRS?

☐ Do you regularly handle tax cases, other than tax planning and pre-audit problems?

☐ What is your experience with the IRS Collections Division?

☐ What tactics should be used in my case? Why?

FINDING PROFESSIONAL ASSISTANCE

Use of common sense is important in searching for a tax professional. Often, people evaluate a tax professional by the size of fees the professional charges. Research indicates that fees charged have little relationship to the ability of the individual. Many good tax professionals have very reasonable fees, and unfortunately, there are some inept professionals who charge high fees.

Many taxpayers wrongly consider gray hair or maturity on the part of the tax professional as an indication of experience and competence. A problem with this indicator is that some professionals fail to keep themselves current and thus may be outdated. Others have one year's experience repeated 20 times rather than 20 years of varied experience. An inept attorney or accountant is too expensive at any price.

Attorneys and accountants who advertise may be good salespersons and inept professionals. Competent attorneys and accountants rely on referrals rather than advertising to obtain new clients. Fancy offices are often wrongly used by clients to evaluate the quality of the professional. (He-must-be-good-to-afford-this-office concept.) One of the most competent criminal tax attorneys I know has his offices in an old rundown building.

It is important to shop for a tax professional. Check with others who have had tax problems regarding their recommendations, check with local universities or law schools, the bar association, law directories, or directories of CPAs. The time invested in locating the correct tax professional for you is normally time well invested. The key thing is to find the right person for your situation. Common sense should be your best guide. Interview the person before you retain him/her. The questions listed above should be utilized during the interview.

If you feel uneasy with the professional during this first interview, trust your intuition and do not retain him/her. The reverse, however, is not true. Do not make a quick judgment in hiring.

RELATIONSHIP WITH TAX PROFESSIONAL

Whether the taxpayer hires a tax attorney or an accountant, the relationship with the professional should be a professional one. Obtain a clear understanding of the fee arrangements, including how you will be billed and for what you will be billed. In tax problems, the common fee arrangement is a retainer plus an hourly rate. It will not be cheap.

Because the professional's time is the standard measurement of his/her fee, the taxpayer should do as much as possible to reduce the amount of time that the professional will expend on the case. If certain records are needed, the taxpayer should provide them or obtain them to save the professional's time. Keep an accurate record of your dealings with the attorney or accountant. If you feel that his/her fees are too high, discuss it with the professional.

FIRING YOUR TAX PROFESSIONAL

Both the client and the tax professional have certain basic rights that each other should honor. You have the right to be treated fairly, honestly, and courteously. You also have the right to a fair billing. If, for some reason, it is not working out between you and your professional assistance, consideration should be given to retaining a new professional. The earlier this is accomplished, the better.

If the conflict is based on serious breeches of duty by the attorney or the accountant, consideration should be given to reporting the problems to the local bar association or professional accounting board of the State.

When you discharge the attorney or accountant, you have a right to obtain your files from the professional. If the professional fails to turn them over, report the individual. The files pertaining to your case belong to you, not the professional. In most states, an attorney has no right to retain your files until you have paid him/her.

IRS INVESTIGATIONS OF PROFESSIONALS

A negative aspect of hiring a tax professional is that in some cases, the IRS will take action against a taxpayer because the taxpayer is a client of a targeted tax professional. See the discussion in Chapter 5 regarding IRS's list of problem tax preparers. There are many cases where the IRS has conducted investigations of taxpayers because they retained certain attorneys and CPAs. One attorney sued the IRS in 1985 in an attempt to prevent the IRS from investigating his clients. He was unsuccessful. Accordingly, if during prehiring discussions with the tax professional, he or she indicates that he or she has had problems with IRS investigations, do not hire that person.

TO TELL THE TRUTH

After the tax professional has been selected, the next decision is how open to be with the professional. The general rule is that with your attorney, tell him/her everything. Any information you provide the attorney regarding past events can not be used against you. They are considered privileged communications. Only with full disclosure will the attorney be able to adequately prepare the taxpayer's case.

With your accountant or enrolled agent, the taxpayer should be careful not to disclose any information that may tend to incriminate him/her. The taxpayer, however, should not deliberately mislead his/her tax professional.

The privileged communications rule between an attorney and his/her client does not apply to the below situations:

☐ Information disclosed by the client as to future misconduct. For example, if the taxpayer tells his/her attorney that he/she intends to commit perjury, the attorney may be under an obligation to report this fact.

☐ Information that is overheard by others not associated with the attorney. For example, discussions in public under circumstances where it is clear that the conversation was not meant to be confidential.

☐ Records provided to the attorney. (Keep records in your possession. These records may be subject to court orders to turn them over if they are in the possession of the attorney. There is greater protection available to the taxpayer when the records are in the taxpayer's possession. This is discussed later.)

CHAPTER 7

Appealing IRS Decisions

Some key concepts in appealing IRS decisions are listed below:

☐ IRS decisions may be appealed administratively within the IRS, and if unsuccessful, the taxpayer can still pursue Tax Court or a refund suit.

☐ If the taxpayer does not agree with the auditor, he/she may request a conference with the auditor's supervisor.

☐ Normally the IRS issues a 30-day notice after an audit. This 30-day letter provides the taxpayer with an opportunity to prepare his/her case for an administrative appeal.

☐ There is no statutory requirement to issue a 30-day letter. Accordingly, the taxpayer may not contest an assessment on the failure of the IRS to issue a 30-day letter.

☐ A formal protest must be in writing and addressed to the District Director. It will then be forwarded by the Director to the Appeals Office of the Regional Director.

☐ In most cases where the taxpayer's tax liability is under $10,000, there is no requirement for a formal protest.

☐ In most cases, the 90-day notice is effective when it is mailed.

☐ There is no particular form required for the 90-day notice.

☐ The 90-day notice suspends all collection action until the 90-day period has expired.

☐ Indicating a new address on the next year's tax return is not considered as formal notice to the IRS of an address change.

☐ The Problem Resolution Program is used to assist taxpayers who have been unable to resolve their problems using the normal channels.

In this chapter methods to attack IRS decisions will be discussed. The first part of the chapter focuses on IRS requirements that must be complied with before collective action may be taken against a taxpayer. In the second part, whether to take the administrative or judicial route is discussed.

TAKING THE ADMINISTRATIVE ROUTE

In this section, using appellate procedures within the IRS are discussed. The procedures may be used whether or not the taxpayer has received a 90-day notice. (Note: although the taxpayer may use the administrative procedures after receiving a 90-day notice, the time period within which to file a case with the Tax Court continues to run.) See discussion on filing a case with Tax Court for additional information regarding the effects of the 90-day letter. See detailed discussion later in this chapter regarding effects of the 90-day letter.

If You Do Not Agree With the Examiner

If the taxpayer does not agree with the examiner's findings at the conclusion of the audit, the taxpayer may request a meeting with the examiner's supervisor to discuss the findings. If no agreement is reached with the supervisor, the taxpayer may file an appeal using the IRS's administrative appellate system or litigate the issues in court. One advantage of using the administrative route is that if the taxpayer loses, he/she can still litigate the issues in court. (Note: if the grounds for the appeal involve disagreement with the Internal Revenue Code, the IRS administrative route may not be used.)

Appeal Within the Service

There is a single level of appeal from the findings of the examiner (other than the informal conference with the supervisor). The appeals within the IRS are handled by the Office of Regional Director of Appeals.

30-Day Letter

In most cases, after the conclusion of the audit, if there is no agreement between the examiner and the taxpayer, the District Director will issue a 30-day letter (preliminary notice of deficiency). (Note: there is no statutory requirement to issue a 30-day letter. In addition, the District Director can extend the 30-day notice to allow the taxpayer to prepare his/her case for administrative appeal.)

The purpose of the 30-day letter is to notify the taxpayer that unless he/she submits an administrative appeal within 30 days, a statutory notice of tax deficiency will be issued (the 90-day letter).

In some cases, the Director will forego the preliminary 30-day notice and issue the statutory 90-day letter (Notice of Deficiency). In these cases, the taxpayer must file a petition in Tax Court within the 90 days or lose the right to litigate the issues in Tax Court. For example, in those cases where the statute of limitations is about to run out, and the taxpayer fails to waive the time period, the Director will immediately issue the 90-day letter.

An important factor to keep in mind is that the 30-day letter and the 90-day each have their own time frames. In some cases, the IRS has mailed a 30-day letter one day and a 90-day letter two weeks later. In these cases, taxpayers must monitor the 90-day statutory period for filing with the Tax Court.

Written Protest

A formal protest must be in writing and addressed to the District Director. The protest should contain as a minimum:

- ☐ Statement that an appeal is desired.
- ☐ Taxpayer's name, address, and tax identification number.
- ☐ The IRS symbols that were in the 30-day letter (if one was received).
- ☐ Date of the 30-day letter.
- ☐ The taxyear in issue.
- ☐ Itemized schedule of the adjustments that are being protested.
- ☐ A statement of facts supporting the taxpayer's position on any issues with which the taxpayer does not agree. (Statement must be sworn to.)
- ☐ If a 90-day letter has been received, similar information from the 90-day letter.

The statement of facts, as noted above, must be sworn to. The following declaration will be accepted by the IRS:

> Under the penalties of perjury, I declare that
> I have examined the statement of fact presented
> in this protest and in any accompanying schedules
> and, to the best of my knowledge and belief, it is
> true, correct, and complete.

When Formal Protests Are Not Required

Formal written protests are not required in the following cases:

- ☐ The proposed increase or decrease in tax, or claimed refund is not more than $10,000 for any of the tax periods involved. (The value of $10,000 was increased in 1986 from $2,500.)

☐ The examination was conducted by correspondence or in an IRS office by a tax auditor.

In those cases where formal protests are not required, the taxpayer may request the appellate procedures by letter.

Conduct of the Appeal

As can be noted from Fig. 7-1, after the protest is filed the case goes to the Appeals Office in the Office of the Regional Director. The Appeals Office will arrange for an appeals conference at a convenient time and place.

The proceedings at the appeals conference are informal, and no testimony is taken. There will normally be a representative of the audit division of the District Director's office present at the conference. In most cases, the representative will not be the same examiner who audited the taxpayer's case.

Any additional evidence is normally presented by affidavits (sworn statements). In most cases, new or unrelated issues not raised by the original examiner are not raised. If any issues were settled by agreement with the examiner, those issues are also not considered at the conference.

Settlement

The Appeals Office has more latitude to settle a case than does an examiner. For example, the appellate officer can consider the problems and costs of litigation when evaluating a settlement offer with the taxpayer. In many cases, the appeals officer may be under pressure to settle cases. This makes them more likely to accept reasonable offers of settlement.

If there is no resolution of the case, or if the appeals officer agrees with the examiner, then the IRS will usually issue the statutory notice of tax deficiency (the 90-day letter). As discussed in Chapter 8, at this point the taxpayer may either pay the tax, file for a refund, and then (after the refund claim is denied), sue in District Court or the Court of Claims; or delay paying the tax and file a petition with the Tax Court within the statutory 90 days.

Partial Settlement

If the taxpayer agrees with part of the appellate decision but not all of it, the taxpayer may make a payment for the partial amount in order to stop the interest penalty on it.

Representation

A taxpayer may represent him/herself or may be represented by an attorney, certified public accountant, or an enrolled agent. The representative must have a power of attorney if he will not be accompanied by the taxpayer.

Income Tax Appeal Procedure

Internal Revenue Service

At any stage of procedure:
You can agree and arrange to pay
You can ask the Service to issue
you a notice of deficiency so you
can file a petition with the Tax Court.
You can pay the tax and file a claim
for a refund

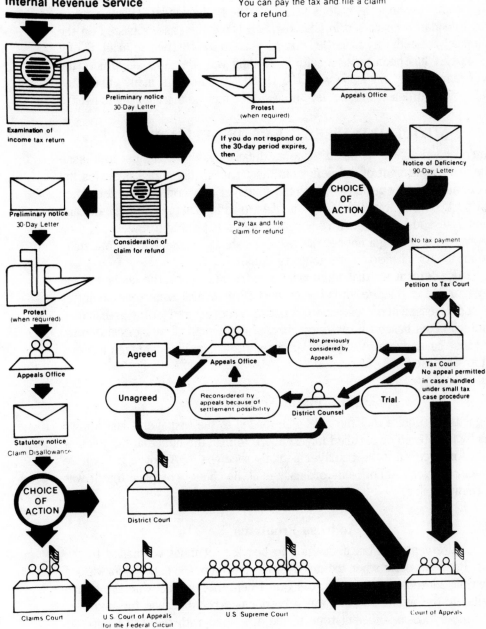

Examination of income tax return

Preliminary notice 30-Day Letter

Protest (when required)

Appeals Office

If you do not respond or the 30-day period expires, then

Notice of Deficiency 90-Day Letter

Preliminary notice 30-Day Letter

Consideration of claim for refund

Pay tax and file claim for refund

CHOICE OF ACTION

No tax payment

Protest (when required)

Appeals Office

Petition to Tax Court

Statutory notice Claim Disallowance

Agreed

Unagreed

Appeals Office

Reconsidered by appeals because of settlement possibility

Not previously considered by Appeals

District Counsel

Trial

Tax Court No appeal permitted in cases handled under small tax case procedure

CHOICE OF ACTION

District Court

Claims Court

U.S. Court of Appeals for the Federal Circuit

U.S. Supreme Court

Court of Appeals

IRS SETTLEMENTS AFTER 90-DAY LETTER

Once the IRS has issued a 90-day letter, it can still continue to attempt to settle the case. In fact, for four months after a petition is filed in Tax Court, the Appeals Office has exclusive settlement authority over most tax cases. This settlement authority continues until the case is placed on the trial calendar. (Placement on the trial calendar is discussed in Chapter 12.) Once the case is placed on the trial calendar, the authority to settle is transferred to the District Counsel. (Note: if the taxpayer has been unsuccessful in settling with the Appeals Office, the taxpayer may wish to try again with the District Counsel. In many cases, the counsel is over-burdened with numerous cases and may be more willing to listen.)

NOTICE AND ASSESSMENT OF DEFICIENCY

Before collection activity is taken for a tax deficiency, the IRS must first issue a notice and assessment of deficiency. In most cases, this notice provides the taxpayer with a 90-day period in which the taxpayer may contest the deficiency in Tax Court. (Note: "tax deficiency" applies to additional taxes, interests, and penalties assessed.) The notice requirement does not apply to taxes listed on the return. On receiving a notice, the taxpayer should examine it to determine whether it meets all the requirements to constitute due notice.

If the IRS determines that additional taxes are due against the taxpayer, and the taxpayer does not agree, then the District Director will issue a 90-day letter (Notice and Assessment of Deficiency). A notice is not required for the assessment of additional taxes based on the correction of mathematical or clerical errors. (Note: those cases where the taxpayer agrees to the additional taxes are discussed in Chapter 5.)

Mailing of Notice

The regulations require that the notice be mailed to the taxpayer's last-known address by registered or certified mail. Failure to mail the notice in the manner prescribed is excused if the taxpayer actually receives it. Accordingly, where a taxpayer receives the notice by ordinary mail, he cannot complain that it was not correctly mailed.

Address Problems

For the assessment of a tax deficiency to be valid, it must be mailed to the taxpayer. Problems occur when the taxpayer has moved or the notice is forwarded to the wrong address. In one case, the Court held that the fact that the notice was mailed to the wrong address was a harmless error, because the taxpayer received the notice in sufficient time to file a petition with the Tax Court.

The rules do not require that the notice be received by the taxpayer, only that it be mailed to the last-known address of the taxpayer. If the taxpayer has failed to notify the IRS of his/her new address, the IRS can continue to use the last-known one.

In one case, notice was held improper where the IRS mailed via certified mail to the last-known address. The mail was then forwarded to another address and thereafter returned to the IRS marked unclaimed. The Court stated that the IRS had a duty to make an effort to ascertain the correct address. In this case, the Court held that the returned notice put the IRS on notice as to the incorrectness of the address. (Note: apparently if the notice had not been returned, then the IRS could continue the collection action.)

In one case, it was held that the Commissioner did not send the notice to the proper address when the taxpayer had furnished an agent in the District Office with the new address, but not the agent assigned to the case. In another case, the IRS sent a notice to the wrong address and a copy to the taxpayer's accountant, who notified the taxpayer of the notice. The Court held in this case that the notice was not valid even though the taxpayer was informed of it by his accountant.

Notice received by the taxpayer mailed to the correct address is valid even where the IRS failed to send a copy to the attorney named as the representative in a power of attorney in the case.

In cases of joint returns, if either spouse indicates that his or her address is different from the other, then the IRS is required to mail notices to each spouse.

Indicating a new address on the next year's tax return is not considered a formal notice to the IRS of an address change.

Effective Date of Notice

In most cases, the notice is effective when it is mailed. One court held that the 90-day notice period started when the properly addressed notice was mailed to the taxpayer by registered mail. In this case, the mail was delivered to the taxpayer almost two months after mailing. The Court refused to extend the 90-day period, based on the fact that the time period started on the day after mailing. (Note: if the notice is personally handed to the taxpayer, the notice period began on the day after it was given to the taxpayer.)

In one case, the Tax Court held that where a notice was mailed to one address and returned to the IRS because of a change of address, the 90-day period began to run on the date the second notice was mailed. In a case where the 90-day notice was mailed to the warden of a prison for a prisoner, the time did not start until the notice was delivered to the prisoner. (Note: in this last case, if the notice had been mailed directly to the prisoner at the prison, the time would probably start on the day after it was mailed.)

When filing a petition in Tax Court after the 90-day period, the taxpayer must state in the petition any deficiencies in the notice which would lengthen the time period.

Required Notice Form

There is no particular form required for the notice. It must clearly advise the taxpayer that an additional tax deficiency has been determined. In one case, an unsigned notice was held a valid notice.

The IRS normally includes in the 90-day letter advice to the taxpayer regarding the taxpayer's rights of appeal. The failure, however, to include this advice does not render the notice invalid.

Except in cases of fraud, the IRS cannot send additional notices of deficiency for the same taxyear after a taxpayer has filed a petition in Tax Court. If no petition is filed, then the IRS may file additional notices until the 6-year period of limitations expires.

Effects of Notice

The notice suspends the statute of limitations on the assessment and collection of taxes. Unless a jeopardy determination is made, the notice also suspends all collection activity until the 90 days have expired.

Military Personnel

In most cases, the Soldiers' and Sailors' Civil Relief Act extends the time in which a military person has to answer or file a petition in court. In tax deficiency cases, however, the provisions of the Soldiers' and Sailors' Civil Relief Act is expressly made inapplicable to any limitation periods under the Internal Revenue Code.

IRS Motives

Many taxpayers have attempted to invalidate the 90-day notice based on improper motives of the IRS personnel in issuing the notices. In most cases, the courts have refused to question the motives of the IRS in issuing such notices. One court indicated that only in an "extraordinary misconduct" situation would the court question the motive of IRS in issuing a notice.

Withdrawal of Notice

If both the taxpayer and the IRS agree, the IRS can rescind the statutory notice of deficiency prior to the expiration of the 90 days. If this occurs, the legal effect is the same as if no notice was ever issued. Accordingly, a new notice could be issued if the statute limitations has not expired.

Notice Relating to Several Years

The statutory notice can cover several years in one notice. In one case, the IRS issued a statutory notice covering years 1979, 1980, and 1981. At the time that the taxpayer received the notice, the statute of limitations had expired for the taxyear 1979. The taxpayer contended that because the notice was illegal for 1979, it was not a valid notice for the taxyears 1980 and 1981. The Court disagreed and held that a notice relating to several years is divisible. Accordingly, the notice was valid for taxyears 1980 and 1981.

Based on Invalid Information

Some taxpayers have been successful in attacking the deficiency notice if the basis for the notice was based on invalid information. For example, in one case, the IRS made a determination that the individual had $100,000 of unreported income from a labor racketeering payoff. The Court ruled that the IRS could not base the notice on any illegal payoff without evidence of a payoff.

In a somewhat similar case, however, the Court upheld the notice issued by the IRS based on grand jury testimony. (Note: there is a statute which makes the use of grand jury testimony for this purpose illegal. The Court stated that the IRS violated the statute in basing the notice on this evidence, but the notice was not null and void.)

PROBLEM RESOLUTION PROGRAM

The IRS Commissioner, in 1977, established a Problems Resolution Program (PRP). There is a Problems Resolution Officer and supporting staff in each tax district. The Officer has direct access with the District Director.

The PRP assists taxpayers who have been unable to resolve their problems using normal Internal Revenue Service channels. The PRP does not handle appeals of decisions made in tax examinations, Freedom of Information Act requests, and Privacy Act inquiries. The program also does not handle complaints regarding the hiring practices of the IRS.

The PRP can assist taxpayers with computer foul-ups, missing refund checks, etc. When referring a matter to the PRP office, the taxpayer must establish that he or she has exhausted the normal channels to solve the problem. The IRS states that the PRP office will solve the problem within five days of its referral to that office. The offices, however, are flooded with requests, and the five-day rule is not being complied with.

RULES OF PRACTICE BEFORE THE IRS

This section contains a summary of the rules of practice before the IRS. The majority of the material for this chapter is taken from the *Federal Register*, Volume 31, beginning at page 10,773. If the reader needs a more in-depth discussion of the rules, he/she may refer to the Register and to *IRS Circular 230.*

Authority to Practice

"Practice before the Internal Revenue Service" refers to all matters connected with the representation of a taxpayer before the IRS and includes the preparation and filing of documents, correspondence, etc. with the IRS. It also includes the representation of taxpayers at conferences, hearings, and meetings.

Who May Practice

Taxpayers have a right to represent themselves in any matter pending with the IRS or any court. Traditionally, the right of self-representation has been a basic right in our society. The big problem with self-representation is the fact that individuals have a tendency to be emotional when dealing with personal tax problems. Accordingly, a reasonable, detached unemotional approach rather than an impassioned plea is difficult to accomplish when one is defending one's self. There is an old saying regarding self-representation that goes: "The attorney who represents himself has a fool for a client."

Tax Professional

As discussed in Chapter 6, there are three types of tax professionals that are permitted to represent a taxpayer before the IRS. They are an attorney, a certified public accountant, and an enrolled agent. An attorney no longer needs to be admitted to practice before the tax court as long as he is licensed to practice in his home State. Similar requirements exist for certified public accountants. Enrolled agents are persons who have passed an IRS examination on tax matters. Chapter 6 discusses when to hire a professional and who to hire.

Government Employees

Government employees may not practice before the IRS on behalf of a taxpayer unless the taxpayer is the employee or is part of the immediate family of the government employee.

Tax Return Preparers

Persons who prepare tax returns may not practice before the IRS unless they qualify as an attorney, CPA, or an enrolled agent. In some cases, they may be called as a witness at a hearing for either the IRS or the taxpayer.

General Rules and Limitations

Listed below are some of the general rules and limitations for persons practicing before the IRS. They are:

- [ ] The person cannot also serve as a notary public and take the acknowledgments or perform the official services of a notary in any matter before the IRS in which he/she is involved as a taxpayer or tax professional.
- [ ] No tax professional shall represent a client before the IRS in any matter in which there is a conflict or potential conflict of interest.
- [ ] Tax professionals cannot make uninvited solicitations for the business of practice before the IRS.
- [ ] Tax professionals cannot, except in cases involving themselves as taxpayers, endorse or otherwise endorse any check issued by the government pertaining to a tax matter.
- [ ] The Secretary of the Treasury, after due notice and an opportunity for a hearing, has the authority to suspend any person from practicing before the IRS who is incompetent, refuses to comply with rules and regulations, or who is involved in unethical conduct.

Records

The IRS is required to maintain a roster of all persons enrolled as ''enrolled agents'' to practice before the IRS, and a roster of all persons disbarred or suspended from practice before the IRS.

PREPARER PENALTIES

The IRS estimates that approximately one-half of all taxpayers use some form of professional or commercial tax advice in preparing their returns. Accordingly, a great degree of compliance with the tax code and administrative regulations depend on tax preparers. To prevent abuses in the system, the IRS has, since 1976, imposed penalties on preparers as one method to encourage voluntary compliance with the tax requirements.

The penalties apply to any person who received compensation for tax assistance or who employs others to prepare tax returns. In one case, the IRS held an attorney liable as a tax preparer when the attorney reviewed the return for a fee prior to the return being mailed. Persons who, without pay, review or prepare returns for friends, relative, etc., are not considered as tax preparers.

Some of the standard penalties are:

- [ ] $100 for failure of tax preparer to sign the return.
- [ ] $500 for willfull attempts to understate the tax liability.

☐ $1,000 for aiding a taxpayer to illegally evade taxes.

☐ $500 for endorsing a tax refund check other than his/her own.

☐ $25 for failure to furnish the taxpayer with a copy of the tax return.

☐ $25 penalty on the tax preparer if taxpayer fails to sign the return or fails to put a social security number on the return.

☐ $25 penalty for failure of the tax preparer to put his or her identifying number on the return.

In addition to the above penalties, in some cases the tax preparer may be liable for criminal penalties.

CHAPTER 8

Taking the IRS to Court

You have the right to appeal any decisions made by the IRS in a court of law. Some key concepts in litigating tax cases are listed below:

- ☐ The taxpayer has a choice of three courts, the Tax Court, the U.S. Court of Claims, and the U.S. District Courts.
- ☐ The Tax Court is the most popular because the alleged tax deficiencies are not required to be paid prior to instituting suit, and the Tax Court's procedures are the simplest.
- ☐ Before filing a claim in District Court or Court of Claims, the taxpayer must first pay the alleged taxes and then file a refund suit in either of these courts.
- ☐ In cases pending before the Tax Court, the interest on the alleged unpaid taxes continue to run. If the taxes are determined to be valid, then the accumulated interest must also be paid.
- ☐ In cases before the District Court or the Court of Claims, because the taxes have been paid and the taxpayer is claiming a refund, interests on the taxes do not continue to accumulate.
- ☐ It may be easier to settle tax disputes during litigation in Tax Court than with the Assistant U. S. Attorneys who handled the cases in the District Courts.
- ☐ Cases pending in Tax Court may be reconsidered by the Appellate Division of the IRS and settled to the taxpayer's benefit.
- ☐ All three courts have a backlog of cases, especially the Tax Court. This increases the pressure on both the IRS and the taxpayer to settle the case.

☐ Tax Court has a small claims division that handles matters where the amount in issue is less than $10,000.

☐ The small claims division of Tax Court has summary procedures. Taxpayers have no right to appeal cases decided in the small claims division.

CHOICE OF COURTS

In determining whether or not to take the IRS to court and to which court, several factors must be considered. One key question involves the chances of a taxpayer winning in court compared to the administrative route. The below listed percentages are presented as an indicator of chances of winning in the various courts.

In Tax Court—Taxpayer wins approximately 7 percent of the time. IRS wins approximately 51 percent of the time. In approximately 42 percent of the cases, the court finds partially for each.

In District Court—Taxpayer wins approximately 31 percent of the time. IRS wins approximately 56 percent and the remaining 13 percent are split decisions.

In U.S. Claims Court—Taxpayer wins approximately 46 percent of the time. IRS wins about 46 percent, and about 8 percent are split decisions.

WHICH COURT?

In a dispute with the IRS that cannot be settled by using the IRS's administrative procedures, the taxpayer must decide which of three judicial routes that he/she wishes to take. As noted above, the taxpayer wins more often in the U.S. Court of Claims and less often in Tax Court. There are, however, other factors involved that should be considered before the final decision on the appropriate judicial route to take.

In most cases, the only way that a taxpayer can get his/her case before the U.S. Court of Claims or a U.S. District Court is to pay the alleged tax deficiency and file a refund suit in either court. The taxpayer, however, does not pay the deficiency prior to instituting a petition with the Tax Court. For cases involving small deficiency amounts, there are summary procedures available in Tax Court that are not present in the other two courts.

Cases will be tried quicker in Tax Court than in U.S. District Courts or the U.S. Court of Claims. The legal fees will probably be much higher for cases tried in District Court and less in Tax Court because of the more complex procedural rules used in District Courts. The taxpayer has a right to a jury trial in either the District Court or Court of Claims, but not in Tax Court. In all of the courts, attorney fees may be awarded the taxpayer.

The U. S. Tax Court is considered a court of record as are the District and Claims Courts. (A court of record is one that keeps a formal record of its proceedings.) The Tax Court is not in any way connected with the IRS.

REFUND SUITS

If the taxpayer pays the deficiency alleged by the IRS, then he/she may bring suit in either a U. S. District Court or the Court of Claims. The basis for suits in either the District Court or the Court of Claims is on an overpayment of taxes. If, for some reason, the claim of overpayment of taxes, interests, or penalties by the taxpayer is not present, the case will be dismissed.

The rules governing suits by taxpayers in a District Court or the Court of Claims are set forth in the *Judicial Code (Title 28)*. Suits may not be brought in both courts for the same refund claim. A suit for refund was at one time maintained against the District Director of Internal Revenue. Now, the suit must state the United States as the defendant.

In a refund suit, the taxpayer is the plaintiff. Accordingly, the burden of proof to establish that a refund is due rests with the taxpayer. There is, however, no presumption of correctness of the tax assessment.

As noted earlier, the taxpayer must pay the tax alleged before bringing a refund suit. In addition, the taxpayer must file a claim for refund with the IRS. The requirement to file for a refund with the IRS can, in some cases, delay the processing to the case by six months.

The U.S. Supreme Court held that before a taxpayer could bring a refund suit, the taxpayer must pay the entire amount alleged due by IRS. In this particular case, the taxpayer had made a partial payment and then filed a suit for refund. The Court did not consider the fact that the taxpayer was unable to pay the entire amount due. (Note: in any refund suit, the IRS can assert a counterclaim for taxes due in other years.)

If the amount paid by the taxpayer is in the form of an advance payment or deposit, a refund suit is not permissible. Until the IRS has assessed and collected the taxes, a refund suit may not be maintained.

Requirements for Filing a Refund Suit

As noted earlier, there must be an allegation that an overpayment of taxes, etc. has been made and that the IRS has refused to refund this amount as requested by the taxpayer. The taxpayer can consider that his/her request for refund from the IRS has been refused if he/she has not received an answer within six months of filing the request.

The refund suit must be filed in the appropriate court within two years after receiving notice of disallowance.

USING THE U.S. COURT OF CLAIMS

The U.S. Court of Claims has jurisdiction in any taxpayer suits against the government, regardless of the amount of refund at issue. The Court of Claims cannot issue declaratory judgments because it has jurisdiction only for actions seeking money judgments from the government.

The Court of Claims is located in Washington, D. C. It does, however, hold hearings at other locations in the United States. The taxpayer has no right to a jury trial in this court. Its procedures are similar to those of the Tax Court.

USING THE U.S. DISTRICT COURT

The U.S. District Courts have jurisdiction in refund suits as discussed earlier in this chapter.

Writ of Mandamus

The District Courts have jurisdiction in actions to compel any IRS officer or employee to perform a duty owed to the plaintiff. These actions, called *writs of mandamus*, if successful, will result in the District Court ordering the IRS to perform the act requested. For the taxpayer to be successful in these types of cases, the act must be one that the IRS officer or employee has a clear duty to perform.

Which District Court

Suits brought in the U.S. District Court should be filed in the judicial district in which the taxpayer lives or has his/her principle place of business. If the taxpayer filed the return in a different jurisdiction, a check should be made as to which District Court would be appropriate.

Declaratory Judgments

As a general rule, the District Courts are prohibited from entering declaratory judgments in respect to federal income taxes. Declaratory judgments are court decisions on the validity of proposed actions of one party to the lawsuit, i.e. governmental actions. The courts have refused to allow the taxpayer to file declaratory judgments on the legality of tax deficiency assessments, including those where the taxpayer is claiming that the statute of limitations has run against the government. Accordingly, to obtain a District Court ruling on whether or not the statute of limitations has run against the government, the taxpayer would be required to pay the tax assessment and file a refund suit.

TAX COURT

The Tax Court was established in 1924 as an executive agency. It was originally known as the Board of Tax Appeals. In 1942, the agency was renamed the U.S. Tax Court. It became a constitutional court in 1969. The present Tax Court is composed of 19 judges, plus judges in retired status who sit on a limited number of cases. In this chapter, only a brief review of the Tax Court is presented. In Chapter 12, a detailed discussion of how to win your case in Tax Court is presented.

Tax hearings are held before solitary judges, sitting in various parts of the country. Only those decisions considered as advisable by the Chief Judge are reviewed by the entire court. Approximately one-half of the court decisions are published in the *Tax Court Reports*. Only the published reports are considered as precedent in future tax issues.

Tax Court Jurisdiction

The Tax Court is empowered to hear only cases involving federal income taxes, self-employment taxes, federal estate taxes, and federal gift taxes. It does not have jurisdiction to decide matters involving employment, excise, or other miscellaneous federal taxes. Lack of jurisdiction to hear the case may be raised at any time by any party to the case.

The basis of the Tax Court jurisdiction in income tax cases is the Statutory Notice of Deficiency. In one case, the IRS issued the taxpayer a Statutory Notice of Deficiency based on the calendar taxyear. The taxpayer, however, was on a fiscal year basis. The Court ruled that the Tax Court had no jurisdiction to uphold the assessment of additional taxes, because the notice was fatally defective.

Once the Tax Court obtains jurisdiction, it is retained until the case is decided by the Tax Court. In one case, the IRS attempted to withdraw its statutory notice of deficiency to deprive the Tax Court of jurisdiction. The Court concluded that they retained jurisdiction until the issue was decided.

In another case, the taxpayer appealed to the Tax Court. The IRS, in their answer, alleged a larger deficiency than stated in the statutory notice of deficiency. The taxpayer paid the amount stated in the notice and contended that the Tax Court no longer had jurisdiction in the case. The court retained jurisdiction.

SMALL CLAIMS COURT

The special procedures for the small claims division of the Tax Court applies to those cases where the amount in dispute does not exceed $10,000. (Note: the taxpayer may elect to have his/her case tried as a regular tax case even when the amount in dispute is less than $10,000. If there are reasonable grounds for determining that the amount in dispute is in excess of $10,000, the IRS may request that the small claims proceedings be discontinued.)

A taxpayer may represent him/herself or use a tax professional qualified to practice before the Tax Court. The petition need not be verified unless otherwise ordered by the Court. An answer is not required to be filed by the IRS unless there are issues where the burden of proof is on the IRS. The taxpayer is not required to reply to the IRS's answer (if any) unless directed to by the Court.

Trials of small tax cases are conducted as informally as possible, consistent with orderly procedure, and any evidence deemed by the Court to have probative value shall be admissible. Neither briefs nor oral arguments are required. The transcript of a small tax case is recorded but not transcribed unless so ordered by the Court. In most cases, a summary of the proceeding shall be reported. Special judges will normally be used in small claims cases.

Any decision made by the Tax Court pursuant to the small claims rules is not reviewable in any other court and shall not be treated as a precedent for any other case.

NEW ISSUES

In a 1986 case, the IRS was allowed, in Tax Court, to raise new questions and issues and therefore recover a larger deficiency than originally assessed. In this case, it appeared that the taxpayer did not object to the evidence of prior tax years. In most cases, however, the IRS is limited to the amount of the deficiency claimed to that set forth in the 90-day letter.

A refund suit in either the District Court or the Court of Claims involves the question of whether or not the government owes the taxpayer any money. Accordingly, a suit in either of those courts opens the entire issue of tax liability, and the IRS may raise additional issues and make additional claims not previously raised.

CLASS ACTIONS

In class actions, court suits are brought on behalf of a certain class of people who are similarly situated. The courts have not allowed class actions on behalf of taxpayers against the IRS. The decision is based on the theory that because each taxpayer must submit a claim for refund, that the taxpayers are not similarly situated and therefore do not constitute a class.

ATTORNEY FEES

In some cases, the taxpayer can recover attorney fees from the IRS if the IRS's position is "not substantially justified." For example, in one case, the government was required to pay a taxpayer's attorney fees when the IRS's position was contrary to an earlier Tax Court decision to which the IRS had agreed. (Note: for cases filed prior to 1986, before a taxpayer could obtain attorney fees, he or she had to establish that the IRS position was unreasonable.)

In one 1987 case, attorney fees were not awarded when the IRS conceded its mistake shortly after the suit was filed. The government contended that its conduct was reasonable in conceding defeat quickly. The taxpayer contended that the prelitigation conduct of IRS personnel should be considered, including the fact that the government had failed to communicate with the taxpayer's attorney prior to the filing of the suit. (Note: there are several other court decisions which allow consideration of the prefiling conduct of IRS personnel in awarding attorney fees.)

In another 1987 case involving the failure of the IRS personnel to communicate with the taxpayer's attorney prior to filing suit, the court held that the IRS had not acted unreasonably, and therefore, no attorney fees were awarded where the conduct involved was the delay of the IRS in conceding an issue. In this case, the IRS had failed to notify the taxpayer that the issue was administratively decided in the taxpayer's favor.

A taxpayer was denied attorney fees based only on a 15-month delay in receiving refunds after the refund suit was filed.

In addition to attorney fees, the taxpayer may also recover expenses for prelitigation and postlitigation costs.

CHAPTER 9

How IRS Gets Information About You and How to Stop Them

The IRS functions on information gathered from many sources. To protect your rights, several key concepts about this information gathering network are noted below:

☐ There is no requirement that the IRS be logical and fair.
☐ Your bank records and safe-deposit boxes are not private to the IRS.
☐ Through the use of computers, IRS can develop a complete profile of a taxpayer.
☐ IRS pays for information by using paid informers.
☐ For a summons to be effective, it must be valid and must be served on the taxpayer.
☐ For a summons to be valid, it must be issued for a proper purpose.
☐ In cases of doubt regarding the validity of the summons or its manner of service, consult an attorney.
☐ Under the provisions of the Privacy Act of 1974 and the Paperwork Reduction Act of 1980, IRS must tell you what major purposes they have in asking for information from you.

ADMINISTRATIVE SUMMONS

The IRS has considerable authority to issue administrative summons. The scope of their summons is limited only by the requirement that they establish a legitimate purpose for the investigation. A summons is a judicial order.

In the context of IRS litigation, normally the summons is an order to produce books, records, or other information regarding the taxpayer's business, income, or expenses. The IRS code provides that the summons issued by the IRS can require the taxpayer to produce for examination "books, papers, records, or other data." The statute also requires the taxpayer to appear for "testimony."

The IRS can issue a summons to examine records and books pertaining to the taxpayer that are in possession of a third party. For example, the IRS can summon the bank records from your bank that your bank retains on your account. (Note: any time the IRS summons records in possession of a third party, the IRS must notify the taxpayer of the summons.)

Purpose of Summons

The Internal Revenue Code lists five purposes for which the IRS can issue an administrative summons. Those listed purposes are:

- ☐ To determine the correctness of any tax return.
- ☐ To prepare a constructive return for a taxpayer.
- ☐ To determine the tax liability of a taxpayer.
- ☐ To assist in the collection of any federal tax.
- ☐ To determine any transferee liability.

What IRS Cannot Do with a Summons

The purposes for which the IRS may issue a summons are listed above. As can be noted, their purposes are very broad. There are, however, limits to the summons power of the IRS. The limitations include inability to require the taxpayer to prepare his/her own return and to force the taxpayer to give information that is protected by constitutional rights. The protected rights include prohibition against self-incrimination and protection against unreasonable searches and seizures. These protections are discussed more in detail later in this chapter.

Who May Be Summoned

The tax law allows the IRS to summon any person liable for a tax, any person who has information regarding the tax liability of the taxpayer, any employee or officer of any person or tax entity whose tax liability is under investigation, and anyone who has information that will assist in the collection of a tax liability. (Note: the reason for the summons must be to promote the assessment and collection of federal taxes. It cannot be a "fishing expedition.")

Subject of a Summons

The summons must specify which records are being requested. In one case, a court held that an IRS summons which directed the taxpayer to produce all records, memos, and workpapers pertaining to the taxpayer's tax returns for the past three years was too broad. One court, however, upheld an IRS summons that requested all the names of clients of a certain tax preparer.

There are several court cases which hold that business records that were not used in tax return preparation or to substantiate business income or expenses could not be the subject of a summons. In one case, the IRS attempted to obtain the proposed budget from a business. The court held that the proposed budget was a planning tool only and therefore was not subject to the summons. A similar ruling was made when the IRS requested a copy of a business memo, which listed the possible liabilities of the company.

The IRS can examine property on which the taxpayer has claimed depreciation. One court limited this authority in a case where the property in question was needed to conduct the business. In this case, the taxpayer was in the business of renting video tapes. The IRS requested possession of the tapes for examination. The court concluded that turning over the tapes would destroy the taxpayer's business.

A summons by the IRS for the taxpayer to provide examples of his handwriting was upheld by the courts. In that case, there were some questions regarding the validity of certain records used by the taxpayer to substantiate business deductions. The court opened that the statutory duty to appear and give testimony included the duty to provide nontestimonial evidence.

In a case involving corporate books, the court allowed the IRS to examine all corporate stockholder meetings minutes for the year being audited. The taxpayer had contended that the IRS should be allowed to examine only those minutes that were the subject of a tax issue.

Enforcement of a Summons

The Internal Revenue Code provides that "If any person is summoned under the internal revenue laws to appear, to testify, or to produce books, papers, or other data, the District Court of the United States in which such person resides or may be found shall have jurisdiction by appropriate process to compel such attendance, testimony, or production of books, papers, or other data." Accordingly, when a taxpayer fails to produce books, etc., when ordered to do so by an IRS summons, the agent can then apply to the local District Court for an order requiring the taxpayer to comply with the summons.

Failure to comply with the court order to produce records, may be punished by contempt. The contempt may be civil or criminal. If the taxpayer is punished by criminal contempt, he/she can be ordered to jail as punishment. In civil contempt cases, normally the remedy ordered by the court is the attachment of property or the assessment of a tax liability against the taxpayer. Before a taxpayer can be punished for criminal contempt, the IRS must establish that the records are in existence and that the taxpayer has the ability to produce them.

In one case, the taxpayer was held in criminal contempt for failing to obey a court order to produce his tax records, despite the fact that he relied on the advice of his attorney not to produce the records. In some cases, self-incrimination is a justification for not producing records or books. This aspect is discussed later in this chapter.

In any proceeding before a District Court where the IRS is seeking court enforcement of a summons, the taxpayer has an opportunity to present evidence as to why the summons should not be issued and to depose (ask questions of) the agent.

In most cases, before the taxpayer can be ordered to comply with a summons, the taxpayer must have been served with the summons. Service is normally accomplished by having a process server or other person handing the taxpayer a copy of the summons. In some cases, the service may be by posting at the taxpayer's residence or place of business. If the taxpayer appears in court regarding the summons, this court appearance will normally constitute a waiver of the service requirement.

United States vs. Rylander

One of the leading U.S. Supreme Court decisions on the enforcement of a summons is *United States v. Rylander*, decided in 1983. In January 1979, the IRS issued a summons to Rylander, ordering him to appear before an agent of the Service in Sacramento, California, and to produce for examination, and testify with respect to, books and records of two corporations. Rylander was president of both corporations. When he failed to appear, the District Court issued an order to show cause why the summons should not be enforced.

He was able to evade the service of the summons for several months. He finally appeared before the Court in January, 1980, but failed to produce the records as ordered. At the contempt hearing, he stated that he did not possess the records and had not disposed of them to other persons. He refused to answer other questions regarding the records. He was held in contempt.

The Supreme Court held that a proceeding to enforce an IRS summons is an adversary proceeding, in which the defendant may contest the summons on any appropriate grounds. In civil proceedings for contempt, a defendant may assert the defense of present inability to comply with the order.

The Court also held that the shield against self-incrimination could not be used by a defendant to shift the burden of proof to the government. Because the burden of proof was on the defendant to establish that he did not have the records in question and by refusing to answer questions as to the location of the books, the defendant's conviction for contempt was upheld.

Third Party Summons

As noted earlier, the IRS may issue a summons to a third party to produce records, books, etc., pertaining to an individual taxpayer. There are special procedures that the IRS must use to enforce a third party summons. For the most part, the special procedures are designed to allow the taxpayer to contest the production of third party books, records, etc. (Note: the special rules do not apply to testimony of a third party nor to collection action after a valid assessment.)

The IRS is required to provide sufficient information in the summons to the third party that will allow the third party to identify and locate the records in question. If the third party is a "record-keeper," the taxpayer may bring court proceedings to cancel the summons.

In any third party summons which identifies the taxpayer by name, the taxpayer is required to be notified within three days after the summons is served and at least 23 days before the date set for the production of the documents.

The taxpayer may, within 20 days of receiving notice, bring an action in court to cancel the summons. The taxpayer, if contesting the summons, must, within the 20 days, notify the third party in writing not to comply with the summons. A certified copy of the notice not to comply must be mailed to the IRS person who issued the summons. (Note: the IRS cannot examine the records within the 20-day period, thus giving the taxpayer an opportunity to object to the summons.)

The IRS can issue a "John Doe" summons if the IRS has knowledge that a particular transaction with tax aspects has been made and that the records are in possession of a third party, but does not know the name of the taxpayer. A "John Doe" summons, however, may not be issued without court approval to prevent IRS "fishing expeditions."

Contesting the Summons

In the court proceedings to enforce the summons, the taxpayer will be provided an opportunity to establish why the summons should not be enforced. In one case, for example, the court refused to order the taxpayer to comply with the summons where there was evidence that the agent issuing the summons was being arbitrary. In several cases, the courts have refused to enforce summons where the IRS agents had refused to answer valid questions by the taxpayer.

Often, when the taxpayer refuses to produce records, books, etc., as demanded by IRS, the IRS will merely assess a tax liability against the taxpayer, rather than use court proceedings. This is based on the theory that the taxpayer is required to substantiate any information included on the taxpayer's tax return.

Grounds which taxpayers have used in the past to prevent the enforcement of a summons include:

☐ Establishing that the summons was issued merely to harass the taxpayer.
☐ Failure of the IRS to establish a legitimate purpose for issuing a summons.
☐ Information was already available to the IRS.
☐ The IRS has failed to follow required procedural steps in issuing summons.
☐ The records that are subject to the summons are privileged. (This is discussed later in this chapter under self-incrimination.)
☐ Agent refused to answer taxpayer's relevant questions.
☐ Inability to produce subject demanded records.
☐ Production of documents are requested for unnecessary re-examination purposes.

INFORMATION FROM STATE AGENCIES

In most cases, the rules involving third party summons do not apply to State agencies. State agencies apparently can turn over information to the IRS without the necessity of a formal summons or notification to the taxpayer.

The leading case involving this issue was decided by the U.S. Court of Appeals for the Ninth Circuit in 1987. In that case, *United States v. Joseph*, the taxpayer was investigated by the Clark County, Nevada, District Attorney's Office for practicing dentistry in Las Vegas without a license. Joseph's case was concluded with a plea of guilty by Joseph. During the investigation, the Assistant District Attorney obtained possession of Joseph's records. It appeared that Joseph may have also failed to comply with the federal income tax requirements.

At the conclusion of the case, Joseph's records were turned over to the Attorney for the Board of Dental Examiners. Next, the records were given to a special agent of the IRS. The taxpayer filed a notice to suppress the records and to prevent the IRS from using them. He claimed a violation of his rights and that the IRS had failed to comply with the notice requirements prior to obtaining the records.

The Court stated that evidence obtained by one police agency may be made available to other agencies without a warrant, even for a use different from that for which it was originally taken. Federal examination of evidence in the State's possession does not constitute an independent search requiring the execution of a search warrant.

The Court next discussed the requirement that the IRS provide notice to the taxpayer of a request for records from a third party. The Court stated that for this requirement to be applicable, the third party must be a recordkeeper for the taxpayer. The Dental Board and the District Attorney's Office were not third-party recordkeepers, and thus the IRS was under no duty to issue a summons or to notify Joseph that it was seeking the records. (Note: as discussed later in this chapter and in Chapter 10, there are additional restrictions on the IRS providing information to other agencies. The restrictions, however, do not apply to other agencies providing information to the IRS.)

SELF-INCRIMINATION

Violation of the Internal Revenue Code can be a criminal act. Accordingly, in certain situations, the taxpayer can claim the privilege against self-incrimination when ordered to produce certain records, etc. For the taxpayer to assert the privilege against self-incrimination the following conditions must be present:

- ☐ A real risk of self-incrimination.
- ☐ The privilege cannot be a blanket one—it must refer to specific books, records, questions, etc.
- ☐ The books, records, etc., must be in the hands of the taxpayer at the time the summons is issued.

The records, books, etc. in most cases must be items prepared by the taxpayer. For example, if the items were prepared by someone other than the taxpayer, then they can be the subject of a summons even if they are in possession of the taxpayer.

Records, etc. in possession of a third party are not normally protected by the self-incrimination privilege. In one case, records in possession of a corporation were required to be produced and were used against the only stockholder of the corporation. The court stated that the corporation and the stockholder were two separate parties, even though the stockholder owned all the shares of the corporation.

The IRS is restricted from using an administrative summons if the case has been referred to the Justice Department for prosecution. For purposes of this restriction, each taxyear is considered as separate. Accordingly, if the case on one taxyear has been referred for criminal prosecution, the IRS can still use the administrative summons for other taxyears.

The Supreme Court requires that the taxpayer raise the defense of self-incrimination at or prior to the court proceedings to enforce an IRS summons. The taxpayer cannot wait until contempt proceedings to raise this issue for the first time.

One of the leading cases on requiring the taxpayer to produce records is the case of *United States v. Bellis*. This case, decided by the U.S. Supreme Court in 1974, involved a partner in a small law firm who was held in contempt for failure to comply with a subpoena requiring production of the partnership's financial records. Mr. Justice Marshall held that Fifth-Amendment privilege against compulsory self-incrimination is limited to its historic function of protecting only natural persons from compulsory incrimination through his own testimony or personal records.

The Court held that a person could not rely on the privilege against self-incrimination to avoid producing the records of a collective activity, even if the records might incriminate him personally. One of the key factors discussed in the case was the fact that the defendant (taxpayer) held the records in his representative capacity of a partner in the partnership. The Court stated that the rights against self-incrimination were personal rights, that individuals, when acting as representative of a collective group, cannot be said to be exercising their personal rights and duties.

ATTORNEY-CLIENT PRIVILEGE

Any communications between a taxpayer and his attorney are normally *privileged*, and the government cannot force the attorney to testify regarding the communications. Although the attorney cannot refuse to testify, he/she can refuse to answer specific questions because of this privilege. The attorney-client privilege is separate from the privilege against self-incrimination discussed above.

Exceptions to this attorney-client privilege include situations where the attorney was retained in furtherance of continuing criminal activity. Another exception is where the communications are overheard or disclosed to persons not included within the privilege. (Note: secretaries, etc. employed by an attorney are included in the privilege.)

The privilege applies to both oral and written communications between the attorney and the taxpayer. It does not apply to taxpayer records being retained by the attorney. In most cases, the attorney can be required to turn over the taxpayer records.

The work product of an attorney made during a tax examination or litigation cannot be summoned by the IRS. Work product includes memos, notes, or conclusions, regarding a taxpayer's case. The working papers of the person who prepared the taxpayer's taxes can, however, be summoned by the IRS.

In many situations, the attorney can be required to testify regarding the date and general nature of services performed for a taxpayer and on the fee received from a client.

ACCOUNTANT-CLIENT PRIVILEGE

The IRS does not recognize any privileges between an accountant and taxpayer. Even those privileges available to accountants under State law are not available in IRS proceedings. If the accountant is an employee of the taxpayer, any records in possession of the accountant are considered to be in possession of the taxpayer. Accordingly, the privilege against self-incrimination may be available.

WITHDRAWAL OF CONSENT

If the IRS's possession of the records are the result of a voluntary turnover by the taxpayer, and if the taxpayer withdraws his/her consent, the IRS must promptly return the records. In many cases, the IRS may then issue a summons for the records.

INFORMANTS

In criminal cases, the U.S. Supreme Court has stated that the IRS is not required to provide the taxpayer with the name or names of any informants who have provided information to the IRS regarding a taxpayer's tax situation. There is one U.S. Court of Appeals case which held that in civil proceedings, like criminal proceedings, the IRS is not required to reveal the source of its information. Accordingly, in many cases, the taxpayer has no indication of the extent of knowledge in possession of IRS auditors who are acting on tips from informants.

Tips from informants account for about 15 percent of all government fraud investigations. Many times the informants are ex-spouses, former girlfriends, and former employees. The problem in many cases is that the informants provide information that the government would otherwise not have available. Accordingly, conducting an audit defense can be difficult in these cases.

OBTAINING RECORDS FROM IRS

In some situations, the taxpayer may need to obtain records from the IRS or other governmental offices. The Internal Revenue provides that a taxpayer has the right to inspect his/her tax returns including any amendments, attachments, etc. In addition, under the *Freedom of Information Act*, the taxpayer may obtain many documents from the IRS. For example, under the Freedom of Information Act, taxpayers have been able to obtain IRS policy manuals, audit manuals, etc. Much of the information used in research for this book was obtained from the IRS under this act.

Courts have required the IRS to provide the taxpayer with documents that indicate how the IRS arrived at certain positions with regards to the taxpayer's tax liability. (Note: in some cases, discovery has been refused as an exception to the Freedom of Information Act. An example of the latter involved an auditor's report; the court stated that it was prepared for litigation purposes and therefore not subject to discovery.)

In an 1987 U.S. Supreme Court case (*Church of Scientology of California vs. IRS*), the Court rejected an appeal from the Church of Scientology to obtain government tax records and ruled that the public has no right to get information kept by the IRS. The Court stated that even if the IRS could delete the names of the taxpayers involved, there was no duty to turn over the requested tax records. The defendant was attempting to establish that the IRS was harassing them and therefore requested "copies of all records, correspondence, or any form of information relating to the defendant or its founder." The defendants contended that they were put on the "enemies list" by the Nixon Administration and that they were harassed for political reasons. The question before the Supreme Court was whether or not the IRS should be required to produce the records of taxpayers after deleting their names. The Court stated that the tax return itself, after removal of identification information is still protected from disclosure under the Freedom of Information Act.

RELEASE OF INFORMATION IN NON-TAX SITUATIONS

In this section, how others can get information from the IRS on individual taxpayers will be discussed. Listed below are the major methods by which others can obtain information on taxpayers from the IRS files.

Nontax Criminal Investigations

A federal judge or magistrate may order that any tax return or return information in possession of the IRS be turned over to officers or employees of any federal agency conducting an investigation pursuant to nontax criminal proceedings. The Secretary of the Treasury may also release information within the possession of the IRS that indicates that persons are involved in nontax criminal activity. In addition, the Secretary can release information where it appears that there is imminent danger of an individual's death, physical injury, or flight from prosecution.

The IRS will release information to the Social Security Administration to prevent the payment of social security benefits to illegal aliens. The IRS can also release information in order to assist in the locating of fugitives from justice. The IRS will not, as a matter of policy, release any information that will hamper or impair a criminal or civil fraud tax investigation. Nor will the IRS release information that will identify an informant.

Any federal or state agency that administers certain social security and food stamp programs may obtain information regarding unearned income of individual taxpayers.

Deceased Taxpayers

The IRS often relaxes the rules on the disclosure of information in the cases of deceased taxpayers. In one recent case, the IRS was forced to release information regarding the tax return of a deceased taxpayer. In this case, the requester of the information was the mother of an illegitimate child. She was trying to locate assets of the deceased taxpayer who was the father of the child.

Unauthorized Disclosure by IRS

If the taxpayer's returns or any information from his/her return is disclosed, either knowingly or negligently except as permitted by law, the taxpayer may sue both the IRS and the individual who released the information. Court actions brought regarding unauthorized disclosure must be commenced within two years of the taxpayer discovering the disclosure.

Taxpayers may receive compensation for their damages for the unauthorized disclosure in the amount of their actual damages or $1,000 for each disclosure, whichever is greater. If the disclosure was willful or the results of gross negligence, then actual damages plus an additional sum (punitive damages) to punish the person disclosing the information can be levied.

In one case, a chief criminal investigator was held liable for the unauthorized disclosure of tax information when he indicated that the taxpayer was subject to a criminal tax investigation regarding "oil thefts." The indication that the taxpayer was involved was based on information from the taxpayer's Form 1040. In another case, the IRS mailed out information that the taxpayer was a promoter in an abusive tax shelter. In this case, the court held that the information on which the conclusion was based was taken from the tax records of the taxpayer. Because the release was not made pursuant to a court order or other exception, the release by IRS was wrong.

IRS INFORMATION GATHERING GUIDELINES

The IRS has issued guidelines for IRS personnel gathering information regarding taxpayers. The guidelines are set forth in the *IRS Manual 4100-217 (Classification, Screening, and Identification for Examination of Tax Returns, Claims, and Information Items)*. The guidelines are set forth below:

☐ All examination employees will be alert for indications of noncompliance with the tax laws. They will continue to seek facts and evidence necessary to resolve issues in assigned cases and projects; however, care must be taken to ensure that only directly tax-related information is sought. Employees will not maintain any individual files or background information on taxpayers other than project files which they have been specifically authorized to maintain by the District Director.

☐ Tax related information, other than potential fraud and informants' communications, received by examination employees will be forwarded with a Form 5346 to the Chief, PSP for processing.

☐ Information received indicating noncompliance by a large number of taxpayers should be forwarded through channels to the Chief, Examination Division, and as appropriate, to the District Director, the ARC (Examination) or Assistant Commissioner (Examination), for consideration and appropriate action.

IRS investigators are prohibited from using lie-detector (polygraph) tests unless the taxpayer or the informant has "fully agreed to cooperate with the government and provide information." The IRS guidelines provide that the tests will be used only after the subject signs a waiver of his/her rights and only to help determine the credibility of the person. No adverse conclusions or determinations may be made based on a refusal to take the test. A refusal is to be noted only in the administrative file and not in the correspondence used to determine the tax liability of a person.

All polygraph tests must be approved by the Chief of the Criminal Investigation Division and should only be used selectively. Polygraph examiners from other agencies or commercial firms will not normally be used. Only school-trained persons may be used to administer the test.

PRIVACY ACT AND PAPERWORK REDUCTION ACT NOTICES

Under the provisions of the *Privacy Act of 1974* and the *Paperwork Reduction Act of 1980*, when the IRS requests information from a taxpayer, they must advise the taxpayer of the below listed items:

☐ The legal right to ask for the information.
☐ The major purposes in asking for the information and how the information will be used.
☐ What the penalties or results are if the information is not provided.
☐ Whether a response is voluntary or required by statutes to obtain a benefit.

In most cases, IRS's legal authority to ask for information is contained in the Internal Revenue Code, sections 6001 and 6011.

CHAPTER 10

Tax Fraud and Other Criminal Problems

Some of the key concepts regarding tax fraud and criminal problems are listed below:

☐ The taxpayer may be prosecuted for civil or criminal fraud involving the same taxyear.

☐ It is the government's policy to pursue only one course of action.

☐ If the taxpayer has an indication that he/she is being investigated for civil or criminal fraud, the taxpayer should cease all communications with the government and retain an attorney.

☐ The taxpayer cannot administratively appeal the IRS's determination that criminal fraud is present.

☐ If a taxpayer is tried for criminal fraud, he/she will be tried in U.S. District Court or before a U.S. Magistrate.

☐ The taxpayer has a constitutional right to be tried in the federal court district in which the return was filed.

CIVIL AND CRIMINAL LIABILITIES

Although in many cases the taxpayer may be prosecuted by the government for criminal fraud and at the same time by civil proceedings for civil penalties, it is the government's policy not to prosecute both criminal and civil liabilities against a taxpayer. The U.S. Supreme Court, in one case, however, found that the government's prosecution of the taxpayer, although contrary to the IRS's published policy, was not an unconstitutional denial of the taxpayer's due process rights.

Cases involving possible criminal or civil fraud charges are investigated by special agents from the Intelligence Division of the IRS.

PROOF OF CIVIL FRAUD

The Internal Revenue Code provides for civil penalties for cases involving civil fraud, negligence, delinquency, and substantial understatement of tax liability. For penalties other than for civil fraud, the IRS has allowed a "reasonable cause" defense to abate penalties against taxpayers.

If the taxpayer fails to comply with the IRS's valid request for discovery of the taxpayer's records, the Tax Court has allowed a default judgment to be entered against the taxpayer for civil fraud. The Court stated that in applying the Federal Rules of Civil Procedure, where one party fails to respond to valid requests for pretrial discovery, the burden of proof is transferred to the person refusing the discovery requests.

In one case, the Tax Court considered the fact that the taxpayer, a sheriff, had a history of failing to report income and had consistently underpaid his taxes as evidence of a fraudulent intent on the part of the taxpayer regarding the failure to report income other taxyears.

CRIMINAL PENALTIES

Included below is a list of some of the methods that IRS has used in the past to establish criminal conduct on the part of a taxpayer. The *bank deposit method* to prove gross income was sufficient proof to establish that the taxpayer had willfully attempted to avoid the payment of his income tax. In this case, there were substantial unaccounted-for deposits in the taxpayer's bank account. Under the bank deposit method, the IRS considers any unaccounted for deposits as gross income. Once the IRS establishes that the deposit was made, it is up to the taxpayer to establish that the money came from nontaxable sources.

The fact that an individual was an active tax protester was used, along with the fact of his failing to file a return, to establish that the individual had "willfully" failed to file his tax return.

A taxpayer cannot use the Fifth Amendment privilege against self-incrimination as a justification for failing to file income tax returns. In this case, the taxpayer had failed to file for several years. He claimed that after the first year, any filing would have alerted the IRS of the previous nonfiling. The court held that the Fifth Amendment does not excuse the failure to file.

GENERAL RULES IN CIVIL FRAUD AND CRIMINAL CASES

Listed below are some of the rules and concepts of which individual taxpayers should be aware when faced with possible civil fraud or criminal tax violations.

☐ As a matter of policy, the IRS does not attempt to prosecute the taxpayer for both criminal and civil liabilities.

☐ Failure to claim the benefits of the statute of limitation may be considered as a waiver of it.

☐ The six-year statute of limitations does not start until April 15, even though the taxpayer may have filed earlier.

☐ The taxpayer may not use the Freedom of Information Act to obtain additional information not available under ordinary court discovery methods.

☐ Evidence illegally seized from a third party may be used against the taxpayer in a tax evasion trial as long as the taxpayer's rights were not violated.

☐ Although the constitutional immunity against self-incrimination does not apply to excuse a taxpayer from failing to file tax returns, it may be used in a tax examination procedure.

☐ The constitutional immunity against self-incrimination applies only to those records that are in possession of the taxpayer. Those in possession of an accountant are not normally protected.

☐ The failure of a special agent to inform the taxpayer prior to interrogation of the taxpayer's right not to answer questions normally does not prevent any statements made from being used against the taxpayer.

☐ The IRS cannot use an administrative summons against a taxpayer if the case has been referred to the Justice Department for possible prosecution.

☐ The "work product" doctrine of an attorney generally makes the notes, conclusions, etc. of the attorney protected from forced disclosures.

☐ The attorney, in most cases, may be compelled to disclose the identity of his/her client and the general nature of the services performed for the client.

☐ There is no accountant-client privilege against disclosure of information.

TACTICS IN QUESTIONS OF CIVIL OR CRIMINAL FRAUD

If the taxpayer discovers that he/she is being investigated for civil or criminal fraud, certain steps should immediately be taken. First, stop all communications with the IRS. There is nothing to be gained and a lot to be lost in cooperating with the government in this situation. Second, get an attorney. (Note: an IRS agent is not required to warn the taxpayer that he/she is being investigated for fraud purposes. Nor is the agent required to give a taxpayer a warning regarding self-incrimination before questioning him.)

In most fraud investigations, the special agent already has the answer to the questions that he is asking. In this situation, the agent is attempting to strengthen the government's case. Do not assist the agent in proving a case against you.

APPEALS FROM THE IRS DETERMINATION OF CRIMINAL FRAUD

The administrative appeal discussed in Chapter 7 is not available to the taxpayer to challenge an IRS determination that criminal fraud is involved. Once the IRS makes this determination, the case is then referred to the Department of Justice for trial. The taxpayer, of course, has an opportunity to present his/her defense in criminal court proceedings.

TRIAL OF A CRIMINAL TAX CASE

The trial, in this case, will be either in Federal District Court or before a U.S. Magistrate. The government will be represented by an Assistant U.S. Attorney. The taxpayer has the right to be represented by either an attorney of his/her choice or, if the taxpayer cannot afford an attorney, one appointed by the court. The taxpayer has a right to be tried in the federal judicial district in which the return was filed.

CHAPTER 11

Researching Tax Issues

In this chapter, the various administrative regulations and rulings that constitute the administrative law involving income taxes are covered. A discussion on how to obtain private rulings is also included. A careful review of this chapter should assist you in researching any tax issues. The reference material reviewed in this chapter may be researched at the local county law library or local university library. The material for the first part of this chapter was extracted from *IRS Publication 1140*.

TREASURY REGULATIONS

Treasury regulations are used to provide explanations, definitions, examples, and rules that explain the language of the Internal Revenue Code (normally referred to only as the code). Any research of a particular code section is not complete without referring to the regulations which interpret it.

Most income tax regulations are issued under the general authority of code section 7805(a). These regulations are considered as interpretative regulations. In addition, some other code sections specifically authorize regulations to provide the details of the meaning and rules for that particular code section. Regulations issued under this authority are considered as legislative regulations. The courts have tended to rely on regulations when the code is ambiguous or incomplete.

Classes of Regulations

There are three basic classes of regulations: temporary, proposed, and final. All IRS regulations are written by the Legislation and Regulations Division of the Office of the Chief Counsel, IRS, and approved by the Secretary of the Treasury.

Temporary regulations are issued to provide guidance for both the IRS and the public until final regulations are adopted. Being temporary in nature, there is no requirement for a public hearing prior to adopting them.

Proposed regulations are issued to solicit public written comment. If any written comments are received, then public hearings will be held on them. If there are temporary and proposed regulations on the same subject, the temporary regulations are binding unless specifically superseded by the proposed regulations.

Final regulations are issued only after public comments, if any, on the proposed regulations are evaluated. Final regulations replace both temporary and proposed regulations.

Regulations involving federal income taxes are published in the *Federal Register, Code of Federal Regulations* (C.F.R.), Treasury Decisions (T.D.), *Internal Revenue Bulletin* (I.R.B.), and *Cumulative Bulletin*.

REVENUE RULINGS

Revenue rulings are published opinions of the IRS concerning the application of tax law to an entire set of facts. Revenue procedures are official statements of procedures that either affect the rights or duties of taxpayers or other members of the public, or should be a matter of public knowledge.

The purpose of revenue rulings is to promote a uniform application of the tax laws, and therefore are required to be followed by IRS employees. Taxpayers can rely on them or can challenge them in the Tax Court or other federal courts. How to obtain private rulings is discussed later in this chapter.

Revenue rulings and revenue procedures are published by the IRS in the *Internal Revenue Bulletin* (I.R.B.), which is issued weekly and is available to the public. The contents of the I.R.B. are consolidated at least semi-annually into a permanent, indexed *Cumulative Bulletin* (C.B.). The IRS also publishes a *Bulletin Index-Digest System* and publications 641, 642, 643, and 644, which comprise a research system that lists the rulings by subject and code section. A brief explanation of each ruling is included.

BULLETIN INDEX-DIGEST SYSTEM

As noted above, the *Bulletin Index-Digest System* provides a method for researching matters published since 1952 in the *Internal Revenue Bulletin*. It is divided into four sections:

1. Income Tax (Service One)
2. Estate and Gift Taxes (Service Two)
3. Employment Taxes (Service Three)
4. Excise Taxes (Service Four).

Each of the above services consists of a basic volume and the latest cumulative supplement. Service One (income tax) is published quarterly. The others are published semiannually.

Digests (brief summaries) of currently applicable revenue rulings and procedures constitute a major part of the system. The digests are arranged under topical headings and subheadings. Also included are digests of Supreme Court tax cases and Tax Court decisions in which the IRS Commissioner has announced either acquiescence or nonacquiescence, Executive Orders, Treasury Department Orders, and miscellaneous items published in the I.R.B.

As a research tool, each digest is preceded by descriptive *key words* that further identify the subject matter, followed by a citation to the code and regulations section under which the item was published, and also a citation to the item and the I.R.B. or C.B. in which the full text may be found. This arrangement of the digest under topical headings makes it possible to use the "subject matter" research approach to find the revenue ruling or procedure directly on point. (Note: public laws and Treasury Decisions are not digested, but are listed in a separate topical index.)

Supreme Court Decisions

All Supreme Court decisions involving federal tax issues are published in the I.R.B. and C.B. They can be located using either the subject matter method or the code section method. If the name of the decision is known, its citation can be located by checking the list of Decisions of the Supreme Court, which are listed in alphabetical order followed by court decision number and digest number.

Tax Court Decisions

The *Internal Revenue Bulletin* does not publish Tax Court decisions. It does publish announcements concerning the Service's acquiescence or nonacquiescence on adverse Tax Court decisions. (Note: digests of Tax Court decisions to which the IRS has acquiesced or not acquiesced are published in the index system. Included with each case digest is the citation to the Tax Court volume in which the decision is published and the notation of "Acq" (acquiescence) or "Nonacq" (nonacquiescence).

Current Status of Rulings

The Listing of Revenue Rulings and Revenue Procedures contains a list of all revenue rulings and procedures that have been published in the I.R.B. and that have not been superseded or otherwise modified. The listing gives a citation to the digest for each current ruling or procedure.

Actions on Previously Published Rulings

The *List of Actions on Previously Published Rulings and Revenue Procedures* contains a list of every revenue ruling and revenue procedure that has been modified, superseded, or otherwise acted upon, and gives the number of the later ruling or procedure, together with a citation to the appropriate I.R.B.

Cumulative Supplements

Cumulative supplements are issued quarterly for the income tax service and semiannually for the others. After you have researched the basic volume, you should check the cumulative supplement for later developments. Information on items published in the Bulletin after the cutoff date for the basic volume is presented in the same format used in the basic volume, that is, in finding lists, digests, etc.

COURTS

Within the IRS the taxpayer may appeal an examination decision and request an appeals conference. If the taxpayer is not satisfied with the appeals decision, he or she may appeal to the Tax Court by filing a petition within 90 days of the Notice of Deficiency or may pay the amount that the IRS claims is due and file a refund suit in either U.S. District Court or U.S. Court of Claims.

Tax Court

Decisions of the Tax Court are issued as either a regular report or a memorandum decision. Regular reports are printed in bound volumes by the government. Memorandum decisions are not published by the government.

District Court and Claims Court

Decisions of the U.S. District Courts and U.S. Court of Claims are published by three commercial printing houses, West Publishing Company, which publishes the Federal Supplement (a bound volume series). The *Federal Supplement* (F.Supp.) notes selected U.S. District Court decisions. West also publishes the *Federal Reporter* (F.). U.S. Court of Claims decisions are published in this bound volume series.

Prentice-Hall publishes *American Tax Reports* (A.F.T.R.). This bound volume series publishes selected tax case decisions from the various courts. Commerce Clearing House publishes the *United States Tax Cases* (U.S.T.C.). This series also publishes selected tax case decisions from the various courts.

Appellate Courts

Decisions of the Tax Court and the District Courts may be appealed to one of the thirteen U.S. Courts of Appeal. All recent decisions of the Courts of Appeal are published by West in the *Federal Reporter*, second series (F.2d). In addition, tax cases are published by Prentice-Hall (A.F.T.R.) and Commerce Clearing House (U.S.T.C.).

Supreme Court

Decisions of the Courts of Appeals may be reviewed by the U.S. Supreme Court. The Supreme Court is not obligated to review most decisions of the Courts of Appeals. The most common type of tax issue that the Court reviews is where a tax statute is held invalid. Decisions of the Court are published in *U.S. Reports* (U.S.) and the *Supreme Court Reporter* (S.Ct.).

Significance

Decisions of courts other than the Supreme Court are binding on the IRS only for that particular taxpayer and for the years litigated. Thus, decisions of the lower courts do not require the IRS to alter its position for all other taxpayers.

The Commissioner may decide to acquiesce to an adverse regular Tax Court decision. Decisions by the Commissioner on Tax Court decisions are published in the *Internal Revenue Bulletin*, which later becomes part of the *Cumulative Bulletin*. Acquiescence (Acq.) by the Commissioner generally means that the IRS will follow the Tax Court decision in cases involving similar facts. The Commissioner may also file nonacquiescence (Nonacq.), which is notice that the IRS does not accept an adverse decision and will not follow it in cases on the same issue. Generally, these cases are appealed to a higher court. An acquiescence or nonacquiescence may be subsequently revised by the Commissioner of IRS.

SUGGESTED RESEARCH PROCEDURES

It is important to properly research all the information pertinent to your case. A step-by-step list of procedures is given below:

1. Develop the fact of the case.
2. **Internal Revenue Code**. Research the Internal Revenue Code first, because it is the highest authority and should be used in lieu of any other tax source.
3. **Treasury (Internal Revenue) Regulations**. The regulations provide an in-depth probe of many issues and often examples of computations. If the IRS Code or regulations do not address the issue specifically, go to step 4.

4. **Revenue Rulings**. Generally, the easiest method in researching for applicable rulings is through the Bulletin Index-Digest System. Rulings provide factual situations which may be "on point," that is, substantially identical in facts to an issue with which you may be currently involved. The Bulletin Index Digest System also provides a list of cases which have been decided by the Tax Court to which the Commissioner has issued acquiescence or nonacquiescence. These cases are listed by Code section.

5. **Court Cases**. Look to the courts for guidance in resolving the issue. It is at this point that your judgment becomes especially crucial. In researching a tax issue, obtain case citations within situations as close as possible to the issue in question. The *commercial tax services* provide synopses of court cases and allow you to find the applicable citations easily. In addition to the synopses, the tax services provide references to similar or related cases and, for Tax Court cases, indicate whether the Commissioner has issued an acquiescence or nonacquiescence.

6. **New Matters.** Almost all of the commercial tax services have a section entitled "New Matters," which provides information concerning recent developments.

7. **Court Decisions.** Because the commercial tax services provide only a synopsis of court decisions, the particular facts of an issue may not be clear. Thus, you must pursue the matter to the case-book. Only in this way are you sure that the case is appropriate and similar to your own.

   A word of caution is necessary: Courts write their rulings using both decision and dictum. Decision is the court's formal answer to the principal issue in litigation. It has legal sanction and is enforceable by the authority of the court. Dictum is a court's statement of opinion on a legal point other than the principal issue in the case. Dictum does not have legal sanction and is not enforceable.

   Dictum and decision are often both addressed in a court's ruling and are not identified as such. Read the ruling carefully to determine where decision ends and dictum begins. Decisions are often prefaced by "we find" or "we hold," however, this is not a hard and fast rule.

8. **Citator.** Checking the citator is a critical step in the research process. The citator contains case histories and recent case developments such as appeals, *writs of certiorari,* and related cases. The denial of a writ is not the equivalent of a reversal or disagreement. Its only significance is to show that the Supreme Court has refused to review the case.

   The citator traces the case history from its original entry into Tax Court, District Court, or Claims Court and, if the decision is appealed, continues through the Supreme Court.

Decisions reached in a lower court are sometimes reversed in the appellate or Supreme Courts. A lower court's decision which has been reversed on appeal has no legal sanction.

Courts also sometimes reverse themselves; this action may indicate a shift in legal opinion and will have precedential value. The term "precedence" means a legal decision that serves as an example, reason, or justification for a later decision. Precedence is a cornerstone of law. If a series of courts reverse a case in question, the case will quickly lose precedence.

9. **Research Glossary**. *Interpretative Regulations*—Treasury regulations issued under the general mandate of IRS Code 7805(a).

Legislative Regulations—Treasury regulations issued when a specific code section authorizes the Secretary of Treasury to write regulations giving details of the application of that code section.

Regular Report—A report of the Tax Court decision thought to be of some value as a precedent.

Memorandum Decision—A report of a Tax Court decision thought to be of little value as a precedent, because the issue has been decided many times.

Acquiescence—Notice given by the Commissioner of Internal Revenue of intent to follow, to the extent indicated in the Cumulative Bulletin, an adverse Tax Court decision.

Nonacquiescence—Notice given by the Commissioner of intent not to follow an adverse Tax Court decision.

OBTAINING PRIVATE LETTER RULINGS

A *private ruling* is a request to the IRS to obtain a ruling regarding the tax aspect of planned transaction. For example, a taxpayer is considering a large transaction that would involve possible substantial tax liability. The taxpayer may request a private letter ruling to determine how the IRS would decide the issue. As noted earlier, private rulings are not precedent in other cases. They are, however, binding on the IRS in regards to the specific taxpayer to whom they are issued.

Whether or not to request a private ruling is a critical question in this regard. By requesting a private ruling, the taxpayer is putting the IRS on notice as to a possible tax liability. The taxpayer is also bound on an adverse IRS ruling, whereas if he or she is not audited, the IRS may never rule on it. Normally, a taxpayer should ask for a private ruling when:

☐ When required by tax law involving certain tax-free transactions with foreign corporations.

☐ When the law is not clear and the chances of the taxpayer being audited are good.

☐ When the law appears to be favorable to you, and the transaction depends on the tax treatment it will receive.

There are no required forms to request a private letter ruling. The normal method is to write a letter to the IRS requesting the private letter ruling. The letter should include: a *statement of the facts* of the transaction, the *purpose* of the transaction, the *points and authorities involved* in the legal issue, and a definite statement of the *nature of the ruling* requested.

Requests for private rulings must be made to Internal Revenue Service, Assistant Commissioner, (Technical), Attn: T:TP:T, 1111 Constitution Ave. N.W., Washington, D.C. 20224.

The IRS can revoke a private ruling at any time. Rarely will the IRS change its position on a transaction made in reliance on the ruling. The IRS will not issue a private ruling on the below areas:

☐ Questions involving court decisions which the IRS has not decided whether to accept or appeal.

☐ Hypothetical transactions.

☐ Questions of a political nature.

☐ How estate taxes will apply to living persons on their death.

☐ Questions of a factual nature such as the value of a gift.

☐ Issues on Internal Revenue Code sections where regulations are being adopted.

Normally, within one month of filing the letter, an agent will discuss it with the taxpayer (by telephone). If the request will be disapproved, the taxpayer is usually notified in writing within 90 days. If the request for a ruling will be approved, it may take the IRS up to 120 days to issue the ruling.

CHAPTER 12

Winning Your Case in Tax Court

In this chapter, a detailed discussion of Tax Court litigation is presented. As noted in Chapter 6, any person may represent him/herself in Tax Court. Although the employees in the Clerk's office of the Tax Court will not give you legal advice, they are very helpful in explaining the Court's administrative requirements to taxpayers.

TAX COURT INFORMATION

The mailing address of the Tax Court is:

United States Tax Court
400 Second Street, N.W.
Washington, D.C. 20217

In case of questions, inquiries may be made by telephone to the below listed offices of the Court.

Office of the Clerk of the Court: *(202) 376-2754*
1. For general information regarding procedure in and practice before the Court.
2. For general information.

Admissions Section: *(202) 376-2736*
1. For information on admissions procedures for practice before the Court.

Appellate Section: *(202) 376-2757*
  1. For information regarding the filing of notice of appeal from Tax Court decisions.
  2. Other procedures relating to appellate review of cases decided by the Tax Court.

Docket Section: *(202) 376-2777*
  1. For information relating to documents and pleadings filed subsequent to petitions.
  2. For information regarding action taken on documents filed.
  3. For information regarding the status of pending cases.

Petitions Section: *(202) 376-2764*
  1. For information regarding petitions.

Business Hours

The normal business hours of the Tax Court for the purpose of receiving petitions, pleadings, motions, and other papers are from 8:30 A.M. to 5:00 P.M. The Court is closed on Saturdays, Sundays, and legal holidays.

Payments to Court

All payments to the Court may be by cash, check, or money order, or other draft. The checks, etc. should be made payable to the "Clerk, United States Tax Court" and mailed or delivered to the Clerk of the Court at the above address.

Filing Fees
  Filing a Petition..$60.00
  Application for admission to practice.....................25.00
  Photocopies (plain)—per page...............................25
  Photocopies (certified)—per page..........................50
  Transmitting record on appeal—actual cost of insurance and postage

Information on costs for copies of transcripts can be obtained from the trial clerk at the trial session.

Tax Court Rules

Any taxpayer trying a case before the Tax Court will find the Tax Court Rules a valuable, inexpensive resource tool. For a copy of the Tax Court Rules, contact the Clerk of the Court for current cost and ordering instructions.

Tax Court Forms

Appendix G contains copies of most of the standard forms used in Tax Court.

Places of Trial

Appendix F contains the list of cities where regular sessions of the Tax Court are held.

FILING PROCEDURES

To file a case with the U.S. Tax Court, the taxpayer must file a petition within 90 days after the date that the notice of deficiency is mailed. If the 90th day is a legal holiday in the District of Columbia, a Saturday, or Sunday, then the petition must be filed by the next business day.

Filing is accomplished by mailing the document to be filed to: United States Tax Court, 400 Second St., N.W. Washington, D.C. 20217. All pleadings or other papers to be filed with the Court must be filed with the Clerk in Washington, D.C., during business hours or by mail, except if the judge presiding at any trial or hearing permits or requires documents pertaining thereto to be filed at that particular session of the Court.

If the petition is mailed prepaid by registered mail and correctly addressed, the document is considered as filed on the date indicated by the registration mark. If the document is filed by certified mail, prepaid and correctly addressed, then the document is considered as filed on the date indicated by the postmark. (Note: when mailing by registered or certified mail, the document is considered filed even if lost in the U.S. Mails, provided the document was mailed prepaid and correctly addressed.)

If the document is placed in regular U.S. Mail (not registered nor certified), is correctly addressed and mailed prepaid, the document is considered as filed if it is received by the Tax Court. In this case, the filing relates back to the date the document is postmarked by the post office. (Note: the date on the postmark is the controlling date, even if that date is wrong.) In one case, where the envelope was correctly addressed but with the wrong zip code, it was received by the Court on the 92nd day. The court held that the petition was correctly addressed and thus was considered as timely filed, because the letter was postmarked on the 89th day. (See Chapter 7 for an in-depth discussion on the 90-day letter.)

In the following situations, the Tax Court held that the documents were not properly filed:

☐ Where the taxpayer mailed the petition to the IRS.
☐ When the taxpayer mailed the petition to the Tax Court in New York.

☐ When delivered by a private delivery service. (In this case, the court had received the letter on the 91st day. Had it been sent by certified mail, it would have been considered as filed on the date mailed.)

☐ Documents which are electronically transmitted.

☐ Presenting the petition to a judge of the Tax Court sitting at a temporary location.

If the taxpayer's notice of deficiency is addressed to the taxpayer whose address is "outside the States of the Union and the District of Columbia," the taxpayer has 150 days in lieu of 90 to file a petition.

The filing of the petition within the required time is a jurisdictional requirement. Failure to file in the required time leaves the Tax Court no alternative but to dismiss the petition. An exception to this was allowed in one case where the notice of deficiency was not mailed to the taxpayer's last known address, and the taxpayer did not receive the notice. In that case, the Tax Court held that the taxpayer had not received a valid notice.

Form of Petition

The purpose of the petition is to provide all parties with notice of the matters in controversy and the basis for the taxpayer's positions. The petition should be submitted on *Tax Court Form 1*. (Appendix G contains a copy of Form 1.) Prior to submitting a petition, the taxpayer should review the *Tax Court Rules*. For a copy of the rules or a copy of Form 1, the taxpayer may contact the Clerk of the U.S. Tax Court at (202) 376-2754.

The pleadings should be simple, concise, and direct. No technical forms of pleadings are required. All pleadings will be construed by the Court in a manner to do substantial justice. A party may plead the case in the *alternative* or *hypothetical*. In this regard, the alternative pleadings are not required to be consistent with each other. As a minimum, the petition must contain:

☐ A statement indicating the jurisdiction of the Tax Court. This is normally accomplished by a statement in the petition that the taxpayer disagrees with the Notice of Deficiency issued on (within the past 90 days).

☐ A clear and concise statement of each error which the taxpayer claims to have been committed by the IRS.

☐ In those issues where the taxpayer has the burden of proof, there must be a statement of fact which supports the taxpayer's position.

☐ Any affirmative defense such as waiver, duress, statute of limitation, etc. must be alleged by the taxpayer.

Other requirements that pertain to the petition and all other documents filed with the Court include:

☐ Caption, date, and signature required on all papers. (Caption is the first part of the document that identifies the parties involved and the case number.)

☐ All prefixes and titles such as Dr. and Mr. shall be omitted from the caption.

☐ The date on the document should be the date that the document is signed, not the date filed.

☐ After a court number is assigned, that number must appear on all documents presented for filing.

☐ All copies must be legible.

☐ Documents shall be typed on one side only and only on plain white paper, 8½ inches by 11 inches and weighing not less than 16-pound per ream. All papers must have an inside margin not less than 1¼ inches.

☐ All documents shall be fastened together on the upper left-hand side only and shall have no covers or binders.

☐ All case citations shall be underscored when typewritten and shall be in italics when printed.

☐ Documents failing to meet the above requirements will be returned without being filed.

At the time the petition is filed, the taxpayer should also file a request indicating the place where he would prefer to have the case tried. A list of cities where trials are conducted is included in Appendix F.

In cases where the petition is defective, the court may either order that the taxpayer submit a more definite statement or may dismiss the petition. The Tax Court, however, cannot dismiss a petition without providing notice to the taxpayer.

Service of Papers

Unless otherwise directed by the Court, all pleadings, motions, orders, decisions, notices, etc. shall be served on each of the parties involved in the case. All petitions will be served by the Clerk of the Court. Other papers will, in most cases, be served by the Clerk unless the party submitting the document has forwarded a certified mail copy of the document to the other parties and has completed a certificate of service.

If the taxpayer is represented by a counsel of record, then the papers will be served on the counsel. If the taxpayer or other party is acting without counsel, then the papers will be served on the taxpayer or other party.

Service and execution of writs or similar directives of the Court will be served by a United States Marshall or deputy marshall. In some cases, the Court will appoint an individual to serve writs, etc.

Answer

Within 60 days after service of a copy of the petition on the IRS Commissioner, the IRS will need to file an answer to the taxpayer's petition. The Court can extend the 60-day period if requested prior to expiration of the original time period. Any allegations in the petition that are not denied in the answer are considered as admitted by the government.

In those issues in which the government has the burden of proof, fraud for example, the IRS answer should contain sufficient facts to support those allegations. The taxpayer must then file a reply within 45 days on those allegations. If no reply is filed, then those allegations are deemed admitted.

Amended Pleadings

Any party may amend his/her pleadings once before any responsive pleading are served. This means that the taxpayer may amend his/her petition one time before the government has served its answer. Normally, an amendment is made to cure a defect discovered in the pleadings. After a response is served, a party may amend the pleadings only with permission of the court.

Motions

Any requests to the Court for an order is made in the form of a motion. The motion shall be in writing and shall state with particularity the basis for the request and the nature of the relief requested. The motion should show that prior notice has been given to other parties involved in the case. (Note: motions made during actual court sessions are not required to be in writing unless directed by the Court.)

If a hearing will be held on the motion, a party may submit a statement together with any supporting documents prior to the hearing date in lieu of actual appearance at the hearing. The filing of a motion does not act to delay or postpone the trial of the case, unless the motion requests such action and the Court approves the requested delay.

If the motion is directed to defects in a pleading, prompt filing of a plea correcting the defects by the other party may obviate the necessity of a hearing on the motion.

The more common motions are:

☐ Motion for a continuance or other delay.

☐ Motion for more definite statement. This motion is made when the other party feels that the pleadings are so vague or ambiguous that the party cannot reasonably be required to frame responsive pleadings. If the party toward whom the motion is directed fails to submit a more definite statement, the Court may strike the original pleadings or take such other action as appropriate.

☐ Motion to strike. This is a request to strike (cancel) any pleadings or portion of pleadings by the other party. This is normally made when the pleadings contain redundant, immaterial, impertinent, frivolous, or scandalous matter.

☐ Motion to dismiss. This motion is based on the concept that, from the pleadings, it is clear that one party should prevail without the necessity of taking any evidence or that, for some statutory reason, the case should not continue.

Counsel

The government is represented by an attorney assigned to the Chief Counsel's office. The taxpayer may represent him/herself before the Tax Court or be represented by retained counsel. (Note: a corporation may not appear without a representative admitted to practice before the Tax Court.) As discussed later in this chapter, in some cases the taxpayer may be awarded attorney fees.

Computation of Time

In computing any time requirements for cases pending before the Tax Court, the first day that an event or act occurs shall not be included. If the period of time is computed with respect to documents mailed, the time starts on the day after the date of mailing. Saturdays, Sundays, and holidays are counted unless the total period is less than seven days. If the last day of the period is a Saturday, Sunday, or Court Holiday, then the period runs until the end of the next business day. Using the above rules, if a 90-day notice is mailed on a Friday, the 90-day period begins on Saturday and ends on the 90th day, unless that day is a non-Court day.

Except for those cases where time is a jurisdictional requirement, the Court may extend the period on the motion of a party or on its own motion. (Note: the period fixed by statute, within which to file a petition with the Tax Court to redetermine a deficiency or liability [the 90-notice given by the IRS] cannot be extended by the Court.)

COURT PROCEDURES

After the pleading is completed, the Court will direct each party to submit a trial status report. The purpose of the status report is to assist the court in attempting an out-of-court settlement of the case. If the case cannot be settled, each party will then receive notice of hearing date and place of hearing. Parties will be given at least 90 days advance notice of hearing date.

The court may grant a delay in the hearing date if promptly requested to by either party. Delays requested within 30 days of the hearing date will probably be refused. If a party fails to appear at the hearing, the court may enter judgment for the other party without hearing any evidence.

The parties are required to stipulate to the fullest extent possible in order to limit the issues required to be established. Either party may request the other party to admit certain facts. This is accomplished by serving a request for admissions on the other party. Unless the served party files a reply denying the admissions within 30 days, the admissions will be considered by the Court as having been admitted. The purpose of these procedures is to eliminate the requirement to prove facts that neither party disputes.

Discovery

Discovery is the method used by the parties to discover the evidence that the opposing parties have regarding the case. The normal methods of discovery are by written interrogatories, production of documents, and depositions. Discovery may not, in most cases, be until 30 days after pleadings are completed and at least 45 days before the date set for the trial to be started. The Court may approve variations in the above time schedule.

The scope of the discovery may concern any matter not privileged and which is relevant to the subject matter of the case. It is not grounds to refuse to provide the information, because the information is not admissible in Court.

Written interrogatories (questions) may be served on the other parties without permission of the Court. The Court will be involved only if there is a dispute regarding them. Normally, a party has 45 days in which to answer interrogatories.

Any request for the production of documents must be in writing and set forth the items to be inspected. Normally, a party has 30 days to respond to any request for the production of documents.

Depositions for discovery purposes may be taken of any party and any nonparty witness. A deposition is the taking of a witness's testimony out of court, but under oath, and the testimony is recorded. A deposition may be entered in evidence if it meets the requirements for admission. The person to be disposed must be issued a notice of deposition, which states the time and place that the deposition will be taken. A copy of the notice must be served on all other parties to the trial. The party taking the deposition is responsible for paying all expenses, fees, etc. associated with the taking of the deposition. (Note: other parties are usually required to pay for copies of the transcript if they want a copy.)

If a person fails to answer interrogatories, produce documents, or fails to appear for the taking of a deposition without good and sufficient cause, the Court may sanction (penalize) such person.

Burden of Proof

Burden of proof is with the taxpayer on all matters except for fraud, transferee liability, and any new allegations contained in the IRS's answer. The burden of proof in Tax Court is that of preponderance of evidence. This burden is substantially less than the "clear and convincing" or "proof beyond a reasonable doubt" used in criminal cases.

The IRS cannot support their allegations with evidence obtained in violation of the taxpayer's constitutional rights. In addition, if the taxpayer can establish that the tax deficiency was also based solely on tainted evidence, the burden of proof shifts to the IRS to establish by untainted evidence the tax deficiency of the taxpayer. A recent court case holds that for the evidence to be considered as tainted for Tax Court proceedings, the violation of any constitutional rights in obtaining the evidence must be by federal officers.

The taxpayer needs only to establish that the IRS's determination of a tax deficiency is "arbitrary and excessive." The taxpayer is not required to establish the exact amount of tax due. (Note: if the taxpayer establishes that the notice is incorrect and fails to establish that it was arbitrary, the burden does not shift to the IRS.)

Often the evidence to support the taxpayer's position is the taxpayer's own testimony. The Tax Court may completely disregard the unsupported testimony of the taxpayer where it is incomplete, inconsistent, or partially rebutted by other evidence.

COURT CALENDARS

Calendars are used by the Court to schedule the cases. The Tax Court has three basic calendars; report, trial, and motion. The *report calendar* is used to require the parties to report the status of any pending case. Questions usually asked in this regard concern if the case will be tried, when it will be ready for trial, and any possible settlements of the issues.

The *motions calendar* is used to schedule hearings on motions and requests for defaults, etc. Normally, the motions calendar is held only in Washington, D.C.

The *trial calendar* is the schedule of cases set for trial. When a case is ready for trial, the Clerk will notify the parties of the trial date. The notification will include time, date, and place of trial. Ordinarily, the Clerk will provide 90 days notice of trial date.

Each case appearing on a trial calendar will be called at the time and place scheduled. Normally, more than one case will be set for the same time and place. At the call, counsel or parties without counsel will be requested to provide the court with an estimate of the time required to hear the case. The cases then will be tried in the order determined by the judge. In most cases, the judge will try the shortest cases first. Accordingly, do not overestimate the time required to try your case if you want early trial.

EVIDENCE

In trials before the Tax Court (except for small tax cases discussed later in this chapter), the rules of evidence applicable in trials without juries in the U.S. District Court for the District of Columbia will be used. These rules include the Federal Rules of Civil Procedure.

Ex parte affidavits, statements in briefs, and unadmitted allegations in the pleadings do not constitute evidence. Any testimony taken by deposition is not considered evidence until the deposition is actually entered in evidence by the Court. (Note: in some cases, the Court will admit only parts of a deposition. In these situations, only those portions of the deposition admitted into evidence will be considered by the Court.)

In regards to documentary evidence, the Court requires that the original document be submitted unless this is impractical. (Note: after the original is admitted in evidence, with permission of the Court, a clearly legible copy may be substituted for the original.)

If interpreters are needed, the parties will be expected to make their own arrangements for obtaining and paying interpreters.

Any party calling an expert witness will be expected to cause that witness to prepare a written report for submission to the Court. The opposing parties must be served with a copy of the report prior to calling the expert witness. The report shall set forth the qualifications of the expert, state his or her opinions and the facts or data on which the opinions are based. The written report does not excuse the presence of the expert witness at trial.

SUBPOENAS

Subpoenas are court orders for witness to attend the trial. In certain cases, the subpoenas are used to require persons to produce records or other documents. Tax Court subpoenas are issued under the seal of the Court. They must state the name of the Court and the caption of the case. In addition, the subpoena must command the person to whom it is directed to attend and give testimony at the time and place specified. In the case of a subpoena for records, it must command the person to appear with the specified records. Subpoenas are issued by the Clerk's office or from a trial clerk at a trial session.

Any witness summoned to a hearing or trial or whose deposition is taken is entitled to witness fees and mileage, the same as a witness in United States District Courts. The party calling the witness has the original responsibility to pay the witness fees and mileage.

FAILURE TO APPEAR

The unexcused failure of a party or counsel to appear for trial is not a grounds for delay of the case. The case may be dismissed for failure to prosecute, or the trial may proceed without the presence of the absent party or counsel.

RECORD OF PROCEEDINGS

All hearings and trials before the Tax Court shall be stenographically reported or otherwise recorded. A transcript shall be made of the proceedings on order of the judge when a permanent record is deemed necessary. Parties may receive copies of the record on payment of such charges as assessed by the Clerk.

BRIEFS

Unless otherwise directed by the judge, parties are required to submit briefs after the trial. The purpose of the brief is to set forth the issues in the case, apply the facts presented at the hearing to those issues, and set forth the law which applies to the case to help the judge reach a decision in the case. The prosecuting party (normally the taxpayer) files an opening brief within 75 days after trial, and the defending party (normally the IRS) must file a reply brief within 45 days after receiving of a copy of the opening brief.

CONSOLIDATION OF TRIALS

When cases involving the same or a common issue of law or fact are pending before the Court, the Court may order that the cases be heard jointly. In addition, the Court may join only a portion of the trial.

DECISIONS WITHOUT TRIAL

After the pleadings are completed, any party may move for judgment on the pleadings. In addition, any party may move for summary judgment. These motions are based on the contention that there are no valid issues for the Court to hear. A motion for judgment on the pleadings is based solely on the pleading in the case, whereas in a motion for summary judgment, the parties may attach supporting affidavits to establish that there are no issues to be decided based on evidence.

Default and dismissal may also end the case without the necessity of a trial. A default is where the other party fails to file any required pleadings. Dismissal occurs where the petitioner fails to properly prosecute the case or comply with the Court rules and orders.

POST-TRIAL PROCEEDINGS

Any motion for reconsideration of any findings or decisions of fact by a trial court must be filed within 30 days after a written opinion is received or the decision is stated orally in court session. Any motion to vacate or revise a Tax Court decision must also be made within 30 days.

APPEALS

A decision of the Tax Court can be appealed to the U.S. Court of Appeals for the circuit in which the taxpayer has his/her legal residence. In the case of a corporation, this is the U.S. Court of Appeals for the circuit in which the corporation has its principal place of business or office. Appeals of decisions of the Courts of Appeal may be made to the U.S. Supreme Court only via a writ of certiorari or certificate.

The parties involved may agree to take the appeal to any U.S. Court of Appeals. A notice of appeal must be filed with the appropriate court of appeals within 90 days of the Tax Court decision. If one party appeals, the other may appeal other issues in the same case within 120 days of the Tax Court decision.

SMALL TAX CASES

In those cases where the tax deficiency is less than $10,000, the taxpayer may choose to litigate the case in the small claims division of the Tax Court. These cases, called S-Cases, are litigated using special simplified procedures. The advantages of using the small tax procedures are that the case is tried with informal procedures and normally will be tried quicker. The big disadvantage is that neither the taxpayer nor the IRS can appeal the Tax Court decision. Small tax case proceedings are very similar to small claims cases in most states. The Clerk's office publishes a pamphlet entitled ''Election of Small Tax Case Procedure and Preparation of Petitions.'' A copy may be obtained from the Clerk.

Small Tax Case Defined

The term ''small tax case'' for Tax Court purposes means:

1. Neither the amount of the deficiency, nor the amount of any claimed overpayment placed in dispute (including penalties, additional taxes, etc.) exceeds:

a. $10,000 for any one taxable year in the case of the income taxes;
b. $10,000 for any one calendar year in the case of gift taxes;
c. $10,000 in the case of estate taxes; or
d. $10,000 for any one taxable period or, if there is not taxable period, for any taxable event.

2. The petitioner must make a request to have the proceedings conducted under the small tax case procedures.

Procedure for the Election of Small Tax Case Procedure

The request for small tax case procedure for those cases that meet the above restrictions may be submitted at the time the petition is filed or at any time before trial. When such a request is made and approved by the Court, the case will be docketed as a small tax case. The Court may, at any time before trial, order that the small tax case designation be removed and the case placed back on the regular calendar.

Small Tax Case Pleadings

The petition in a small tax case should be substantially the same as in other cases. (Note: Appendix G contains a form for filing a petition in a small tax case.) There is no requirement that the pleadings be verified (sworn to). The normal filing fee may be waived if the taxpayer can establish that he/she is unable to pay the fee without incurring a substantial hardship.

No answer is required in these cases unless requested by the Court. There is an exception to those cases where the IRS has the burden of proof. In those cases, the IRS must file an answer. Normally, a reply is not required.

Preliminary Hearings

Normally, preliminary hearings shall not be required in small tax cases unless so ordered by the Court. If the Court deems one necessary, the parties will be notified by the Clerk.

Trial

At the time of filing the petition, the taxpayer may designate the place where he/she desires the trial be conducted. If the taxpayer fails to request one at that time, he/she may do so by submitting a written request to the Court. If the taxpayer has not designated a place of trial within 30 days after the petition is filed, the IRS may file a designation indicating the location of trial preferred by the IRS. The general rule is that the Court will attempt to conduct the trial at a location most convenient to both the taxpayer and the IRS.

Appendix F contains a list of cities where the Tax Court normally holds trial. In addition to those cities, there are other cities where only small tax case proceedings are conducted. Prior to requesting a specific location, call the Clerk's office to determine the locations most convenient to you.

The actual trial proceedings will be conducted as informally as possible, consistent with orderly procedure. The formal rules of evidence are relaxed, and any evidence deemed by the Court to have probative value is admissible.

Briefs and oral arguments are not required unless specially requested by the Court. The hearing of the case shall be stenographically reported or otherwise recorded, but a transcript normally will not be made.

On any papers filed with the Tax Court in small tax cases, only an original and two copies need be filed. If other cases are consolidated with the case, then an additional copy is needed for each additional case.

Finality of Decisions

A decision entered in any case tried under the small tax case proceedings is not reviewable in any other judicial court. This limitation precludes both the government and the taxpayer from filing an appeal from a small tax case. The decision, also, is not a precedent for any other case.

DISCLOSURE ACTIONS

Disclosure actions in Tax Court are to accomplish one of the following actions:

- ☐ Actions to prevent any disclosure of Tax Court records pertaining to certain taxpayers. For example, if a business is prosecuting a case before the Tax Court, and its records or books are evidence in the case, an action may be brought to prevent any disclosure to others of the business records.
- ☐ Actions to obtain information regarding past IRS determinations, rules, regulations, etc.
- ☐ Actions to require the IRS to disclose third party contacts regarding the taxpayer's case. This is often used to attempt to determine how and what information the IRS has regarding a taxpayer's case.

CLAIMS FOR LITIGATION COSTS

When a taxpayer has prevailed in the trial of a case, he/she may request an order from the Court imposing litigation costs on the IRS. The motion for costs must be made within 30 days of the decision.

The motion should contain a statement indicating that the taxpayer has substantially prevailed with respect to the amount in controversy. A clear and concise statement of each reason that the IRS's position was not substantially justified must be included. Costs that are recoverable include attorney fees, court costs, and witness fees and mileage.

CHECKLIST FOR FILING A PETITION

Your petition should include at least the below information. Forms that may be used are included in Appendix G.

- ☐ Your full name (both husband's and wife's if you are filing a joint return).
- ☐ The years of claimed deficiencies.
- ☐ The name of the city and State from which the Internal Revenue Service sent your Notice of Deficiency (90-day letter).
- ☐ Your social security or other taxpayer identification number. The year, the amount of the disputed deficiency, the amount of any disputed addition to tax (additional amount or penalty), and, for an overpayment, the amount claimed.
- ☐ A statement of the Internal Revenue Service's proposed changes with which you do not agree.
- ☐ Your reasons for disagreement with the proposed changes.
- ☐ Your signature, date, present address, and telephone number at the bottom of the petition.
- ☐ Your spouse's signature, date, present address, and telephone number if you are filing a joint petition.
- ☐ In your mailing to the Clerk of the Court include:

   a. check for filing fee
   b. original and two copies of petition
   c. complete copy of the Notice of Deficiency attached to the original and each copy
   d. the designation of place of trial (see form in Appendix G).

CHAPTER 13

An Overview of the
Internal Revenue Code

In this chapter, the key aspects of the Internal Revenue Code concerning the administration and collection of income taxes are summarized. The actual reference to the code section is included to permit an in-depth examination of the specific reference if needed by the taxpayer. (Note: Only those sections considered as key sections are listed.) The procedure and administration portion of the code is contained in Subtitle F of Code.

If you wish to obtain more information regarding any code section, visit your local library, county law library, university law library, or the local IRS office. When using the library, please ensure that you are using the latest edition of the code. Frequently, libraries will retain outdated codes for historical purposes.

INFORMATION AND RETURNS
Section 6001

This section requires every person liable for any tax imposed by this code to keep such records, make such returns, and comply with such rules that the Secretary of the Treasury may from time to time prescribe.

Section 6011

This section provides that the Secretary of the Treasury may prescribe regulations regarding the making of returns and the collection of taxes.

Section 6020

This section empowers the Secretary to have returns prepared for those required taxpayers who do not prepare returns.

Section 6021

Section 6021 directs the Secretary to maintain a list of all taxable objects in any internal revenue district owned by non- U.S. residents.

Section 6031

Partnerships are required to submit tax returns under the provisions of this section.

Section 6032

Section 6032 requires banks to submit returns on all common trust funds they maintain.

Section 6033

This section requires tax-exempt organizations to file tax returns.

Section 6035

In this section, persons who are officers, directors, and/or shareholders of interests in foreign personal holding companies are required to provide certain types of information in their tax return.

Section 6037

S Corporations (certain small corporations) are required to file tax returns under the provisions of section 6037.

Section 6038

Section 6038 requires U.S. residents and citizens to provide the IRS with certain information with respect to their holdings in certain foreign corporation.

There is a maximum penalty of $1,000 for each annual accounting period for which the information is not filed. If, after formal notification, the person still fails to file the information, the penalty increases to $24,000 per period.

Section 6038B

Failure to file information regarding certain transfers to foreign persons or foreign corporations may subject the person of a penalty equal to 25 percent of the profit from such transfer.

Section 6039

This section requires corporations to report transfers of stock to any person pursuant to the exercise of a qualified stock option, an incentive stock option, or a restricted stock option.

Section 6039C

Any foreign person holding any interest in real property (land) in the United States must provide certain information to the IRS.

Section 6039D

Employers are required to maintain certain records and make reports when required by the IRS on certain fringe benefit plans for their employers.

Section 6039E

Any person who applies for a passport, renewal of a passport, or resident visa must provide his/her taxpayer identification number and, in cases of those seeking residential status in the U.S., information on previous income tax filings for the past three years.

Individuals failing to provide the above information when required are subject to a $500 penalty for each failure.

Section 6041

Section 6041 is the heart of the IRS matching program discussed in Chapters 4 and 5. This section requires all persons engaged in a trade or business who, in the course of this business, pays to a third person any rent, salaries, wages, premiums, annuities, compensations, renumerations, etc. of $600 or more in any one taxable year, report this to the IRS. With the information returns submitted pursuant to this section, the IRS can match the money received with the reported income of a taxpayer. Currently, the IRS claims they can match over 80 percent of the information received under this requirement to individual taxpayers.

Information required to be reported under this section includes the name and address of the person receiving the payment and the aggregate amount paid during the tax year. In addition to reporting the information to the IRS, a copy is required to be provided to the person who received the money.

Section 6041A

Section 6041A is similar to section 6041 except that it applies to remuneration for services and direct sales. Payment for services of $600 or more in any tax year are required to be reported. Persons who sell consumer products for resale are also required to report sales of $5,000 or more in any one year. The information required to be reported under this section is the same as under section 6041.

Section 6042

Section 6042 requires persons who makes payments of *dividends* aggregating $10 or more during any calendar year to file an information return similar to one required under section 6041.

Section 6043

Within 30 days after the dissolution of a corporation, the corporation must submit a return regarding the distribution of assets, stating the names and addresses of those persons receiving assets from the corporation.

Section 6045

This section requires stock brokers to provide information returns on sales and purchases of stock. In addition, the broker is required to furnish his/her customers with informational statements.

Section 6047

This section requires trustees to trusts and annuities to provide information statements to persons receiving funds from trusts or annuities. In addition, information statements are provided to the IRS.

Section 6049

Every person who makes payments of interest aggregating $10 or more per calendar year is required to provide both the IRS and the person receiving the interest with information statements. (Note: interest on any obligation issued by a natural person is exempt from this requirement. There are certain other exceptions listed in this section.)

Section 6050B

Payments of unemployment compensation aggregating $10 or more to any one individual is required to be reported to the IRS.

Section 6050E

States and cities are now required to report state and local income tax refunds in excess of $10 to the IRS.

Section 6050F

Information on individual accounts is required to be submitted to the IRS by the Social Security Administration regarding any social security payments made by individuals.

Section 6050H

Mortgage interest payments received by any person who is regularly involved in such trade or business must be reported. The informational return must identify the individual paying the interest.

Section 6050I

Any business or person engaged in a trade or business who has cash receipts of more than $10,000 in any one transaction or two or more related transactions must file a report with the IRS.

Section 6050N

Payments of royalties aggregating $10 to any one individual must be reported on an information return.

Section 6051

Any employer who withholds income taxes is required to provide each employee with a receipt for the withholding.

Section 6064

A taxpayer's signature on a tax return shall be presumed to be authentic and shall be considered as prima facie evidence that the return was actually signed by the taxpayer.

Section 6091

The Secretary may prescribe the place for filing any tax returns or other documents unless otherwise required by the code.

TIME AND PLACE FOR PAYING TAX

Section 6103

Returns and return information shall be confidential and except as authorized by the Code shall not be otherwise disclosed.

Section 6107

Tax preparers must furnish a copy of the return to the taxpayer.

Section 6109

Taxpayers must provide identifying numbers on returns and other correspondence when directed by the IRS. (In most cases, identifying numbers are the social security numbers of the taxpayer.)

Section 6110

Written determinations and background files (less taxpayer identification data) are public records and must be disclosed when requested.

Section 6111

This section requires the registration of certain tax shelters.

Section 6112

Organizers and sellers of potential abusive tax shelters must keep lists of investors.

Section 6151

The time and place for paying tax shown on return, unless otherwise specified by the code, shall be determined by the Secretary.

Section 6161

The Secretary may, for reasonable cause, extend the time for payment of the amount of tax shown due on the return. In most cases, the extension of time shall not exceed six months.

ASSESSMENT

Section 6201

The Secretary is authorized and required to make the inquires, determinations, and assessments of all tax, penalties, and interest imposed by law.

Section 6202

If the time and mode for the assessment of any internal revenue tax is not otherwise provided for, the Secretary may establish the same by regulations.

Section 6203

Assessments shall be made by the recording of liability of the taxpayer in the Office of the Secretary. Except as otherwise provided for in this code, the Secretary shall publish rules and regulations for the recording of assessments. When any assessment is recorded against any taxpayer, the taxpayer shall be furnished with a copy of the record of assessment.

Section 6211

This provides rules for defining deficiencies.

Section 6212

This section prescribes the procedures for issuing notices of deficiencies by the IRS.

Section 6213

This prescribes the time for filing a petition with the Tax Court after receiving notice of tax deficiency.

Section 6215

This section provides that if the taxpayer files a petition with the Tax Court, the entire amount determined by the decision of the Tax Court (which is final) shall be paid upon notice by the Secretary.

Section 6223

This provides, in most cases, that notice provided to one partner of a partnership shall be considered as notice to all partners.

Section 6229

The general rule is that the period for the assessment of additional taxes against a partnership must be made within three years of the last regular day for filing the return in question.

COLLECTION

Section 6301

The Secretary shall collect the taxes imposed by the internal revenue laws.

Section 6302

The time and mode for the collection of taxes that is not otherwise provided for in the code shall be as directed by the Secretary.

Section 6303

When not otherwise provided by the code, the Secretary shall publish rules for the notice and demand for the payment of the tax.

Section 6311

The Secretary may accept checks in payment of internal revenue tax. If the check is returned unpaid, the taxpayer shall remain liable for the unpaid taxes and any penalties added.

Section 6314

As a general rule, the Secretary must, when requested, provide a receipt for any sums collected.

Section 6316

The Secretary may, at his discretion, allow the payment of tax liability in foreign currency.

Section 6321

If any person liable to pay any tax neglects or refuses to pay the same after demand, the amount due shall be a lien on all the property of the taxpayer.

Section 6322

Unless otherwise prescribed by the code, any such tax lien shall continue until the liability is paid.

Section 6323

This section discusses the priority of liens against the taxpayer's property before and after the notice of a tax lien is filed.

Section 6325

The Secretary is required to provide a certificate of release for a tax lien not less than 30 days after the tax liability is satisfied.

Section 6331

The Secretary may levy on any taxpayer's property if the taxpayer fails to pay any amounts due after the period of assessment or other determination of liability within 10 days after notice and demand.

Section 6331 (c)

This section gives the Secretary of the Treasury the authority to levy against additional property of taxpayer if the property first seized and sold does not satisfy the deficiency owed the U.S.

Section 6331 (d)

Levy may be made on the salary or wages or other property of the taxpayer only after the Secretary has notified the person in writing of the intention to make such a levy.

The notice required shall be 10 days unless the Secretary has made a finding that the collection of the tax is in jeopardy. Except for jeopardy cases, the notice must be given in person, left at the person's dwelling or usual place of business, or sent by registered or certified mail at least 10 days before the levy.

Section 6331 (e)

Any levy on wages or salary shall continue until the liability is satisfied or becomes unenforceable because of lapse of time.

The Secretary has a duty to promptly release the levy when the liability has been satisfied or becomes unenforceable.

Section 6332

Any person in possession of any property that has been levied on by the IRS has a duty to surrender the property as demanded by the IRS.

If the levy is on a life insurance policy or endowment contract, unless the Secretary demands the contract document, it is not required to be turned over. No payments on it, however, may be made to the taxpayer or others without IRS or judicial approval.

Any person who refuses to turn over property pursuant to a valid IRS levy and demand is personally liable to the government in a sum equal to the value of the property or the liability owed to the U.S., whichever is less.

Any person holding property belonging to a taxpayer who is the subject of an IRS levy, shall be discharged from any obligation or liability to the delinquent taxpayer with respect to the property turned over to the IRS.

Section 6333

Any person in possession of books or records containing evidence or statements related to property or right to property subject to levy, shall, upon demand of the Secretary, exhibit such books or records to the secretary.

Section 6334

The following property is exempt from levy:

☐ Wearing apparel and school books.
☐ Fuel, provisions, furniture, and personal effects (that do not exceed $1,500 in value).
☐ Livestock, poultry, and firearms for personal use (that do not exceed $1,500 in value).

- ☐ Books and tools of a trade, business, or profession that do not exceed in the aggregate $1,000 in value.
- ☐ Undelivered mail addressed to any person.
- ☐ Certain annuity and pension payments (including railroad pensions, most military pensions).
- ☐ Workmen's compensation.
- ☐ Judgments for the support of minor children.
- ☐ Minimum (weekly) exemption for wages, salary, and other income of $75, plus $25 for each dependent and for spouse. (Note: if delinquent taxpayer is paid on other than a weekly basis, the exemption is computed as near as possible to the weekly rate).
- ☐ Certain service-connected disability payments.

Section 6335

As soon as practicable after the seizure of property, notice in writing of the seizure shall be given by the Secretary. Notice of sale must also be given in writing at least 10 days prior to the sale. In addition to personally serving the owner of the property with the notice of sale, such notice must also be placed in some newspaper of general circulation in the county in which the property was seized. If there are no newspapers in the county, then the notice must be posted in the post office nearest the place of seizure and in two other public places. A ten-day notice is not required for perishable goods.

If the property is valued greater than the amount of the liability owed to the government, and the property is not divisible, the IRS may sell the entire property. In this case, after the liability is satisfied and the costs of sale subtracted, the excess must be forwarded to the delinquent taxpayer.

Except for perishable goods, the sale shall be not less than 10 days nor more than 40 days from the date of notice. The place of sale shall be within the county in which the property is seized, except on special order of the Secretary.

Prior to the sale, the IRS must determine a minimum price for the property, taking into account the expense of making the levy and conducting the sale. If no minimum bid is received, under most conditions, the property becomes the property of the government with an amount equal to the minimum bid deleted from the liability owed or the property is returned to the owner with the expenses of levying and attempted sale added to the liability of the delinquent taxpayer.

Sale must be by either public auction or public sale under sealed bids.

Section 6339

Except for real property, the certificate of sale issued by the IRS shall be prima facie evidence of ownership of any person purchasing at the sale.

In cases involving sale of real property, the Secretary shall issue a deed of title which shall be prima facie evidence of ownership of the real property.

Section 6341

The expenses of levy and sale shall be charged against the proceeds from the sale. Any money realized after that shall be applied to the liability owed to the government. If there is any surplus money, it shall be, on application, forwarded to the person or persons legally entitled to it.

If the sale of the property fails to satisfy the liability to the government, the delinquent taxpayer still remains liable for the balance due.

Section 6343

The Secretary may release the property seized before sale if the delinquent taxpayer otherwise satisfies the liability owed to the government.

Section 6361

The Secretary may transfer to the State any sums due a taxpayer to satisfy any state tax liability for those states that have entered into agreement for joint cooperation in collection cases.

Section 6337

Any person whose property has been levied upon shall have the right to pay the amount due, together with the expenses of proceeding, if any, at any time prior to the sale and redeem the property.

The owners of any real estate sold under this code shall be permitted to redeem any particular tract of property at any time within 180 days after the sale thereof. (Note: in redeeming the property, the amount paid for the property and interest at the rate of 20 percent per annum shall be paid to the purchaser or the assignees of the purchaser.)

ABATEMENTS, CREDITS, AND REFUNDS

Section 6402

In case of overpayment, the Secretary may credit the overpayment as: credits against estimated tax, debts owed to federal agencies, past-due family support as per judicial order, and/or refund to the taxpayer.

The priorities for crediting overpayment by taxpayer shall be first to debts owed for prior tax years, then to debts due to other federal agencies, next to past-due family support, and last to future tax liabilities (estimated tax credits).

Section 6404

The Secretary shall abate any interest or penalties attributable in whole or in part by any employee of the IRS unless there is also some fault on the part of the taxpayer or the error was caused by the taxpayer.

The Secretary shall abate any interest caused by an erroneous refund check unless the taxpayer caused the erroneous refund or the amount of the refund exceeds $50,000.

Section 6406

In the absence of fraud or mistake in mathematical calculation, the findings of fact in and the decision of the Secretary upon the merits of any claim presented under or authorized by the internal revenue laws shall not be subject to review by any other administrative or accounting office, employee or agent of the United States (except for tax court petitions).

LIMITATIONS

Section 6501

Except as otherwise provided, the amount of any tax imposed by the Internal Revenue Code must be assessed within three years of the date the return was due to be filed. If the return is filed late, the time limit is three years from actual date of filing.

In the case of false or fraudulent returns with the intent to evade tax, the tax may be assessed and proceedings to collect such tax may be begun without assessment at any time.

If there has been a willful attempt to evade tax or if no return is filed, then tax may be assessed or collection without assessment may begin at any time.

The three-year limitation period may be extended by agreement of taxpayer, if the agreement is made prior to the expiration of the three-year period.

If an amended return is filed within 60 days of the expiration of the three-year period, the period is extended at least 60 days after the filing of the amended return.

If a substantial amount of gross income is omitted from the return (normally 25 percent), the assessment period is six years.

Section 6502

Collection by levy or by proceeding in court is begun within six years after the assessment, unless taxpayer agrees to an extension before the period runs.

For purposes of this limitation period, the date of levy is considered as the date the notice of seizure is given.

Section 6503

The running of the period of limitation shall be suspended during the period that the proceedings are being considered by the Tax Court or other judicial court and for 60 days after the court decision or determination.

Section 6511

Any claim for refund or credit by a taxpayer must be filed within three years from the date the return was originally required to be filed or two years from the date the tax was paid, which ever is later.

Section 6512

No suit may be filed in any court for refund if, after receiving notice of deficiency, the taxpayer files a petition with the Tax Court, unless an overpayment is determined by a final decision of the Tax Court. (Note: this section prevents the taxpayer from filing both a petition with the Tax Court and also filing a refund suit in another court.)

Section 6513

Tax returns filed early are considered as filed on the last day prescribed for filing. Any estimated payments of taxes shall be considered as paid on the last day for filing the returns for purposes of the three- or two-year limitation period.

Section 6531

No person shall be prosecuted, tried, or punished for any offense under the Internal Revenue Code (except as noted below) unless the indictment is found or the information is instituted (charged) within three years after the commission of the offense.

There is a six-year limitation period for the following offenses under the internal revenue code:

- ☐ Offenses involving fraud or conspiracy to commit fraud.
- ☐ Willfully attempting to evade taxes.
- ☐ Willfully aiding or assisting in the preparation of a false or fraudulent document or return.
- ☐ Willfully failing to pay any tax or file a return.
- ☐ Offenses relating to the intimidation of officers and employees of the government.
- ☐ For offenses committed by officers and employees of the government.

Section 6532

No refund suit may be brought until the expiration of six months from the date of filing of the claim for refund unless the Secretary has made a decision on the claim. The claim for refund must be brought within two years of the time the Secretary renders a decision on the claim or the six-month period expires.

The two-year period may be extended by agreement between the IRS and the taxpayer.

Any reconsideration by the Secretary of any refund claim shall not operate to extend the two-year period.

Suits by the United States to recover erroneous refunds must be started within two years of the refund, unless the erroneous refund is caused by fraud or misrepresentation of the taxpayer or someone acting for his/her benefit. In the latter case, the suit to recover an erroneous refund must be started within five years of the refund.

Suits by persons other than the taxpayer against the government must be commenced within nine months of the levy or action complained about.

INTEREST

Section 6601

Interest on any tax imposed by the Internal Revenue Code normally starts on the date that the tax is due.

The last date prescribed for payment of taxes in determining interest due is determined without regard to any extensions of time for payment. (This means that if you are given an extension of time to pay the tax, interest still accrues from the date it was originally due.)

Interest on penalties, additional amounts, and additions to tax liability shall start on the date of notice and demand of the penalty or of the additional amount.

Section 6602

Interest shall be due on any erroneous refund from the date of the refund.

Section 6611

Interest may be payable to the taxpayer on any overpayment of taxes. Interest on income tax refunds is payable if the refund is not paid within 45 days after the last date prescribed for filing the return. If the return is filed late, 45 days after the return is filed.

Section 6621

The interest rate for underpayment of taxes is the short-term Federal rate plus 3 percent points. The interest rate for the overpayment of taxes is 2 percent points over the short-term Federal rate.

The short-term Federal rate is determined by the Secretary during the first month of each calendar quarter. The rate is based on the average market yield on outstanding marketable obligations of the United States with remaining periods of maturity of 3 years or less.

If the underpayment is the results of a tax motivated transaction, the interest rate shall be 120 percent of the underpayment interest rate.

Tax motivated transactions include:

☐ Any valuation overstatements.
☐ Any loss disallowed by certain sections of the code.
☐ Any tax straddles.
☐ Any use of an accounting method which may result in a substantial distortion of income.
☐ Any sham or fraudulent transaction.

Section 6622

Interest shall be compounded daily.

PENALTIES AND ADDITIONS TO THE TAX
Section 6651

There are two types of penalties that may be imposed on taxpayers. In the case of failure to file most tax returns, the penalty shall not be less than $100 or 100 percent of the amount required to be shown as tax on the return. This penalty may be waived by establishing that the failure to file was due to reasonable cause and not due to willful neglect.

For other returns, the penalty is 5 percent for each month or partial month thereof, not to exceed 25 percent of the amount required to be shown as tax on the return. This penalty is also waivable as noted above. An additional penalty may be assessed for failure to pay within ten days after formal notice is given.

Section 6652

Failure to file information returns for certain payments aggregating less than $10 shall be $1 per individual statement, not to exceed $1000 per calendar year.

Failure to report tips by an employee to an employer may cause the assessment of a penalty not to exceed 50 percent of the tax due on the tips.

The penalties for failure to file other information returns can be as much as $5,000 per calendar year.

Section 6653

If any part of the tax underpayment is due to negligence or disregard of rules and regulations, the penalty may be 5 percent of the underpayment and 50 percent of the interest payable.

For purposes of this section, negligence is defined as any failure to make a reasonable attempt to comply with the provisions of the Internal Revenue Code. The term "disregard" includes careless, reckless, or intentional disregard.

In cases of fraud, the penalty may be 75 percent of the underpayment and 50 percent of the interest payable on the underpayment.

Section 6654

The Secretary may waive the penalty for good and sufficient causes in most cases.

Section 6672

As a general rule, any person required to collect taxes who willfully fails to collect such tax is liable for a penalty equal to the total amount of tax evaded or not collected.

Section 6674

This section makes it a crime to furnish fraudulent statements to employees or failing to furnish required statements.

Section 6676

The failure of any person required to supply taxpayer identification numbers (TIN) is punishable by a penalty from $5 to $50 for each failure, and the total cannot exceed $100,000 in each calendar year.

Section 6682

Giving false information with respect to withholding of federal taxes may be punished by civil fraud penalties in addition to criminal sanctions.

Section 6686

Failure to file returns or supply information as required may be punished by civil penalty and/or criminal sanctions.

Section 6701

The penalties for aiding and abetting in the understatement of tax liability is punishable by a penalty of not more than $10,000 and/or criminal sanctions.

CIVIL ACTIONS BY THE UNITED STATES
Section 7402

The District Courts of the United States have the jurisdiction to make and issue orders as may be necessary for the enforcement of the Internal Revenue Code. The District Court also has the power to enforce summons.

Section 7405

The District Courts have the authority to issue the necessary orders to enforce the recovery of erroneous refunds.)

Section 7408

The District Court has the authority to issue injunctions against promoters of abusive tax shelters.

PROCEEDINGS BY TAXPAYERS
Section 7421

The District Courts have no jurisdiction to restrain the assessment of a tax liability.

Section 7422

This section deals with the authority of District Courts to accept refund suits by taxpayers against the government.

Section 7431

This section permits the taxpayer to sue in District Court employees of the U.S. government who make unauthorized disclosures of personal information on taxpayers.

CHAPTER **14**

Keeping Records to Support Your Case

It is vitally important to maintain good records to support your tax position. Some key concepts in keeping records are given below:

- ☐ The code and IRS regulations require the taxpayer to keep adequate records.
- ☐ The burden of proof to establish income tax elements, deductions, adjustments, etc. is on the taxpayer.
- ☐ Failure to keep adequate records may result in the taxpayer being required to pay more tax than necessary.
- ☐ Certain types of records are required to support certain tax transactions.
- ☐ Tax records should be retained for a minimum of six years.
- ☐ Missing copies of tax returns may be obtained from the IRS service center where the returns were filed.
- ☐ Most taxpayers are required to use the cash accounting method.

As noted in Chapter 5, good record keeping is the best proof to substantiate your tax return. Records are necessary when your returns are audited. As discussed in Chapters 8 and 12, the burden is on the taxpayer to establish the correctness of his/her return. Usually, an examination of a taxpayer's return does not occur until one to three years after the return is filed. It is almost impossible, without good records, to establish the correctness of the return filed by the taxpayer.

TYPES OF RECORDS REQUIRED

The IRS regulations require the taxpayer to keep sufficient and adequate records to determine the proper tax due. Records must be kept accurately. No particular form is required. As a rule, the non-business taxpayer should keep at least the following records:

☐ All sales slips that are tax deductible.
☐ Invoices and sales slips pertaining to tax deductible purchases.
☐ Canceled checks.
☐ Stock brokerage statements.
☐ Form W-2, Wage and Tax Statements.
☐ Form W-2P, Statement for Recipients of Annuities, Pensions, Retired Pay, or IRA Payments.
☐ Form 1099s on interests, dividends, distributions, etc.
☐ Pay statements.
☐ Automobile logs to establish business use of automobile.
☐ Copies of tax returns from prior years.
☐ Any other documents that establish either income or tax adjustments transaction.

The use of running records (kept up daily) are more acceptable to the IRS and, in many cases, can be the difference between a successful and unsuccessful audit. In addition, keeping good records helps prevent the taxpayer from overlooking deductions or adjustments.

At one time, IRS regulations attempted to require the keeping of contemporaneous records to support travel, transportation, entertainment, and business gift expenses. This requirement was disapproved by Congress before it became effective. The requirement now is that the taxpayer must establish the deductions or credits by adequate records or by sufficient evidence corroborating the taxpayer's statements. In one case, the courts held that entries on a desk calendar not supported by other evidence was not sufficient proof to support claimed deductions.

Some of the considerations used by the courts and the IRS in determining whether or not to accept the taxpayer's records as sufficient to uphold the deduction or credit include:

☐ Timely recording. Record the expense item in an account book at or near the time of the expense. Late entries are considered as suspect.
☐ Keep copies of any expense records or travel claims presented to your employer. Statements the taxpayer gives to his/her employer, client, or customer are considered as an adequate record of the expenses. In most cases, the statement may be a copy of your account book or other record.
☐ Deductions are not allowed for approximations or estimates, or for expenses that are lavish or extravagant.

☐ Not only must the taxpayer establish the cost of the expense, but also that the expense is deductible.

☐ Separation of expenses. Each separate payment is normally considered as a separate expense. The IRS requires that expenses be recorded separately. An exception to this is that the taxpayer is not required to keep separate records regarding expenses of a similar nature occurring during the course of a single event. For example, the taxpayer may record his/her meal expenses for one day in a single entry.

☐ Receipts are considered as the best item of evidence.

☐ Documentary evidence is required to support all lodging expenses while traveling away from home. It is also required for any expense of $25 or more.

☐ A canceled check does not by itself support a business expense. The check and a bill or invoice is normally sufficient.

Travel

In order to deduct or credit travel expenses, the taxpayer must prove:

☐ Each separate amount that was spent for travel away from home, such as the cost of your transportation or lodging. The taxpayer may total the daily cost of breakfast, lunch, and dinner, and other incidental elements of such travel if they are listed in reasonable categories, such as meals, gas and oil, and taxi fares.

☐ The dates the taxpayer left and returned home for each trip, and the number of days spent on business away from home.

☐ The destination or locality of the travel, described by name of city, town, or similar designation.

☐ The business reason for the travel or the business benefit gained from the travel.

Entertainment

To deduct entertainment expenses, the taxpayer must prove the below listed items:

☐ The amount of each separate expense for entertainment, except for incidental items, such as taxi fares and telephone calls, which may be totaled on a daily basis.

☐ The date the entertainment took place.

☐ The name, address, or location, and the type of entertainment, such as dinner or theater, if the information is not apparent from the name or designation of the place.

☐ The reason for the entertainment or the business benefit gained or expected to be gained from entertaining and, except for business meals, the nature of any activity that took place. (Note: for returns covering taxyears 1987 and later, the Tax Reform Act of 1986 limits the deductibility of certain entertainment expenses.)

☐ The occupation or other information about the person or persons entertained, including name, title, or other designation sufficient to establish the business relationship to the taxpayer. In addition, information regarding whether or not the taxpayer or his/her representive or agent was present.

Office in Home Deduction

The records necessary to establish an office in the home deduction must show:

☐ That part of the home used for business.

☐ That you use this part of the home exclusively and regularly for business as either your principal place of business as a direct seller or as the place where you meet or deal with clients or customers in the normal course of your business.

☐ The amount of depreciation and other expenses for keeping up the part of the home that is for business.

Automobile Expenses

Whether or not the taxpayer uses the standard mileage rates, the taxpayer must keep records to show when the taxpayer started using the automobile for business and the cost or other basis of the car. The records must also show the business miles and the total miles the car was used during the taxyear. In most cases, a log of trips is essential to establish business use of the automobile.

If the actual expenses are claimed, in addition to the above expenses, the records must show the below items:

☐ Cost of operating the car including insurance, personal property, etc. (Note: receipts will be needed.)

☐ The extent the car expenses reflect travel away from home.

Gifts

In order to deduct gift expenses, the taxpayer must prove:

☐ The cost of each gift.

☐ The date of each gift.

☐ The description of each gift.

☐ The reason for giving the gift, or any business benefit gained or expected to be gained from giving it.

☐ The occupation or other information about the person receiving the gift, including name, title, or other designation to establish the business relationship to the taxpayer.

Additional Information

The IRS may require additional information to clarify or to establish the accuracy or reliability of information contained in the taxpayer's records, statements, testimony, or documentary evidence before a deduction is allowed.

INADEQUATE RECORDS

As noted earlier, the Internal Revenue Code requires every person to keep such records as the Secretary of Treasury may require. IRS regulations require taxpayers to maintain such accounting records as will enable him/her to file a correct return. The tax code also requires the taxpayer to maintain records sufficient to clearly reflect income. In addition, the taxpayer is required to maintain sufficient records to establish his/her right to any deductions and adjustments to gross income.

If the IRS determines that a taxpayer's records are "inadequate," then they can use certain methods to arrive at the taxable income of a taxpayer. Methods used include net worth and bank deposits. IRS's methods of arriving at the taxable income of a taxpayer are discussed in Chapter 5.

The IRS has defined "inadequate records" as the lack of records, or records so incomplete that correctness of taxable income cannot be determined. (Note: the IRS has determined that the taxpayer's records were inadequate where they were adequate in all respects except in one area.) If the IRS determines that the lack of adequate records was intentional, then civil or criminal fraud may be pursued.

In most cases, the lack of adequate records causes the IRS to examine deeper into a taxpayer's status. Accordingly, the examiners will look at areas that normally would not be examined. In one recent case, the lack of adequate records was used by the IRS as primary reason to obtain a search warrant to examine the contents of a taxpayer's safe deposit box.

NOTICE OF INADEQUATE RECORDS

In addition to assessing additional taxes, the IRS can issue a *Notice of Inadequate Records*. This is accomplished by IRS's *Standard Letter 978 (DO)*. This letter directs the taxpayer to keep certain records in the future. The required records include:

- [ ] The date and description of each transaction in which the taxpayer engages.
- [ ] The date and amount of each payment made by the taxpayer.
- [ ] The date and amount of each item of gross income received.
- [ ] The date and amount of each payment made.
- [ ] The name and address of each payee.
- [ ] A description of the nature of each payment.

RECONSTRUCTION OF RECORDS

If the taxpayer's records are inadequate, there is nothing illegal in reconstructing them. (Note: this is different from back-dating records, which may be a crime.)

If the records are reconstructed, the examiner should be advised of this fact. In addition, the methods used to reconstruct the records should be explained to the examiner. For example, in a case involving the business use of an automobile by a public school teacher, the use of attendance records at various schools may be used to construct an automobile-use log. Often, the use of third party records will assist in reconstructing tax records.

If the taxpayer claims that the records have been stolen or destroyed, then the examiner will expect a police or fire report to back up the claim. If the report of the loss to fire or theft is dated after notice of audit is received by the taxpayer, the examiner may be suspicious. In most cases, it will be better for the taxpayer to admit the inadequacy of his/her records rather than attempt to falsify receipts, etc.

IRS regulations provide that if a taxpayer does not have adequate records to support an element of an expense, then to support the element, the taxpayer may: submit a statement containing specific information in detail as to the element, and provide other supporting evidence sufficient to establish the element.

HOW LONG TO KEEP RECORDS

Generally, the taxpayer should keep his/her records as long as they are important for any federal tax law. Most records are important for at least three years following the filing to the return.

In some cases, the government can question a return six years after it is filed. For example, the IRS may contend that you underreported your income by more than 25 percent or that fraud was committed. A taxpayer may feel that the six-year period does not apply to him/her, but the essential fact is to prove that to the IRS. Accordingly, the taxpayer should, as a minimum, keep his/her records for six years after the last date the return was filed or due to be filed (whichever is later).

In some cases, as in the receipts for home improvements, the taxpayer may need to establish many years later his/her cost of certain property. The taxpayer should retain those type of records for at least three years after the property is disposed of. For example, a taxpayer who, after owning his home for 20 years, decided to retire and move to a warmer climate, would be required to establish the amount of monetary gain made on the sale of the house. In this regard, all receipts for home improvements, the addition of a pool, etc. will be needed regardless of the date of the expenditure.

RECOMMENDED RECORD KEEPING PROCEDURES

Joseph Narun, a management consultant, recommends the keeping of a four-part system that integrates daily recording, single-item tracking of expenses, filing of receipts, and regular reviews of your tax position. The system uses a daily general diary in which to keep most of the itemized deductions. Separate special diaries are recommended for the recording of single activities such as automobile logs and sideline business activities.

He recommends the use of color coded entries. This requires the taxpayer to keep different colored pens for each type of entry. For example, one color should be used for medical expenses and a different color for taxes paid. A handy reference code is needed to simply the color codings.

Expense receipts should be filed in separate envelopes. (Note: it is helpful to make notes on the receipts as to date and tax consequences of the receipt.) He also recommends at least quarterly totaling up of each expense category.

Other useful hints include:

- ☐ Completing the memo line on checks to help explain the expense.
- ☐ Notations on front and back of charge receipts.
- ☐ Make copies of diary pages on office copier and store them in a different location from other records.
- ☐ If you use a color-code system, use the same system for all your records and checkbook statements.

ACCOUNTING PERIODS AND METHODS

For non-business taxpayers, the normal accounting period is the calendar year. The Tax Reform Act of 1986 limited the right of taxpayers to use other than calendar years in most cases.

A taxpayer can not change his/her accounting period without permission from the IRS.

There are two basic accounting methods, cash and accrual. Most taxpayers are required to use the cash method. Taxpayers are required to use the same method each year unless consent to change is obtained from the IRS.

Under the cash method, the taxpayer reports all items of income in the year that the income is received or made available to the taxpayer. Expenses, in most cases, are deducted in the year that they are paid. In some cases, expenses that are paid in advance can only be deducted in the year to which they apply.

The accrual method accounts for income when earned, not when it is received. Expenses are deducted when incurred rather than when they are paid.

REPLACING MISSING TAX FORMS

If a taxpayer has lost or destroyed his/her copies of tax forms that were previously filed, replacement copies may be obtained from the service center where the forms were originally filed. The taxpayer should file a *Form 4506, Request for Copy of Tax Form* with the service center to obtain the copies. It normally takes about six weeks to get replacement copies.

Appendices

APPENDIX **A**

List of
Toll-Free Numbers
of IRS Offices

To Call Tele-Tax Toll-Free, Use Only The Numbers Listed Below For Your Area

Recorded Tax Information has about 150 topics of tax information that answer many Federal tax questions and a topic for local information such as the location of VITA and TCE sites. You can hear up to three topics on each call you make.

Automated Refund Information is available after March 15. If it has been 10 weeks since you mailed your 1986 tax return, we will be able to check the status of your refund.

Long-distance charges apply if you call from outside the local dialing area of the numbers listed below. **Do not dial 800 when using a local number.** A complete list of these topics and instructions on how to use Tele-Tax are on the next page.

*Note: Cities with a **1** before them have only Recorded Tax Information and can only be called if you have a push-button (tone signalling) phone. Cities with a **2** before them have Recorded Tax Information, including topic 999 for local information, and Automated Refund Information and can be called by using any type of phone.*

ALABAMA
1 Birmingham, 251-9454
1 Huntsville, 534-5203
1 Mobile, 433-6993
1 Montgomery, 262-8304

ALASKA
1 Anchorage, 562-1848

ARIZONA
2 Phoenix, 252-4909

ARKANSAS
1 Little Rock, 372-3891

CALIFORNIA
1 Bakersfield, 861-4105
1 Carson, 632-3555
2 Counties of Amador, Calaveras, Contra Costa, Marin, and San Joaquin, 1-800-428-4032
2 Los Angeles, 617-3177
2 Oakland, 839-4245
1 Oxnard, 485-7236
1 Riverside, 351-6769
1 Sacramento, 448-4367
1 San Diego, 293-5020
1 San Jose, 293-5606
1 Santa Ana, 836-2974
1 Santa Maria, 928-7503
1 Santa Rosa, 528-6233
1 Stockton, 463-6005
1 Visalia, 733-8194

COLORADO
1 Colorado Springs, 597-6344
2 Denver, 592-1118
1 Ft. Collins, 221-0658

CONNECTICUT
1 Bridgeport, 335-0070
1 Hartford, 547-0015
1 New Haven, 777-4594
1 Waterbury, 754-4235

DELAWARE
1 Dover, 674-1118
1 Wilmington, 652-0272

DISTRICT of COLUMBIA
2 Call 628-2929

FLORIDA
1 Daytona Beach, 253-0669
1 Ft. Lauderdale, 523-3100
2 Jacksonville, 353-9579
1 Miami, 374-5144
1 Orlando, 422-0592
1 St. Petersburg, 578-0424
1 Tallahassee, 222-0807
1 Tampa, 229-0815
1 West Palm Beach, 655-1996

GEORGIA
1 Albany, 435-1415
1 Atlanta, 331-6572
1 Augusta, 722-9068
1 Columbus, 327-0298
1 Macon, 745-2890
1 Savannah, 355-9632

HAWAII
1 Honolulu, 541-1185

IDAHO
2 Call 1-800-554-4477

ILLINOIS
1 Aurora, 851-2718
1 Bloomington, 828-6116
1 Champaign, 398-1779
2 Chicago, 886-9614
1 East St. Louis, 875-4050
1 Ottawa, 433-1568
1 Peoria, 637-9305
1 Quad Cities, 326-1720
1 Rockford, 987-4280
1 Springfield, 789-0489

INDIANA
1 Evansville, 422-1026
1 Fort Wayne, 484-3065
1 Gary, 884-4465
2 Indianapolis, 634-1550
1 South Bend, 232-5459

IOWA
1 Cedar Rapids, 399-2210
1 Des Moines, 284-4271
1 Quad Cities, 326-1720
1 Waterloo, 234-0817

KANSAS
1 Wichita, 264-3147

KENTUCKY
1 Erlanger, 727-3338
1 Lexington, 233-2889
1 Louisville, 582-5599

LOUISIANA
1 New Orleans, 529-2854

MAINE
1 Portland, 775-0465

MARYLAND
2 Baltimore, 244-7306
1 Cumberland, 722-5331
1 Frederick, 663-5798
1 Hagerstown, 733-6815
1 Salisbury, 742-9458

MASSACHUSETTS
2 Boston, 523-8602
1 Springfield, 739-6624

MICHIGAN
1 Ann Arbor, 665-4544
2 Detroit, 961-4282
1 Flint, 238-4599
1 Grand Rapids, 451-2034
1 Kalamazoo, 343-0255
1 Lansing, 372-2454
1 Mt. Clemens, 463-9550
1 Pontiac, 858-2336
1 Saginaw, 753-9911

MINNESOTA
1 Duluth, 722-5494
1 Rochester, 288-5595
2 St. Paul, 224-4288

MISSISSIPPI
1 Gulfport, 863-3302
1 Jackson, 965-4168

MISSOURI
1 Jefferson City, 636-8312
1 Kansas City, 421-3741
1 Springfield, 883-3419
2 St. Louis, 241-4700

MONTANA
1 Billings, 656-1422
1 Great Falls, 727-4902
1 Helena, 443-7034

NEBRASKA
1 Lincoln, 471-5450
1 Omaha, 221-3324

NEVADA
2 Call 1-800-554-4477

NEW HAMPSHIRE
1 Manchester, 623-5778
1 Portsmouth, 431-0637

NEW JERSEY
1 Atlantic City, 348-2636
1 Camden, 966-3412
1 Hackensack, 487-1817
2 Newark, 624-1223
1 Paterson, 278-5442
1 Trenton, 599-2150

NEW MEXICO
1 Albuquerque, 766-1102

NEW YORK
1 Albany, 465-8318
1 Binghamton, 722-8426
2 Brooklyn, 858-4461
2 Buffalo, 856-9320
2 Manhattan, 406-4080
1 Mineola, 248-6790
1 Poughkeepsie, 452-1877
1 Rochester, 454-3330
1 Smithtown, 979-0720
2 Staten Island, 406-4080
1 Syracuse, 471-1630
1 White Plains, 683-0134

NORTH CAROLINA
1 Asheville, 254-3044
1 Charlotte, 567-9885
1 Durham, 541-5283
1 Fayetteville, 483-0735
1 Greensboro, 378-1572
1 Raleigh, 755-1498
1 Winston-Salem, 725-3013

NORTH DAKOTA
1 Bismarck, 258-8210
1 Fargo, 232-9360
1 Grand Forks, 746-0324
1 Minot, 838-1234

OHIO
1 Akron, 253-1170
1 Canton, 455-6061
2 Cincinnati, 421-0329
2 Cleveland, 522-3037
1 Columbus, 469-2266
1 Dayton, 225-7237
1 Lima, 224-0341
1 Mansfield, 525-3474
1 Toledo, 255-3743
1 Youngstown, 744-4200

OKLAHOMA
1 Oklahoma City, 235-3434
1 Tulsa, 599-0555

OREGON
2 Portland, 294-5363

PENNSYLVANIA
1 Bethlehem, 861-0325
1 Harrisburg, 236-1356
1 Jenkintown, 887-1261
1 Lancaster, 392-0980
1 Norristown, 275-0242
2 Philadelphia, 592-8946
2 Pittsburgh, 281-3120
1 Reading, 373-4568
1 Scranton, 961-0325
1 Wilkes-Barre, 823-9552
1 Williamsport, 323-4242

RHODE ISLAND
1 Providence, 861-5220

SOUTH CAROLINA
1 Charleston, 722-0369
1 Columbia, 254-4749
1 Greenville, 235-8093

SOUTH DAKOTA
1 Rapid City, 348-3454
1 Sioux Falls, 335-7081
1 Watertown, 882-4979

TENNESSEE
1 Chattanooga, 892-5577
1 Jackson, 664-1858
1 Johnson City, 282-1917
1 Knoxville, 521-7478
1 Memphis, 525-2611
2 Nashville, 242-1541

TEXAS
1 Austin, 479-0391
1 Dallas, 767-1792
1 El Paso, 534-0260
1 Ft. Worth, 334-3888
2 Houston, 850-8801
1 San Antonio, 680-9591

UTAH
1 Salt Lake City, 355-9328

VERMONT
1 Burlington, 658-0007

VIRGINIA
1 Bristol, 669-0565
1 Charlottesville, 296-8558
1 Danville, 797-2223
1 Hampton, 826-8071
1 Lynchburg, 845-6052
1 Norfolk, 441-3623
2 Richmond, 771-2369
1 Roanoke, 982-6062
1 Staunton, 886-3541

WASHINGTON
2 Seattle, 343-7221
1 Spokane, 455-9213

WEST VIRGINIA
1 Charleston, 343-3597
1 Huntington, 523-0104

WISCONSIN
1 Eau Claire, 834-6121
1 Green Bay, 433-3884
1 Madison, 264-5349
2 Milwaukee, 291-1783
1 Racine, 886-1615

WYOMING
1 Cheyenne, 634-1198

Note: *If there is no number listed for your specific area, call **1-800-554-4477**.*

To Call IRS Toll-Free for Answers to Your Federal Tax Questions, Use Only the Number Listed Below for Your Area.

*Caution: "Toll-free" is a telephone call for which you pay only local charges with no long-distance charge. Please use a local city number only if it is not a long-distance call for you. **Do not dial 800 when using a local city number.** Otherwise, use the general toll-free number given.*

We are happy to answer questions to help you prepare your return. But you should know that you are responsible for the accuracy of your return. If we do make an error, you are still responsible for the payment of the correct tax.

To make sure that IRS employees give courteous responses and correct information to taxpayers, a second IRS employee sometimes listens in on telephone calls. No record is kept of any taxpayer's name, address, or social security number.

If you find it necessary to write instead of calling, please address your letter to your IRS District Director for a prompt reply. Make sure you include your social security number or taxpayer identifying number when you write.

The IRS has a telephone service called Tele-Tax. It provides automated refund information and recorded tax information on about 150 topics covering such areas as filing requirements, dependents, itemized deductions, and tax credits. Tele-Tax is available 24 hours a day, 7 days a week, to taxpayers using push-button (tone signalling) telephones, and Monday through Friday, during office hours, to taxpayers using push-button (pulse dial) or rotary (dial) phones. See Tele-Tax Information in the index for the page numbers that contain telephone numbers, available topics, and instructions describing how to use this service.

ALABAMA
Call 1-800-424-1040

ALASKA
Anchorage, 561-7484
  Elsewhere in Alaska, call
  1-800-478-1040

ARIZONA
Phoenix, 257-1233

ARKANSAS
Call 1-800-424-1040

CALIFORNIA
Please call the telephone number shown in the white pages of your local telephone directory under U.S. Government, Internal Revenue Service, Federal Tax Assistance.

COLORADO
Denver, 825-7041

CONNECTICUT
Call 1-800-424-1040

DELAWARE
Call 1-800-424-1040

DISTRICT of COLUMBIA
Call 488-3100

FLORIDA
Jacksonville, 354-1760

GEORGIA
Atlanta, 522-0050

HAWAII
Oahu, 541-1040
All other islands,
  1-800-232-2511

IDAHO
Call 1-800-424-1040

ILLINOIS
Chicago, 435-1040

INDIANA
Indianapolis, 269-5477

IOWA
Des Moines, 283-0523

KANSAS
Call 1-800-424-1040

KENTUCKY
Call 1-800-424-1040

LOUISIANA
Call 1-800-424-1040

MAINE
Call 1-800-424-1040

MARYLAND
Baltimore, 962-2590
Montgomery County,
  488-3100
Prince George's County,
  488-3100

MASSACHUSETTS
Boston, 523-1040

MICHIGAN
Detroit, 237-0800

MINNESOTA
Minneapolis, 291-1422
St. Paul, 291-1422

MISSISSIPPI
Call 1-800-424-1040

MISSOURI
St. Louis, 342-1040

MONTANA
Call 1-800-424-1040

NEBRASKA
Omaha, 422-1500

NEVADA
Call 1-800-424-1040

NEW HAMPSHIRE
Call 1-800-424-1040

NEW JERSEY
Newark, 622-0600

NEW MEXICO
Call 1-800-424-1040

NEW YORK
Bronx, 732-0100
Brooklyn, 596-3770
Buffalo, 855-3955
Manhattan, 732-0100
Nassau, 222-1131
Queens, 596-3770
Rockland County, 997-1510
Staten Island, 732-0100
Suffolk, 724-5000
Westchester County,
  997-1510

NORTH CAROLINA
Call 1-800-424-1040

NORTH DAKOTA
Call 1-800-424-1040

OHIO
Cincinnati, 621-6281
Cleveland, 522-3000

OKLAHOMA
Call 1-800-424-1040

OREGON
Eugene, 485-8286
Portland, 221-3960
Salem, 581-8721

PENNSYLVANIA
Philadelphia, 574-9900
Pittsburgh, 281-0112

PUERTO RICO
San Juan Metro Area,
  753-4040
Isla DDD, 753-4549

RHODE ISLAND
Call 1-800-424-1040

SOUTH CAROLINA
Call 1-800-424-1040

SOUTH DAKOTA
Call 1-800-424-1040

TENNESSEE
Nashville, 259-4601

TEXAS
Austin, 472-1974
Corpus Christi, 888-9431
Dallas, 742-2440
El Paso, 532-6116
Ft. Worth, 263-9229
Houston, 965-0440
San Antonio, 229-1700

UTAH
Call 1-800-424-1040

VERMONT
Call 1-800-424-1040

VIRGINIA
Bailey's Crossroads,
  557-9230
Richmond, 649-2361

WASHINGTON
Seattle, 442-1040

WEST VIRGINIA
Call 1-800-424-1040

WISCONSIN
Milwaukee, 271-3780

WYOMING
Call 1-800-424-1040

Note: *If there is no number listed for your specific area, please call **1-800-424-1040.***

Telephone Assistance Services for Deaf Taxpayers Who Have Access to TV / Telephone—TTY Equipment.

Hours of Operation

8:00 A.M. to 6:45 P.M. EST (Filing Season)

8:00 A.M. to 4:30 P.M. EST (Nonfiling Season)

Indiana residents,
  1-800-382-4059

Elsewhere in U.S., including Alaska, Hawaii, Virgin Islands, and Puerto Rico,
  1-800-428-4732

Toll-Free "Forms Only" Telephone Numbers

If you only need to order tax forms and publications and do not have any tax questions, call the number listed below for your area.

ALASKA
Anchorage, 563-5313
  Elsewhere in Alaska, call
  1-800-478-1040

ARIZONA
Phoenix, 257-1233
Tucson, 882-0730

CALIFORNIA
Please call the telephone number shown in the white pages of your local telephone directory under U.S. Government, Internal Revenue Service, Federal Tax Forms.

COLORADO
Denver, 825-7041

HAWAII
Honolulu, 541-1180
All other islands,
  1-800-232-2511

ILLINOIS
Bloomington, 662-2515

OREGON
Eugene, 485-8286
Portland, 221-3933
Salem, 581-8721

PUERTO RICO
San Juan Metro Area,
  753-4040
Isla DDD, 753-4549

VIRGINIA
Richmond, 329-1052

WASHINGTON
Seattle, 442-5100

Note: *If there is no number listed for your state or specific area, call **1-800-424-FORM (3676).***

IRS Form 433-A
(Collection Information Statement)

Form **433-A**
(Rev. April 1981)

Department of the Treasury — Internal Revenue Service

Collection Information Statement for Individuals

(If you need additional space, please attach a separate sheet.)

1. Taxpayers' names and address *(including County)*	2. Home phone number	3. Marital status

	4. Social Security Numbers	a. Taxpayer	b. Spouse

Section I. — Employment Information

5. Taxpayer's employer or business *(name and address)*	6. Business phone number	7. Occupation
	8. Paydays	9. *(Check appropriate box)* ☐ Wage earner ☐ Sole proprietor ☐ Partner
10. Spouse's employer or business *(name and address)*	11. Business phone number	12. Occupation
	13. Paydays	14. *(Check appropriate box)* ☐ Wage earner ☐ Sole proprietor ☐ Partner

Section II. — Personal Information

15. Name, address and telephone number of next of kin or other reference

16. Age and relationship of dependents *(exclude husband and wife)* living in your household	17. Number of exemptions claimed on Form W-4

	a. Taxpayer	b. Spouse	
18. Date of birth ▶			

Section III. — General Financial Information

19. Latest filed income tax return *(tax year)*	20. Adjusted gross income on return	

21. Bank accounts *(Include Savings & Loans, Credit Unions, IRA and KEOGH accounts, Certificates of Deposit, etc.)*

Name of Institution	Address	Type of Account	Account No.	Balance
Total *(Enter in Item 28)*			▶	

22. Bank charge cards, Lines of credit, etc.

Type of Account or Card	Name and Address of Financial Institution	Monthly Payment	Credit Limit	Amount Owed	Credit Available
Totals *(Enter in Item 34)*	▶				

23. Safe deposit boxes rented or accessed *(List all locations, box numbers, and contents)*

24. **Real Property** *(Brief description and type of ownership)*	**Address** *(Include County and State)*
a.	
b.	
c.	

25. **Life Insurance** *(Name of Company)*	Policy Number	Type	Face Amount	Available Loan Value
Total *(Enter in Item 30)*			▶	

(over)

Form **433-A** (Rev. 4-81)

Section III — continued   **General Financial Information**

26. Additional Information *(Court proceedings, bankruptcies, repossessions, recent transfers of assets for less than full value, anticipated increases in income, condition of health, etc.; include information on trusts, estates, profit-sharing plans, etc., on which you are a participant or beneficiary)*

(Please note: The interviewer will help you complete Sections IV and V.)

Section IV.   **Asset and Liability Analysis**

Description (a)	Cur. Mkt. Value (b)	Liabilities Bal. Due (c)	Equity in Asset (d)	Amt. of Mo. Pymt. (e)	Name and Address of Lien/Note Holder/Obligee (f)	Date Pledged (f)	Date of Final Pymt. (g)
27. Cash							
28. Bank accounts							
29. Stocks, Bonds, Investments							
30. Cash or loan value of Insur.							
31. Vehicles *(Model, year, license)*							
a.							
b.							
c.							
32. Real property a.							
b.							
c.							
33. Other assets							
a.							
b.							
c.							
d.							
e.							
34. Bank revolving credit							
35. Other Liabilities *(Include judgments, notes, and other charge accounts)* a.							
b.							
c.							
d.							
e.							
f.							
g.							
36. Federal taxes owed							
37. Totals			$	$			

Section V.   **Monthly Income and Expense Analysis**

Source	Income (a) Gross	Net	Necessary Living Expenses (b)	
38. Wages/Salaries *(Taxpayer)*	$	$	46. Rent	$
39. Wages/Salaries *(Spouse)*			47. Groceries	
40. Interest - Dividends			48. Allowable installment payments	
41. Net business income *(from Form 433-B)*			49. Utilities	
42. Rental income			50. Transportation	
43. Pension *(Taxpayer)*			51. Insurance	
44. Pension *(Spouse)*			52. Medical	
			53. Estimated tax payments	
			54. Other expenses *(specify)*	
45. Total	$	$	55. Total	$
			56. Net difference *(income less necessary living expenses)*	$

Certification

Under penalties of perjury, I declare that to the best of my knowledge and belief this statement of assets, liabilities, and other information is true, correct, and complete.

57. Your signature	58. Spouse's signature *(if joint return was filed)*	59. Date

· U S GOVERNMENT PRINTING OFFICE 1983-381-541/5202   Form **433-A** (Rev. 4-81)

IRS Form 843
(Claim for Refund)

Form **843**
(Rev. April 1985)
Department of the Treasury
Internal Revenue Service

Claim

▶ **See Instructions on back.**

OMB No. 1545-0024
Expires 3/31/88

If your claim is for an overpayment of income taxes, do NOT use this form (See Instructions)

(Use this form ONLY if your claim involves one of the taxes shown on line 8 or a refund or abatement of interest or penalties.)

Please type or print

Name of taxpayer or purchaser of stamps
ROBERTS, Donald and Marie

Telephone number (optional)
(209) 432-7787

Number and street
4516 West Street

City, town, or post office, state, and ZIP code
Bakersfield, California 93748

Fill in applicable items—Use attachments if necessary

1 Your social security number	2 Spouse's social security number	3 Employer identification number
457 51 1568	257 53 6670	

4 Name and address shown on return, if different from above

same as above

5 Period—prepare separate form for each tax period
From January 1 ,19 XX, to December 31 ,19 XX

6 Amount to be refunded or abated
$ 13,487.20

7 Dates of payment
June 26, 19XX

8 Type of tax or penalty
☐ Employment   ☐ Estate   ☐ Excise   ☐ Gift   ☐ Stamp   ☒ Penalty IRC section ▶ 6653 (b)

9 Kind of return filed
☐ 706   ☐ 709   ☐ 720 IRS No. (s) ▶ _____   ☐ 940   ☐ 941   ☐ 990-PF   ☐ 2290   ☐ 4720
☒ Other (specify) ▶ Form 1040

10 If this claim involves refund of excise taxes on gasoline, special fuels or lubricating oil, please indicate your tax year for income tax purposes.

11 Explain why you believe this claim should be allowed and show computation of tax refund or abatement.

Government erroneously assessed a civil fraud penalty against taxpayers without any proof of intent to defraud or willfully evade taxes legally due.

Taxpayers understatement of tax liability was due to reasonable cause. Accordingly, no penalty should have been assessed.

Under penalties of perjury, I declare that I have examined this claim, including accompanying schedules and statements, and to the best of my knowledge and belief it is true, correct, and complete.

Signature (Title, if applicable)   *Donald Roberts*   Date   July 2, 19XX

Signature   *Marie Roberts*   Date   July 5, 19XX

Director's Stamp
(Date received)

For Internal Revenue Service Use Only

☐ Refund of taxes illegally, erroneously, or excessively collected
☐ Refund of amount paid for stamps unused, or used in error or excess
☐ Abatement of tax assessed (not applicable to estate or gift taxes)

For Paperwork Reduction Act Notice, see instructions on back.

Form **843** (Rev. 4-85)

Instructions

(Section references are to the Internal Revenue Code.)

Paperwork Reduction Act Notice.—We ask for this information to carry out the Internal Revenue laws of the United States. We need it to ensure that taxpayers are complying with these laws and to allow us to figure and collect the right amount of tax. You are required to give us this information.

Purpose of Form.—This form can be used to claim certain refunds and abatements. Use Form 843 to file a claim for refund of overpaid taxes (except in the case of income tax), interest, penalties, and additions to tax. For example, if on your employment tax return, you reported and paid more Federal income tax than was actually withheld from an employee, use this form to claim a refund.

Form 843 is also used to file a claim for abatement of an overassessment or the unpaid portion of an overassessment, if more than the correct amount of tax (except in the case of income, estate, and gift taxes), interest, additional amount, addition to tax, or assessable penalty has been assessed.

General Instructions.—Do *not* use this form to make a claim for overpayment of income tax. Individuals who filed Form 1040, 1040A, or 1040EZ must use **Form 1040X**, Amended U.S. Individual Income

Tax Return, to claim an overpayment. Corporations who filed Form 1120 or Form 1120-A, must use **Form 1120X**, Amended U.S. Corporation Income Tax Return, to claim an overpayment. Other income tax filers should file a claim on the appropriate amended tax return. (Follow the instructions on the appropriate form for filing an amended return.)

Your agent may make a claim for you. In this case, the original or a copy of the power of attorney must be attached to the claim.

If you are filing the claim as a legal representative for a decedent whose return you filed, attach to the claim a statement that you filed the return and are still acting as the representative. If you did not file the decedent's return, attach to the claim certified copies of letters testamentary, letters of administration, or similar evidence to show your authority.

If a corporation is making the claim, the person authorized to act in its behalf must sign the claim and show his/her title.

Specific Instructions.—Lines that are not explained below are self-explanatory.

Lines 1 and 2.—If you are claiming a refund based on an overpayment made on a joint return, such as a refund for overpaid Windfall Profits Tax, each spouse must enter his or her social security number.

Line 8.—Check the appropriate box to show the type of tax or penalty. If you are

filing a claim for refund or abatement of an assessed penalty, check the box and enter the applicable Internal Revenue Code (IRC) section. For example, if the penalty was assessed under section 6700, Promoting Abusive Tax Shelters, check the penalty box and enter 6700 in the space provided for the IRC section. Generally, the IRC section can be found on the Notice of Assessment you receive from the Service Center.

Line 9.—Check the appropriate box to show the kind of return, if any, that was filed. If the box for Form 720 is checked, enter the IRS No.(s) in the space provided. The IRS No. can be found on Form 720 to the right of the entry space for the tax.

Line 11.—Specify in detail your reasons for filing this claim and show your computation for the credit, refund or abatement. Also attach appropriate supporting evidence.

Signature.—If you are claiming a refund based on an overpayment made on a joint return such as a refund for overpaid Windfall Profits Tax, each spouse must sign the refund claim.

Where to File.—File your claim with the Internal Revenue Service Center where you filed your return.

If your claim is for alcohol and tobacco taxes, see the regulations for that particular tax to determine whether you should file with the Regional Director, Bureau of Alcohol, Tobacco and Firearms.

For Internal Revenue Service Use Only

Transcript of Claimant's Account

(Complete only for miscellaneous excise taxes and alcohol, tobacco, and certain other excise taxes imposed under subtitles D and E, Internal Revenue Code.)

The following is a transcript of the record of this office covering the liability that is the subject of this claim.

A—Assessed Taxes

Tax Period and Class of Tax (a)	Document Locator No. (b)	Reference and Date (c)	Amount Assessed (d)	Paid, Abated, or Credited			Remarks (h)
				Date or Sched. No. (e)	Amount (f)	AB. PD. CR. (g)	

B—Purchase of Stamps

To Whom Sold or Issued (i)	Kind (j)	Number (k)	Denomination (l)	Date of Sale (m)	Amount (n)	If Special Tax Stamp, State:	
						Document Locator No. (o)	Period Commencing (p)

Prepared by (initials)	Date		Office	

☆U.S. Government Printing Office: 1987—181-447/40102

IRS Audit Manual

Chapter 100

Introduction

---

110 *(4–23–81)*   4233
Purpose

The Tax Audit Guidelines for Partnership, Estates and Trusts, and Corporations have been prepared for all examiners who make field examinations of income tax returns. They contain techniques relating to the evaluation and disposition of assigned returns and the auditing and reporting on examined returns.

This Handbook should be used in conjunction with IRM 4231, Tax Audit Guidelines for Internal Revenue Examiners, since many of the techniques in that Handbook are also applicable to Partnerships, Estates and Trusts, and Corporations.

120 *(4–23–81)*   4233
Statement of Principles of Internal Revenue Tax Administration

(1) The function of the Internal Revenue Service is to administer the Internal Revenue Code. It is the duty of the Service to correctly apply the laws enacted by Congress; to determine the reasonable meaning of various Code Provisions in light of the Congressional purpose in enacting them; and to perform this work in a fair and impartial manner, with neither a government nor a taxpayer point of view.

(2) The mission of the Service is to encourage and achieve the highest possible degree of voluntary compliance with the tax laws and regulations and to conduct itself so as to warrant the highest degree of public confidence in its integrity and efficiency. (See policy statement P–1–1.) Examination supports the mission of the Service by encouraging the correct reporting by taxpayers of income, estate, gift, employ-

ment, and certain excise taxes. This is accomplished by:

(a) Measuring the degree of voluntary compliance as reflected on filed returns;

(b) Reducing noncompliance by identifying and allocating resources to those returns most in need of examination; and

(c) Conducting on a timely basis quality audits of each selected tax return to determine the correct tax liability.

(3) The purpose of auditing a tax return is to determine the taxpayer's correct tax liability— no more or no less. A quality audit is the examination of a taxpayer's books and records in sufficient depth to fully develop relevant facts concerning issues of merit; ascertaining the true meaning of applicable tax laws; and correctly applying such laws to the relevant facts.

(4) One responsibility of Examination is to conduct on a timely basis quality audits of selected tax returns to determine the correct tax liability. Examination standards were developed as the level of achievement required for you to discharge this responsibility. Examination procedures necessary to achieve the standards are explained in the sections of the Manual indicated. Efforts have been made to define all standards as fully as possible; however, certain terms in the standards are intangible or subjective, and, as such, do not lend themselves to explicit definition. These include terms such as reasonable and professional judgment. Although the explanations have been written in a manner to show you the intended meaning of the terms, you must use your technical knowledge, training, and experience to correctly apply these concepts to the examination process.

Audit Techniques for Business Returns

210 *(4–23–81)*   4233
Preliminary Work at Taxpayer's Office in Corporate and Partnership Examinations

(1) The examination at the taxpayer's office may begin with miscellaneous records other than the actual ledgers and journals. Frequently, these records indicate items which the examiner should be alert for as the examination progresses.

(2) The records and the type of information to be obtained are as follows.

(a) *Minute book*—This corporate record should contain information on officers salaries, real estate leases and sales, construction contracts, law suits, patent applications, the issuance of new stock, the purchase of Treasury stock, and information relating to restricted stock options. As the examiner skims through the minute book, appropriate notes for future consideration should be made.

1 The review of the minute book should not be confined to the taxable year under examination. It is advisable to cover at least some of the period immediately before and after, if necessary, the minute books should be obtained that go all the way back to the inception of the business.

2 The correct name of the corporation should appear on the company charter which is usually kept in the minute book. This name is important when it becomes necessary to prepare a waiver to extend the statutory period of limitations.

3 Large corporations maintain minutes of the executive committee in addition to the minute book.

(b) *Partnership agreement*—The provisions of this document should be noted. The distribution of income including partners salaries and interest on capital and other allowances which it may establish should be checked against the partnership return.

(c) *Audit report of independent auditors*—This report should be read. Where two reports were issued, one in detail for management and the other a condensed one for investors, the former should be secured. Income and net worth per this report may differ from income and net worth per books due to the auditor's adjusting entries not reflected on the books. Where this difference exists, these adjusting entries will be reconciling items between the books and the return. The auditor's workpapers usually explain these entries. They should be checked closely. Any qualifications or unusual comments in the auditor's report or certificates, such as expressions of opinion as to taxpayer's depreciation policy, adequacy of reserves, status of collectibility of receivables and the like, should be noted for consideration later when the items of income and expense are audited.

(d) *Auditor's workpapers*—Audits, particularly of larger companies—may frequently be simplified if the examiner is given access to the auditor's workpapers. Judicious use of such records helps to reduce the time in examining the taxpayer's books. Examples of the types of analyses often found in such workpapers which may prove useful to the examiner are accounts receivable aging schedules, or repair analyses in which each expenditure over a certain amount is described. Guidelines for Requesting Accountants' Workpapers are contained in IRM 4024.

(e) *Retained copy file of income tax returns*—Preceding and succeeding years' tax returns should be inspected. Items to observe are:

1 Significant ratio variations between other years and the current year; such as gross profit ratios or selling expenses to sales. Where they vary widely from the current year the examiner should make a note to determine the cause as the taxpayer's records are being examined. Balance sheet ratios or trends should also be observed.

2 Continuation in the year of examination of prior elections concerning bad debts, inventory valuation methods, depreciation rates and methods, etc.

3 Prior or subsequent year entries in the reconciliation schedules of retained earnings on a corporate return or of partners' capital accounts on a partnership return which affect the year under examination.

4 Retained copies of other prior year returns may be useful in certain cases, such as those requiring determination of the status of the retained earnings account, the basis of assets and depreciation allowed or allowable.

(f) *Stock transfer book*—This book contains the names of present and past stockholders with the number of shares owned and the dates issued or cancelled. It is an essential record where questions of corporate control arise, such as those under IRC 267, 351, 542, and 1239. A general knowledge of the names of the large shareholders is also of value when checking the salary accounts. When the stock transfer book is not available, the record of dividend payments is an alternative source of similar information.

(g) *Statements and schedules filed with regulatory bodies*—Companies in the public utility field are required to file certain data with regulatory agencies, such as the Interstate Commerce Commission, Civil Aeronautics Board, and State and local utility commissions. These schedules are detailed and can at times save the examiner considerable analytical work. Rules of accounting which public utility enterprises are required to adopt by regulatory commissions are not controlling for Federal income tax purposes.

(h) *SEC statements*—Companies with public issued securities are required to file certain statements with the Securities and Exchange Commission (SEC). The statements filed at the time new securities are issued are extremely detailed about the past corporate history, ownership and operations. The annual SEC statements required from such companies are primarily the operating details of past years. Officers' dealings in stock of their own company must be reported to the SEC.

(i) *Financial statement for credit purposes—Financial statements furnished grantors of dealer franchises*—Comparison of such statements with the tax return balance sheet and income schedule may reveal significant variations. For instance the reserve for bad debts on a balance sheet furnished a bank or a credit agency may be smaller than the reserve shown on the return balance sheet. This may indicate the reserve on the return is too high.

(j) *Appraisals*—Engineers' and real estate dealers' appraisals are important in many cases, particularly in allocating real estate costs between land and building. In addition, art dealer appraisals may be useful in valuing works of art.

220 *(4-23-81)* 4233
General Ledger

221 *(4-23-81)* 4233
Examination Approach

(1) The accounts contained in the general ledger will provide the examiner with an insight into the operations of the business. When pertinent, the chart of accounts should be requested from the taxpayer. If a private ledger is maintained, it should also be requested.

(2) The examiner should leaf through the general ledger noting any unusual entries which may need an explanation. Since the individual items on the return are usually summaries of similar items on the books, the examiner should note the details of the items in the summaries.

The majority of the questions noted will be answered later as the examiner goes through the various journals. Concerning questions which pertain to the general journal, some examiners prefer to obtain immediate answers. When this is done, both the ledger and the general journal must be at hand. Other than the mechanical clumsiness of this technique, it is as good a method as accumulating the questions and checking them out later.

(3) As the examiner goes through the ledger unusual or nonrecurring items should be noted. Such items fall roughly into three classes.

(a) *Unusual in Amount*—The examiner should be alert for month-end entries of like amounts which represent large expense items which have been debited to a deferred account and spread over several months to avoid attracting attention. The total amount of an account may be unusual in amount because it appears to be too small. For example, where there is a small repair account total in a year under examination and the taxpayer had substantial fixed assets, the small repair total may be indicative of the practice of charging repairs to other accounts less likely to be checked. The manufacturing expense account is one potential alternative for such repair charges.

(b) *Unusual by source*—Source as used here means the journals from which the account was posted, as indicated in the folio column. There is a normal source pattern for most postings. Repairs or advertising expenses are generally posted from the cash disbursement journal or the purchase journal; if the folio column indicates a cash receipts journal or general journal source it may warrant a further check. Entertainment expense items from the general journal more often than not represent officers' expense. Fixed asset credits from the cash book are unusual, if the assets were sold, a general journal entry is the normal way to eliminate the cost of the asset from the books. A cash book source suggests that the total selling price instead of the cost was credited to the account. These are a few of the possible source variations. The examiner should be alert for the many more items which may be encountered.

(c) *Unusual by nature*—An entry in a ledger account may be unusual by nature as well as by an account itself. Some examples of unusual entries and accounts are:

1 Credit entries in accounts that usually contain only debits or vice versa. As an example a debit to a sales account could possibly be a bad debt write off.

2 Accounts which exist at the beginning of the year but do not exist at the end. For instance, the existence of a supplies inventory at the beginning of the year and no inventory at the end may indicate that the taxpayer had made an unauthorized change in the method of accounting. Conversely, the existence of an account at the end of the year, where none existed at the beginning, such as accrued wages, may indicate a similar unauthorized change.

3 A general ledger in which the nominal accounts are not closed out to the income summary account at the end of the year. Where this situation exists, and the necessary information is not available from the auditor's workpapers, the examiner should trace the account to the tax return. This audit approach is advisable so that the examiner will uncover adjustments to the accounts which are not reflected by entries on the books.

222 (4–23–81)   4233
Net Worth Section

222.1 (4–23–81)   4233
Purpose and Scope of Examiner's Analysis

(1) The principal purpose of an income tax examination is the verification of the taxable income shown on a particular tax return. That taxable income is the end product of the various items of income and expense on the return. Any one of these items may be an accumulation of from one to thousands of individual transactions. These individual transactions do not appear on the tax return. Accordingly, it becomes necessary to examine them in the place where they do appear and that is in the books.

(2) Since the transactions are recorded on the books according to accounting principles rather than tax law, it is likely that there will be some differences between the net income on the books and the net income on the tax return. The examiner must isolate and reconcile these differences.

(3) If a questionable item is noted in the taxpayer's books during the examination of an income or expense account, the examiner should analyze the reconciliation from net book income to net income per return to determine if the item was eliminated from the amount deducted on the tax return.

(4) The net worth section is the starting point in determining the relationship of the books and the return. There are three elements in this section at the end of any given tax year. They are:

(a) the net worth at the beginning of the year;

(b) the operating income or loss of the current year;

(c) the nonoperating transactions of the current year.

(5) The examiner is primarily concerned with the second element. However, since the books and the returns may vary, the examination should not be confined only to the second element. Items which fall in the second element on the books may belong in either of the other two insofar as the tax return is concerned, and vice versa. The examiner must therefore check all three elements.

(6) Having defined the scope and purpose of the net worth analysis and the income reconciliation, the manner in which they are to be accomplished is the next step. In some respects the manner varies depending on the entity involved. The corporate taxpayer will be considered first.

222.2 (4–23–81)   4233
Corporations

(1) The net worth section of a corporate balance sheet is composed of the capital and retained earnings accounts. The examiner of a corporate return will find that most taxpayers have completed Schedules M–1 and M–2 on the return which show a reconciliation of income per books with income per return and an analysis of unappropriated retained earnings and undivided profits per books. (See 232.4 of this Handbook).

(2) Audit techniques include the following:

(a) Analyze and reconcile the retained earnings accounts. Verify correctness of all items, both increases and decreases, appearing on the books or return.

(b) Consider whether the retained earnings has been improperly accumulated beyond the reasonable needs of the business.

222.3 (2–20–86)   4233
Partnerships

(1) There is no great difference in principle between the net worth analysis of a corporation and a partnership. The same technique applies to both.

(2) Schedule M. Reconciliation of Partners' Capital Accounts. Form 1065, is a rough equivalent of Schedule M-1. Reconciliation of Income per Books with Income per Return, and Schedule M-2. Analysis of Unappropriated Retained Earnings and Undivided Profits per Books, on the corporate return, Form 1120.

(3) Schedule K shows total distributive partnership items. Schedule K-1 reflects each partner's share of income, deductions, or credits which are required to be set out separately by the partnership. The schedule provides for the segregation of IRC 1231 transactions. The examiner should remember that the decision on whether gain or loss on such assets is ordinary or capital should be deferred until transferred into the partners' individual returns. For each "at risk" activity, Schedule K-1 requires the entry of the partner's share of partnership liabilities for which the partner is personally liable. Examiners should be aware of "at risk" limitations of losses on certain tax shelter partnership investment—(see IRM 4236, Examination Tax Shelters Handbook.) Examiners should be alert for situations where taxpayers have claimed deductions for accrued interest on existing liabilities and foreclosure proceedings have subsequently occured. Verify that the taxpayer has included the difference between the liability per books and the liability which was relieved by the foreclosure as income.

(4) Since Schedule M on the partnership return is condensed, the examiner should first secure the taxpayer's workpapers showing how various items were grouped for the schedule. Once this breakdown is secured the examiner can reconcile the books with the return. The "per return" column can be prepared solely from Schedule M as allocated in the workpapers; and from Schedule D Sale or Exchange of Property, Form 4797, Supplemental Schedule of Gains and Losses; and Schedule K of the return. The "per books" column detail should be secured from the taxpayer and then checked against the books to see that they agree.

(5) After the reconciliation has been made; the examiner should continue with the examination bearing in mind the effect the above reconciling items have on the transactions appearing in the books. For instance, if there is a $1,000.00 charge to charitable contributions, the examiner should remember that the $1,000.00 was not claimed on the tax return. If the examiner sees an additional $200.00 contribution to another organization the examiner would know that it was claimed on the return and should be adjusted.

(6) The regulations under IRC 6050K require partnerships to file Form 8308 (Report of a Sale or Exchange of Certain Partnership Interests) when a portion of any money or other property given to a selling partner in exchange for all or part of the partner's interest in the partnership is attributable to unrealized receivables or substantially appreciated inventory items (IRC section 751(a)), IRC 6050K is effective for sales or exchanges occurring after 12/31/84. During their examination of partnerships, examiners will verify that all required Form 8308's have been filed. If they have not been filed, the appropriate penalties for failure to file these forms will be imposed, unless reasonable cause is found to exist. Examiners will also give consideration to securing within the district affected partners' returns to determine if examination is warranted, and preparing information reports on out of district partners.

222.4 *(4-23-81)*   4233
Sole Proprietorships

(1) Businesses are sometimes conducted as sole proprietorships, in which case profits or losses are reported in Schedule C (or in the case of a farm, Schedule F) of an individual return. Since this schedule contains no balance sheet the net worth that is to be analyzed is the net worth account on the books including the proprietor's drawing account. All entries in these two accounts should be checked. They may contain items, other than the closing entry which should properly be included as income or expense for tax purposes. If there are, and the taxpayer has not included them, the examiner should make the necessary adjustment in the report.

(2) If the closing entry per books does not agree with the income shown on Schedule C, the taxpayer should be asked to supply the reconciling detail.

(3) After the reconciliation and verification is completed, the examiner should turn to the next phase of the examination. If income per books agree with the return the examiner should go through the books noting items that belong in the other return schedules or the schedule of itemized deductions. Contributions are an example. They are subject to percentage limitations, or to complete disallowance if the standard deduction is used.

230 *(4-23-81)*   4233
Balance Sheet Approach to Examinations

231 *(4-23-81)*   4233
Examination of Asset Accounts

222.3
IR Manual

MT 4233-29

231.1 *(4–23–81)*   4233
Introduction

(1) Thus far, this chapter has presented a series of suggestions on the technique of commencing the examination of a set of books and records. The initial phase includes a verification that the net income per books with appropriate reconciling adjustments, is actually reflected in the tax return under examination, whether it be a corporation, a partnership or a sole proprietorship.

(2) Once this verification is completed, the examiner should turn attention primarily to the books and records, bearing in mind that there are some reconciling items which affect the net income per books.

(3) The following subsections offer guides to the technique of examining the asset, liability, income, and expense accounts normally found in general ledgers.

231.2 *(4–23–81)*   4233
Cash on Hand and in Bank

(1) Review cash disbursements journal for a representative period. Note any missing check numbers, checks drawn to order of cash, bearer, etc.; large or unusual items, and determine propriety thereof through a comparison with vouchers, journal entries, etc.

(a) In the case of a cash basis taxpayer, ascertain if checks were written and recorded which were issued after the close of the year under examination.

(b) Give special consideration to checks issued for cashier's checks, sight drafts, etc., where the payee and nature are not clearly shown.

(2) Obtain bank statements and cancelled checks for each bank account for one or more months, including the last month of the period under examination.

(a) Compare deposits shown by bank statement against entries in cash receipt book.

(b) Note year-end bank overdrafts in case of cash basis taxpayer. This may indicate expenses which are unallowable since funds were not available for payment.

(c) Determine if any checks have remained outstanding for an unreasonable time. This may indicate improper or duplication of disbursements. Old outstanding checks possibly could be restored to income.

(d) Determine whether voided checks have been properly handled.

(e) For a test period, check endorsements to see if they are the same as payee, noting any endorsements by owner, or questionable endorsements.

(3) Review cash receipts journal for items not identified with ordinary business sales, being alert to such items as sales of assets, prepaid income, income received under claim of right, etc.

(4) If records appear unreliable or have not been subjected to a competent independent audit, tests of footings and postings should be made for a representative period.

(5) Investigate entries in general ledger cash account. Look for unusual items which do not originate from cash receipts or disbursements journals. These entries may indicate unauthorized withdrawals or expenditures, sales of capital assets, omitted sales, undisclosed bank accounts, etc.

(6) Test check some cash sales with cash book to ascertain if they have been correctly recorded. Also check cash sales made at the beginning and end of the period under examination to determine if year-end sales have been recorded in the proper accounting period.

(7) Test check disbursements from petty cash to determine if there are any unallowable items included.

(8) Scrutinize cash overages and shortages, being alert to irregularities which may have cleared through accounts.

(9) Review cash on hand account to determine if there are any credit balances during the period under examination. This may indicate unrecorded receipts.

231.3 *(4–23–81)*   4233
Notes and Accounts Receivable

(1) Check entries in general ledger control accounts. Look for unusual items, especially those which do not originate from the sales or cash receipts journals.

(2) Determine if subsidiary ledgers are in agreement with control accounts, and, if not, ascertain the reasons for any differences.

(3) Note any credit balances in the general ledger or subsidiary accounts. This may indicate deposits or overpayments which could be considered as additional income or unrecorded sales.

MT 4233–27

231.3
IR Manual

(4) Some credit sales invoices and postings should be test checked from the sales journal to the subsidiary and control account.

(5) Determine whether accrued income on interest bearing notes or accounts has been included in income.

(6) Where taxpayer reflects an accrual method by subtracting beginning receivables and adding ending receivables to cash collected, consider checking the detailed listing of receivables at the beginning of the period to the cash receipts book. This may disclose diverting of funds, etc. Determine if beginning receivables used in the computation are the same as the ending receivables of the preceding year.

(7) Insure that return conforms to books in terms of method of accounting.

231.4 *(4–23–81)*   4233
Investments

(1) Analyze sales and other credit entries with regard to the following:

  (a) gains or losses (basis, wash sales, interest included in sales price, etc.);

  (b) other (exchanges, write downs, write-offs, transactions with related taxpayers, or controlled foreign entities, etc.).

(2) Review debit entries. Consider such items as:

  (a) Nontaxable securities acquired with borrowed funds.

  (b) Other acquisitions (transactions with related taxpayers, noncash acquisitions, creation, organization or reorganization of a foreign corporation, etc.).

(3) Become familiar with the nature of investments, utilizing any records maintained by the taxpayer. Make necessary test checks to determine if related income has been properly reported (dividends, interest, etc.).

(4) If shares of stock are held in a foreign corporation, determine whether it is a foreign personal holding company.

231.5 *(3–11–85)*   4233
Depreciable Assets

(1) Determine whether assets shown on the depreciation schedule, which have a prior year acquisition date, are the same as shown on the tax return for the immediate preceding period. If not, this would point up depreciation being taken on assets which have previously been expensed or fully depreciated, etc.

(2) Review additions during the period. Test additions by reference to invoices, contracts, etc., giving consideration to the following.

  (a) Note items which appear to have originated from unusual sources such as appraisal increases, transfers, exchanges, etc., and determine propriety thereof. Ascertain if prior earnings were adequate to cover acquisitions.

  (b) Determine if costs relating to the acquisition and installation of assets, leasehold improvements, etc., have been capitalized.

  (c) Ascertain if assets include items of a personal nature.

  (d) Where construction or any other work of a capital nature is performed with the taxpayer's own equipment, labor, etc., for its own use, be certain that the basis of such asset includes the proper elements of material, labor and overhead, including depreciation.

  (e) With regard to the basis of assets, consider such items as trade-ins, acquisitions from related taxpayers, allocations of cost between land and building, etc. Also consider whether the basis has been reduced by the appropriate amount of investment credit for periods after December 31, 1982.

(3) Decreases in the asset accounts during the year should be noted. Gains or losses resulting therefrom should be verified.

  (a) Ascertain if taxpayer has transferred assets to a controlled domestic or foreign corporation for less than fair consideration.

(4) Examiners should be alert for situations where deductions are being claimed by entities leasing property to tax-exempt entities. As a result of the Deficit Reduction Act of 1984, certain tax benefits otherwise available (depreciation, investment credit), have been greatly reduced for owners of property that is leased to tax-exempt entities.

231.6 *(4–23–81)*   4233
Valuation Reserves

(1) Review nature and source of all accounts and ascertain whether they are being used as a means of diverting or understating income, or claiming unallowable deductions.

(2) *Depreciation, Amortization, and Depletion Reserves*—Determine whether any of these are contingent reserves. Check for reasonableness of any addition.

231.7 *(4–23–81)*   4233
Intangible Assets

(1) Verify correctness of deductions claimed, such as amortization, write downs, write-offs, royalties, etc.

(2) Test check current additions to determine if the basis includes the proper elements of cost, such as legal fees, application fees, etc.

231.3
IR Manual

MT 4233–27

(3) Determine if there have been any transactions with related taxpayers, or controlled foreign entities; if so, consider arms-length features.

(4) Determine if income applicable to intangibles has been included in income. In this connection be aware that it is not necessary for an intangible to have a basis or to appear on the records (e.g. subleases, overriding royalties, franchises, etc.).

(5) Analyze any transaction involving transfer of foreign rights to any foreign entity for an equity interest, or for nominal consideration.

(6) Be alert to any situation or transaction which logically could have given rise to an intangible which may have been expensed through inventories, fixed assets, expenses, etc. (e.g. purchase of a going business—which could involve good will, covenant not to compete, etc.).

231.8 *(4–23–81)*   4233
Prepaid Expenses and Deferred Charges

Make check as to the nature and source of these assets, and the manner in which they are charged off to expense. Prepaid expenses are generally present in all businesses. The absence of such items should be considered, since a distortion of income may be involved.

231.9 *(4–23–81)*   4233
Other Assets

The nature and classification of other asset accounts should be considered to determine if they have a bearing on tax liability.

231.(10) *(4–23–81)*   4233
Exchange, Clearing or Suspense Account

Determine nature and purpose of the account. Test check debit and credit entries, being aware of the possibility that such account may be used as a means for diverting sales, padding expenses, etc.

231.(11) *(4–30–87)*   4233
IRC 897—Disposition of Investment in United States Real Property

(1) *INTRODUCTION*—Prior to the enactment of IRC 897, foreign persons could legitimately sell U.S. real property without paying any U.S. taxes. Although investment in U.S. real estate helped the U.S. economy, it was inequitable to U.S. persons and placed U.S. persons at a disadvantage in selling their real estate. Because of this inequity to U.S. persons, Congress passed the Foreign Investment in Real Property Tax Act of 1980 (FIRPTA) IRC, 897, which taxes dispositions of U.S. real property interest by nonresident alien individuals and foreign corporations (including foreign partnerships, trusts, and estates).

(2) *BACKGROUND*—It is helpful to understand the taxability of foreign persons on disposition of interests in U.S. real property before FIRPTA and the techniques used to avoid taxation.

(a) Prior Law—There are two broad categories of income that are taxable to foreign persons.

1 Income effectively connected with the conduct of a trade or business in the U.S. This income is taxed at graduated rates and would include a capital gain from the sale or exchange of U.S. real estate associated with a U.S. trade or business.

2 Income which is U.S. source but not effectively connected with the U.S., trade or business. This income is taxed at a flat rate of 30% or a lower treaty rate. Capital gains that are not associated with the conduct of a trade or business would not fall within this category unless the individual taxpayer (nonresident alien) is physically present in the U.S. more than 182 days during the taxable year.

(b) Techniques Used to Avoid Taxation (Prior to FIRPTA)—For the purposes of this section it is assumed that the capital gain would be taxable as effectively connected with the conduct of trade or business in the U.S. if steps were not taken to avoid the taxable event. These common techniques are:

  1 Sale of stock of a Holding Company
  2 Liquidate a Holding Company
  3 Installment Sale
  4 Like—Kind exchange

(c) Sale of Stock of a Holding Company—A foreign person would transfer real property to a corporation and then on finding a buyer for the real property would sell the stock to the buyer. If the sale were not otherwise effectively connected to a trade or business, the transaction would be tax free.

(d) Liquidate a Holding Company—Again, as in item (c) above, a foreign person would transfer real property to a corporation. Prior to selling the real property, the corporation would adopt a plan of liquidation and liquidate under IRC 337 which provides for nonrecognition of gain. The subsequent capital gain resulting from the exchange of shares in the corporation for the assets would again be tax free to the foreign person.

(e) Installment Sale—Upon the sale of real property, the foreign person would elect installment sale treatment under IRC 453. If the taxpayer was not effectively engaged in a U.S. trade or business in the later years when the proceeds were received and the gain was recognized, the gain would escape taxation.

(f) Like—Kind Exchange—If the foreign person exchanged U.S. real property for real property outside the U.S., under IRC 1031 no gain would be recognized. Also, no taxable gain would be recognized later when the foreign person disposed of the non-U.S. real property.

(g) After FIRPTA—In general, FIRPTA eliminated the simplest method of tax avoidance by deeming that a disposition of a real property interest is always considered to be effectively connected with a U.S. trade or business. This also ended the installment sale technique of avoiding tax on real property sales.

(3) The other techniques for avoiding tax were somewhat more complex and therefore required extensive legislation to eliminate.

(a) Sale of Stock of a Holding Company—The foreign person could still transfer real property to a domestic corporation without a taxable event taking place but the subsequent sale of stock of the domestic corporation would now be taxable. If the foreign person transferred real property to a foreign corporation, the transfer would be taxable at that time (IRC 897(j)). However, the subsequent sale of stock of the foreign corporation would not be taxable. A tax avoidance method still exists when a foreign corporation acquires real property, for then a foreign person could sell the stock of the foreign corporation without tax consequence.

(b) Liquidate a Holding Company—Prior to selling the U.S. real property, a domestic corporation could still adopt a plan of liquidation and liquidate under IRC 337. However, the subsequent capital gain from the exchange of shares in the corporation for the assets would now be taxable to the foreign person. Foreign corporations cannot now take advantage of IRC 337 as it no longer applies to a sale or exchange of U.S. real property interests by foreign corporations (IRC 897(d)).

(c) Like—Kind Exchange—A foreign person can now only exchange a U.S. real property interest for an interest which would be taxable upon later disposition for the nonrecognition provisions of IRC 1031 to apply. Therefore, a foreign person cannot escape taxation by exchanging a U.S. real property interest for a non-U.S. real property interest and then selling the non-U.S. real property interest (IRC 897(e)).

(4) *DEFINITIONS*—IRC 897 contains several terms that are special to this statute. A clear understanding of these terms is essential to the proper interpretation and application of the provisions of IRC 897. Some of the terms are defined below:

(a) Real Property Defined—The term real property includes three types of property:

1 Land and natural products of the land

2 Improvements to land

3 Personal property associated with the use of real property

(b) United States Real Property Interest (USRPI) Defined

1 The term "United States real property interest" means an interest in real property located in the United States or the Virgin Islands or any interest, other than an interest solely as a creditor, in any domestic corporation that is a United States real property holding corporation.

2 Interest in U.S. real property includes a fee ownership, co-ownership or leasehold interest in real property, a time sharing interest in real property and a life estate, remainder or revisionary interest in such property. It also includes options to acquire such interests in real property.

(c) United States Real Property Holding Corporations (USRPHC)

1 A USRPHC is a corporation whose USRPIs constitute 50 percent or more of the fair market value of the aggregate of its USPRPIs, its foreign real property and its trade or business assets.

2 USRPHC status is important for determining whether the disposition of an interest in a domestic corporation by a foreign person is taxable.

3 In the event that the domestic corporation is not a USRPHC and so notifies the foreign persons and the Service, then disposition of an ownership interest in the corporation does not constitute a disposition of a U.S. real property interest. The statement and supporting calculation that foreign persons are relying upon in concluding they do not have a U.S. taxable event will need to be examined to determine their validity.

231.(11)
IR Manual

MT 4233–33

Tax Audit Guidelines, Individuals, Partnerships, Estates
and Trusts, and Corporations

(5) *TAXABLE DISPOSITIONS*—IRC 897 is applicable to dispositions of U.S. real property interests after June 18, 1980, unless the nonresident alien individual or foreign corporation is protected by a tax treaty that allows more favorable treatment. Tax treaties currently in force will not be effected by IRC 897 until January 1, 1985, at which time, IRC 897 will override the treaty provisions.

(6) *IRC 897(i) ELECTION*—A foreign corporation may make an election under IRC 897(i) and its Regulations to be treated as a domestic corporation for purposes of IRC 897 and 6039C if:

(a) The corporation owns a U.S. real property interest.

(b) Under any treaty obligation of the United States the foreign corporation is entitled to nondiscriminatory treatment with respect to that interest.

(c) The corporation submits the election in proper form in accordance with the regulations. A foreign corporation that makes this election shall not be treated as a domestic corporation for purposes of any other provision of the Code or Regulations, except to the extent that it consents to such treatment as a condition to making the election. You may be assigned a return of a foreign corporation reporting income based on an election pursuant to IRC 897(i). Examiners should verify that OP:I:C has approved the election.

(7) *REPORTING REQUIREMENT*—In addition to IRC 897, IRC 6039C, Returns With Respect to U.S. Real Property Interests, was enacted and requires the filing of three information returns: (Note: The due date is to be established when the regulations are final.)

(a) Form 6659—Information Return Under Section 6039C(a)—Domestic Corporations

(b) Form 6660—Information Return Under Section 6039C(b)—Foreign Corporations

(c) Form 6661—Information Return Under Section 6039C(c)—Foreign Persons

(Note: The due date is to be established when the regulations are final.)

(8) *AUDIT TECHNIQUES*—During examinations, the following minimum checks should be made:

(a) Determine if the entity under examination has foreign ownership, either directly or indirectly;

(b) Determine whether dispositions of interests in U.S. real property after June 18, 1980, involve foreign investors. An interest in U.S. real property includes direct or indirect ownership. Indirect ownership could include ownership of real property through a domestic corporation, partnership, trust or estate;

(c) Determine if the information returns required by IRC 6039C were filed; and

(d) Determine if tax havens (e.g., Netherland Antilles) have been used as conduits by foreign investors to disguise purchases of U.S. real property through complex financing arrangements.

1 Foreign investors may form Netherland Antilles corporations to make "participatory loans" with "equity kickers" to disguise foreign purchases in U.S. real property. A participatory loan obligates the borrower to repay the amount loaned, together with a fixed or stated interest, and as additional compensation, pay the lender a portion of gross profits, net profits, or cash flow. Examiners should be aware that interest contingent on the profits, cash flow, or receipts of borrower can convert a loan into an equity investment of the borrower. If the taxpayer has structured their investment in this manner, they may also be claiming that:

a The "equity kicker" is deductible as interest expense; and

b That the foreign "lender" is exempt from the U.S. tax on the U.S. source "interest" of 30 percent rate by virtue of Article XII of the U.S.–Netherland Antilles Tax Treaty.

2 Such investment arrangements would create a filing requirement under IRC 6039C, and upon disposition causes a taxable event under IRC 897. Additionally, if examiners treat these participatory loans as equity investments in a domestic corporation:

a "Interest payments" can be treated as corporate distributions, and to the extent out of current profits or accumulated earnings of the "borrower", the foreign lender would be subject to U.S. tax on a dividend; and

b The U.S. "borrower" will not be allowed an interest deduction.

(e) Audit techniques are not limited to the above checks. This is a new area in which the Service is still gaining experiences. Examiners should employ any other audit techniques that are applicable and should use their ingenuity in examining these issues.

(9) *REFERRALS AND ASSISTANCE*—The Office of Compliance, OP:I:C, has jurisdiction over nonresident alien individuals who have income from U.S. sources. If the case involves disposition of U.S. real property by non-resident alien individuals, a referral should be made to OP:I:C. Because of the involvement of foreign persons and entities using tax havens, examiners should remember that assistance from International examiners in the International Enforcement Program is available when necessary. (See IRM 42(10)3.)

MT 4233–33

231.(11)

232 *(4–23–81)*   4233
Examination of Liability Accounts

232.1 *(4–23–81)*   4233
**Current and Accrued Liabilities,
Including Notes Payable**

(1) Note any debit balances in the general ledger or subsidiary accounts. This may indicate diversion of funds, etc. Also note accounts which have long overdue balances. This may indicate contested liabilities and liabilities which no longer exist such as unclaimed wages, unclaimed deposits, items set up twice, etc.

(2) Review computation of year-end accruals with respect to their allowability as expenses or purchases. Also see that accruals set up at the end of the preceding year were either reversed in the current year or that the actual expenses were charged against them when paid. Be alert to large year-end items which have been shifted between years for the taxpayer's advantage.

(3) Determine if subsidiary ledgers are in agreement with controls, and if not, ascertain the reasons for any differences.

(4) Determine if accrued items payable to related taxpayers, were paid within the time limit prescribed.

(5) Investigate entries in the general ledger control accounts. Look for unusual items, especially those which do not originate from the voucher register or cash disbursements journals. This may disclose unreported income, improper or overstated expense.

(6) Examiners should be alert for situations where taxpayers have claimed deductions for accrued interest on existing liabilities and foreclosure proceedings have subsequently occurred. Verify the taxpayer has included the difference between the liability per the books and the liability which was relieved by the foreclosure as income.

(7) Analyze any newly established liability to a controlled foreign corporation as it may represent a constructive dividend.

232.2 *(3–11–85)*   4233
Officer's Salaries

(1) Determine total compensation paid or accrued to principal officers, taking into consideration any compensation claimed under headings other than officers' salaries, such as manufacturing salaries, supervisory salaries, labor, etc., contributions to pension plans for the officers, payments of personal expenses, year-end or other bonuses, etc.

(2) Determine if and to what extent each principal officer's compensation is unreasonable.

(3) The examiner should take into account such factors as: nature of duties, background and experience, knowledge of the business, size of the business, individual's contribution to profit making, time devoted, economic conditions in general, and locally, character and amount of responsibility, time of year compensation is determined, relationship of stockholder-officer's compensation to stockholdings, whether alleged compensate is in reality, in whole or in part, payment for a business or assets acquired, the amount paid by similar size businesses in the same area to equally qualified employees for similar services, etc.

(4) Be alert to closely held multiple corporation situations in which compensation may be split between two or more related corporations, and which, in the aggregate, may be considered excessive to the officer-stockholder.

(5) In closely held corporations, determine that accruals payable to controlling stockholders are paid within the prescribed time limit.

(6) Determine if executives have received substantial bonuses under the guise that the proceeds would be used by the recipient to make significant political contributions.

(7) Be alert to situations where a corporation has entered into an agreement under which key personnel or other "disqualified individuals" are to receive excessive compensation in the event that control or ownership of the corporation changes. Such payments, commonly referred to as "golden parachute payments", are non-deductible by the corporation and the recipient is subject to an excise tax on the amount of the excess parachute payment in addition to the income tax due.

232.3 *(4–27–83)*   4233
Fixed Liabilities

(1) Financing arrangements such as mortgages, certificates of indebtedness, etc. are areas in which substantial adjustments are quite often found. The examiner should become acquainted with pertinent details with regard to such financing arrangements and consider possible adjustment areas as follows:

    (a) legal, professional and other expenses of issuance;

    (b) refunding of debt;

    (c) transactions with related taxpayers and controlled foreign entities;

232

MT 4233–33

(d) related expense accounts (interest and amortization).

(2) Scrutinize any long term outstanding liability to a controlled foreign corporation as it may represent an equity interest rather than a creditor interest.

(3) Ensure that long term obligations issued after December 31, 1982 are in registered form and are not subject to the exicse tax imposed under IRC 4701 (See IRM 4743).

232.4 (4–23–81)   4233
Other Liabilities

The nature and classification of other liability accounts should be considered to determine if they have any bearing on tax liability.

232.5 (11–3–82)   4233
Capital Stock

(1) Review all capital stock accounts—give adequate consideration to the following.

(a) *No changes during period*—Even though no changes in the total outstanding stock appear on the balance sheet or in the general ledger control accounts, consideration should be given to such features as:

1 Subchapter S Corporations. Is there a valid election, number and changes in stockholders, limitation on losses, etc.

2 Dealings in stock between shareholders. Check gains or losses to the individuals concerned where the corporation ultimately becomes involved in such transactions and consider the possibility of distributions being essentially equivalent to a taxable dividend.

3 Closely held companies should receive special consideration throughout the examination for such items as arms-length features, disguised dividends, etc.

(b) *New issues and additions during the period*

1 Compare date obtained from the corporate minute book and charter with items recorded on books to determine if proper entries have been made.

2 Verify all credit entries. Give consideration to such features as: stock issued for services or properties, stock dividends, employee stock options, stock issued at less than fair market value, reorganizations, taxable and nontaxable exchanges, etc.

3 Determine if expenses relating to the issuance of stock have been properly handled (legal fees, registration fees, etc.).

4 Determine if documentary stamps have been acquired and properly affixed, and cost correctly reflected.

5 Determine during the examination of a recapitalization of the stock in a closely held company that the fair market value of the stock to be received by each exchanging shareholder is equal to the fair market value of the stock surrendered in the exchange. If there is a significant difference, the examiner should be alert to possible gift tax consequences.

(c) *Reductions and cancellations during the period*

1 Compare data obtained from the corporate charter and minute book with items recorded on books to determine if proper entries have been made.

2 Verify all debt entries. Give consideration to such features as, partial or complete redemptions, cancellations, or liquidations; write-offs; distributions essentially equivalent to dividends; etc.

(d) *Treasury stock*

If treasury stock transactions have occurred, consider such possibilities as acquisitions being essentially equivalent to dividends, etc.

232.6 (4–23–81)   4233
Surplus

(1) Analyze and reconcile the surplus accounts. Verify correctness of all items, both increases and decreases, appearing on the books or return.

(2) Consider whether the surplus has been improperly accumulated beyond the reasonable needs of the business.

232.7 (4–23–81)   4233
Surplus Reserves

Review nature and sources of all accounts and ascertain whether they are being used as a means of diverting or understating income, or claiming unallowable deductions.

232.8 (5–14–81)   4233
Schedule M–1

(1) Schedule M–1 is the reconciliation between the net income per books and the taxable income before the net operating loss deduction and special deductions from Schedule I of Form 1120, U.S. Corporation Income Tax Return. (See Exhibit 200–1, Examples of Reconciliation of Income and Analysis of Unappropriated Retained Earnings).

MT 4233–25

232.8
IR Manual

(2) A complete and detailed Schedule M-1 will provide an examiner with the information needed to reconcile income per books and income reported on the return. Variations can arise either because of timing differences or permanent differences between financial accounting and tax accounting. These could surface in lines 4, 5, 7, or 8 of Schedule M-1.

(3) Statement No. 5, Accounting for Contingencies, of the Financial Accounting Standards Board (March 1975), issued by the American Institute of Certified Public Accountants, defines a loss contingency as an existing condition, situation, or set of circumstances involving uncertainty as to the possible loss that will be resolved when one or more future events occur or fail to occur. An estimated loss from such a contingency shall be accrued by a charge to income if the following conditions are met: It is probable that a liability has been incurred at the date of the financial statement; and The amount of the loss can reasonably be estimated. The Standards define "probable" to mean that the future event or events are likely to occur. With respect to unasserted claims, litigation, and assessments, the Standards provide that an enterprise must determine the degree of probability that suit may be filed or a claim or assessment may be asserted, and the probability of an unfavorable outcome. If an unfavorable outcome is probable and the amount of the loss can be reasonably estimated, accrual of the loss is required.

(4) "Tax Accrual workpapers" are produced by the independent auditor in conjunction with the auditing of financial statements required for companies that file financial statements with the SEC. Part of the auditing function is to evaluate the sufficiency of the client's reserves to meet its potential tax liability. This evaluation is based in part on the accountant's analysis of corporate records and in part on its assessment of opinions and projections communicated in confidence by the client. In reaching its conclusion the accountant considers all uncertain tax positions taken by the client and determines the extent of reserves necessary to cover the liability that would result assuming that all such questions were resolved against the client.

(5) Line 2, Federal income tax, may be the actual tax shown on the return or an accrual of the income taxes allocable to the period, which was entered on the books before the return was prepared.

(a) If line 2 is an accrual, an analysis of the taxes payable account and the deferred tax account should be made and explained in the examiner's workpapers. The analysis will require the use of the books, the tax return and tax payment records. The analysis would consist of the reconciliation of the beginning and ending balance of the taxes payable account and the deferred tax account.

(b) After the examination is substantially completed, i.e. the major issues are identified and quantified, and if the examiner determines that a material irreconcilable difference exists in the analysis of line 2, the examiner will ascertain from the taxpayer information to permit reconciliation of the difference. To the extent such difference includes a provision for tax contingencies, the workpapers supporting such provision should only be requested under the guidelines of IRM 4024.4. In any event, tax accrual workpapers as defined in IRM 4024.2:(3) will not be requested as a standard examination procedure.

232.8

IR Manual

Exhibit 200–1

Examples of Reconciliation of Income and Analysis of Unappropriated Retained Earnings

Schedule M-1 -- Reconciliation of Income Per Books With Income Per Return

1.	Net income per books...(g)	$42,000
2.	Federal income tax...(h)	38,000
3.	Excess of capital loss over capital gains.....................(d)	1,000
4.	Income subject to tax not recorded on books this year (itemized)	
	Prior year income.................................(k)	30,000
	Advance rent......................................(l)	10,000
5.	Expenses recorded on books this year not deducted on this return	
	Officer's Life Insurance..........................(i)	9,000
6.	Total of lines 1 through 5.....................................	$130,000
7.	Income recorded on books this year not included in this return..	
	Tax Exempt Interest...............................(j)	20,000
8.	Deductions in this tax return not charged against book income(m)	2,000
9.	Total lines 7 and 8..	22,000
10.	Income (line 6 less 9)..(o)	108,000

Schedule M-2 -- Analysis of Unappropriated Retained Earnings Per Books

1.	Balance at beginning of year (1/1/77).........................(a)	100,000
2.	Net income per books..(g)	42,000
3.	Other increases...	
	Prior year tax accrual reversed...................(p)	10,000
4.	Total of lines 1 through 3.....................................	152,000
5.	Distributions...	
	Cash..(n)	11,900
6.	Other decreases...	
	Prior year expenses...............................(b)	3,500
	Tax deficit (1974)................................(c)	1,200
	Reserve for damages...............................(e)	8,000
7.	Total of lines 5 and 6...	24,600
8.	Balance at end of year (line 4 less 7) (12/31/77)............(f)	127,400

Exhibit 200-1

Exhibit 200–1 Cont. (1)

Examples of Reconciliation of Income and Analysis of Unappropriate Retained Earnings
Examples of Book Income and Taxable Income
Book Income - 1977

Taxable Gross Income	(q)	$300,000
Tax Exempt Interest Income	(j)	20,000
Total		$320,000
Deductible Business Expenses	(r)	230,000
		90,000
Officer's Life Insurance	(i)	9,000
		81,000
Excess Capital Loss	(d)	1,000
		80,000
Federal Income Tax	(h)	38,000
Net Book Income	(g)	42,000

Current Non-Book Income and Expenses

Prior Year Income	(k)	$30,000
Advance Rents	(l)	10,000
Unbooked Expenses	(m)	2,000

Taxable Income - 1977

Taxable Gross Income	(q)	$300,000
Deductible Business Expenses	(r)	230,000
		70,000
Unbooked Expenses	(m)	2,000
		68,000
Prior Year Income	(k)	30,000
Advance Rents	(l)	10,000
Taxable Income	(o)	$108,000
Taxes (approx.)		$ 45,000

Exhibit 200–1 Cont. (2)

Examples of Reconciliation of Income and Analysis of Unappropriated Retained Earnings ◊

Explanatory Notes (Keyed to Schedules M–1 and M–2 and to Book and Taxable Income)

(a) You will note that the balance as of the beginning of the year is $100,000.00. This is the figure that should be entered on line 24, column (B) of Schedule L, of the return. It should also be entered on line 1 of Schedule M–2. If an agent finds a disagreement between the figure reported in Schedule L, with the actual books and also a disagreement between amount report in Schedule M–2 with that of the books, it is an indication that taxpayer is not showing an adjustment made for tax purposes. Unless these figures agree, the amounts reported in Schedule M–2 should be examined.

(b) Prior year expenses represent expenses which had been claimed as a deduction in the 1976 tax return, but not actually booked until 1977. If actually handled properly by the taxpayer, it would have been reported as a Schedule M–1, item 8 of the 1976 tax return. When booked in 1977, it was charged directly to unappropriated retained earnings.

(c) The 1974 Income deficiency was charged directly to retained earnings in 1977, as evidenced in our analysis of unappropriated retained earnings. This should be reported on line 6 of Schedule M–2.

(d) Excess capital loss reported as a charge to Book income is not claimed as a deduction for Income Tax purposes. This should be shown on line 3 on Schedule M–1.

(e) It is apparent that taxpayer set up a liability account Reserve for Damages by charging unappropriated retained earnings and crediting that account.

(f) The end of the year balance amounting to $127,400.00 should be reported on Schedule L, line 24, column (D), and should also be shown on line 8 of Schedule M–2. See comments above about the importance of this figure agreeing with the actual books.

(g) When reconciling income per books with income per return, agents should always use the figure recorded in the Book income account. Many agents make the mistake of working from the return back to the books, rather than the books to the return. The figure appearing on line 1 of Schedule M–1, and line 2 of Schedule M–2 should always be taken from the actual book figure, rather than from a set of workpapers.

(h) In Schedule M–1 the taxpayer adds back the book provision for Federal income tax, because this is not deductible for Federal income tax purposes. The entry may be the actual tax shown on the return or an accrual entered on the books. If the entry is an accrual or a provision for estimated taxes, a reconciliation of the beginning and ending balances in the taxes payable and the deferred tax account(s) should be made using the books, tax return, and tax payment records. An unexplained difference may be due to one or more factors such as:

1. The independent auditor might have computed the tax liability based on certain facts. Someone else may later prepare the tax return and compute the tax without reconciling all aspects of the financial statements.

2. The tax effect on inconsistent positions taken on items shown on lines 4, 5, 7, or 8 of Schedule M–1.

3. An income or expense item might have been treated the same for book and tax purposes but the tax position is questionable.
In those instances the taxpayer's workpapers and/or schedules used in setting up the accrual or provision for taxes may be required to clarify the differences.
An example of Journal Entries, T-Account Entries and reconciliation of taxes payable and deferred taxes are as follows:

Exhibit 200-1 Cont. (3)

Exhibit 200–1 Cont. (3)

Examples of Reconciliation of Income and Analysis of Unappropriated Retained Earnings

Journal Entries

```
Accrued Taxes............................................... $25,000
    Taxes Payable............................................    $25,000
    Provision for Estimated Taxes

Deferred Taxes............................................... $ 5,000
    Taxes Payable............................................    $ 5,000
    Provision for Taxes on Advance Rent Receipts

Accrued Taxes............................................... $10,000
    Deferred Taxes............................................    $10,000
    To Amortize Taxes Paid in Prior Year for Current Book Income

Deferred Taxes............................................... $15,000
    Taxes Payable............................................    $15,000
    To Set Up Actual Tax Liability for Accrual in a Prior Year

Accrued Taxes............................................... $ 3,000
    Deferred Taxes............................................    $ 3,000
    Provision for Tax on Current Income Payable in Future Year

Deferred Taxes...............................................;. $10,000
    Retained Earnings............................................    $10,000
    To Reverse Accrual in Prior Year for Taxes Determined to be Not Payable

Taxes Payable............................................... $35,000
    Cash............................................    $35,000
    Tax Payments for Prior Year Taxes and Current Estimated Taxes
```

Selected T-Accounts
(B) = Beginning Balance

Accrued Taxes			Taxes Payable			Cash	
25,000			35,000	(B) 10,000		35,000	
3,000				25,000			
10,000				5,000			
Dr. 38,000 = Clos. Bal.				15,000			
			Clos. Bal. = 20,000 Cr.				

Retained Earnings			* Deferred Tax		
	10,000		5,000	(B) 15,000	
			15,000	10,000	
			10,000	3,000	
			Dr. 2,000 = Clos. Bal.		

*This is a combined account. In some instances it
may appear as two accounts (Prepaid Taxes &
Deferred Taxes).

Exhibit 200-1 Cont. (4)

**Examples of Reconciliation of Income and Analysis of Unappropriated
Retained Earnings**

Reconciliation of Deferred Taxes and Taxes Payable

Deferred Taxes

	Accrued Taxes...	$38,000	
Plus:	Opening balance in deferred taxes.........................	*15,000	
		53,000	
Plus:	Closing balance in deferred taxes.........................	**2,000	
		$55,000	$55,000

* = A credit balance (+) is added; a debit balance is subtracted
** = A debit balance is added; a credit balance is subtracted.....

Taxes Payable

Taxes Paid...	$35,000	
Less opening balance.......................................	10,000	
	25,000	
Plus closing balance.......................................	20,000	
Taxes current period (approx.).............................	$45,000	$45,000
Difference (see note).................		$10,000

Note: Difference attributable to reversal of prior year accrual determined by taxpayer to be non-payable.

Exhibit 200-1 Cont. (5)

Exhibit 200–1 Cont. (5)

Examples of Reconciliation of Income and Analysis of Unappropriated Retained Earnings ◊

(i) It is indicated that taxpayer had charged book income for a nondeductible Officers' life insurance premium. For tax purposes, the deduction has been eliminated. This should be shown on line 5 of Schedule M–1.

(j) While book income has been increased by receipt of tax exempt interest, it is not taxable for Federal income tax purposes, and so is eliminated in Schedule M–1. It should be shown on Line 7 of Schedule M–1.

(k) Taxpayer has included income in the 1977 tax return which was reported as book income in a prior year. Agents should be alert to the possibility that income of this nature may be entirely omitted in the return. For example, all insurance proceeds over basis on involuntary conversion may not have been reinvested as originally intended. This would result in taxable income in the year the reinvestment period runs out. The item appears on line 4 of Schedule M–1.

(l) This adjustment to taxable income represents rents collected in advance. It must be included on the return in the year received although it will not be recorded on the books until a later period. This item appears on line 4 of Schedule M–1.

(m) Taxpayer is claiming a deduction for expenses which were not booked during the current year. This should be shown on line 8 of Schedule M–1 of the return.

(n) Taxpayer distributed a cash dividend which is charged to unappropriated retained earnings. This item appears on line 5 of Schedule M–2.

(o) This should be the amount shown on line 10 of Schedule M–1.

(p) Taxpayer determined that a prior year provision for taxes was incorrect and has reversed the accrual by crediting unappropriated retained earnings. This is an issue which the agent should examine carefully since it may represent an inconsistent position between the book income and tax income.

(q) This item represents income which is both book and taxable income. It is subject to standard auditing techniques.

(r) This entry represent expenses deductible on the books and on the tax return. It is subject to standard auditing techniques.

IRS Form 2848
(Power of Attorney and Declaration of Representative)

| Form **2848**
(Rev. April 1986)

Department of the Treasury
Internal Revenue Service | **Power of Attorney and
Declaration of Representative**
▶ **See separate instructions.** | OMB No. 1545-0150
Expires : 4-30-88 |

Part I	**Power of Attorney**		**For IRS Use Only**	

(Please type or print)

Taxpayer(s) name(s)	Identification number	**For IRS Use Only**	
		File So.	
		Level	
		Receipt	
Address (Number and street)	Plan number (if applicable)	Powers	
		Blind T.	
City, state, and ZIP code		Action	
		Ret. Ind.	

hereby appoint(s) the following individual(s)*

Name	CAF No.	Address	Telephone No.

as attorney(s)-in-fact to represent the taxpayer(s) before any office of the Internal Revenue Service for the following tax matter(s) (specify the type(s) of tax and year(s) or period(s) (date of death if estate tax)):

Type of tax (Individual, corporate, etc.)	Federal tax form number (1040, 1120, etc.)	Year(s) or period(s) (Date of death if estate tax)

The attorney(s)-in-fact (or either of them) are authorized, subject to revocation, to receive confidential information and to perform any and all acts that the principal(s) can perform with respect to the above specified tax matters (excluding the power to receive refund checks and the power to sign the return, unless specifically granted below). See Regulations section 1.6012-1(a)(5) for information on returns made by agents.

- -
- -

☐ Send originals of all notices and all other written communications in proceedings involving the above tax matters to the appointee first named above, and a duplicate copy of all notices and all other written communications to the taxpayer named above, or

☐ Send copies of all notices and all other written communications addressed to the taxpayer(s) in proceedings involving the above tax matters to:

  1 ☐ the appointee first named above, or

  2 ☐ (names of not more than two of the appointees named above) . . . .

Initial here ▶ . . . . if you are granting the power to receive, but not to endorse or cash, refund checks for the above tax matters to :

  3 ☐ the appointee first named above, or

  4 ☐ (name of one of the above designated appointees) ▶ . . . .

This power of attorney revokes all earlier powers of attorney and tax information authorizations on file with the Internal Revenue Service for the same tax matters and years or periods covered by this power of attorney, except the following:

- -
- - - - - - - - - - - - - - (Specify to whom granted, date, and address including ZIP code, or refer to attached copies of earlier powers and authorizations.)

Signature of or for taxpayer(s)
(If signed by a corporate officer, partner, or fiduciary on behalf of the taxpayer, I certify that I have the authority to execute this power of attorney on behalf of the taxpayer.)

- (Signature) (Also type or print your name below if signing for a taxpayer who is not an individual.)	- - - - - - - - - - - - - - - - - (Title, if applicable)	- - - - - - - - - - (Date)
- (Signature)	- - - - - - - - - - - - - - - - - (Title, if applicable)	- - - - - - - - - - (Date)

* You may authorize an organization, firm, or partnership to receive confidential information, but your representative must be an individual who must complete Part II.

For Privacy Act and Paperwork Reduction Act Notices, see page 1 of the separate instructions.   Form **2848** (Rev. 4-86)

IRS FORM 2848 (POWER OF ATTORNEY AND DECLARATION OF REPRESENTATIVE)

If the power of attorney is granted to a person other than an attorney, certified public accountant, enrolled agent, or enrolled actuary, the **taxpayer(s) signature must be witnessed or notarized below.** (The representative must complete Part II. List representatives there only if they are recognized to practice before the Internal Revenue Service.)

The person(s) signing as or for the taxpayer(s): (Check and complete one.)

☐ is/are known to and signed in the presence of the two disinterested witnesses whose signatures appear here:

_____   _____
(Signature of Witness)   (Date)

_____   _____
(Signature of Witness)   (Date)

☐ appeared this day before a notary public and acknowledged this power of attorney as a voluntary act and deed.

Witness: _____   _____   **NOTARIAL SEAL**
                      (Signature of Notary)   (Date)   (if required by state law)

Part II   Declaration of Representative

I declare that I am not currently under suspension or disbarment from practice before the Internal Revenue Service, that I am aware of **Treasury Department Circular No. 230** (31 CFR, Part 10), as amended, regulations governing the practice of attorneys, certified public accountants, enrolled agents, enrolled actuaries, and others, and that I am one of the following:

1 a member in good standing of the bar of the highest court of the jurisdiction shown below;

2 duly qualified to practice as a certified public accountant in the jurisdiction shown below;

3 enrolled as an agent under the requirements of Treasury Department Circular No. 230;

4 a bona fide officer of the taxpayer organization;

5 a full-time employee of the taxpayer;

6 a member of the taxpayer's immediate family (spouse, parent, child, brother or sister);

7 a fiduciary for the taxpayer;

8 an enrolled actuary (the authority of an enrolled actuary to practice before the Service is limited by section 10.3(d)(1) of Treasury Department Circular No. 230);

9 Commissioner's special authorization (see instructions for Part II, item 9) _____

_____

and that I am authorized to represent the taxpayer identified in Part I for the tax matters specified there.

Designation (insert appropriate number from above list)	Jurisdiction (state, etc.) or Enrollment Card Number	Signature	Date

List of Cities Where U.S. Tax Court Holds Regular Sessions of Trial

PLACES OF TRIAL

(See Rules 140 and 177)

A partial list of cities in which regular sessions of the Court are held appears below.* This list is published to assist parties in making designations under Rules 140 and 177. If sufficient cases are not ready for trial in a city designated by a taxpayer, or if suitable courtroom facilities are not available in that city, the Court may find it necessary to calendar cases for trial in some other city within reasonable proximity of the designated place.

ALABAMA:
  Birmingham
  Mobile
ALASKA:
  Anchorage
ARIZONA:
  Phoenix
ARKANSAS:
  Little Rock
CALIFORNIA:
  Los Angeles
  San Diego
  San Francisco
COLORADO:
  Denver
CONNECTICUT:
  Hartford
DISTRICT OF COLUMBIA
  Washington
FLORIDA:
  Jacksonville
  Miami
  Tampa
GEORGIA:
  Atlanta
HAWAII:
  Honolulu
IDAHO:
  Boise
ILLINOIS:
  Chicago
INDIANA:
  Indianapolis
IOWA:
  Des Moines

KANSAS:
  Kansas City
KENTUCKY:
  Louisville/Frankfort
LOUISIANA:
  New Orleans
MARYLAND:
  Baltimore
MASSACHUSETTS:
  Boston
MICHIGAN:
  Detroit
MINNESOTA:
  St. Paul
MISSISSIPPI:
  Biloxi
  Jackson
MISSOURI:
  Kansas City
  St. Louis
MONTANA:
  Helena
NEBRASKA:
  Omaha
NEVADA:
  Las Vegas/Reno
NEW JERSEY:
  Newark
NEW MEXICO:
  Albuquerque
NEW YORK:
  Buffalo
  New York City
  Westbury
NORTH CAROLINA:
  Winston-Salem

OHIO:
  Cleveland
  Cincinnati
  Columbus
OKLAHOMA:
  Oklahoma City
  Tulsa
OREGON:
  Portland
PENNSYLVANIA:
  Philadelphia
  Pittsburgh
SOUTH CAROLINA:
  Columbia
TENNESSEE:
  Knoxville
  Memphis
  Nashville
TEXAS:
  Dallas
  El Paso
  Houston
  Lubbock
  San Antonio
UTAH:
  Salt Lake City
VIRGINIA:
  Richmond
WASHINGTON:
  Seattle
  Spokane
WEST VIRGINIA
  Charleston/Huntington
WISCONSIN:
  Milwaukee

---

*The Court sits in about 15 other cites to hear Small Tax Cases. A list of such cities is contained in a pamphlet entitled "Election of Small Tax Case Procedure and Preparation of Petitions," a copy of which may be obtained from the Clerk of the Court.

☆U.S. GOVERNMENT PRINTING OFFICE: 1985—497-025

Tax Court Forms

The following forms are listed in this appendix:

The forms marked by an asterisk (*) (Forms 2, 3, 4, 5, and 6) have been printed and are available upon request from the Clerk of the Court. All the forms may be typewritten, except that the subpoena (Form 5) must be obtained from the Court. When preparing papers for filing with the Court, attention should be given to the applicable requirements of Rule 23 in regard to form, size, type, and number of copies, as well as to such other Rules of the Court as may apply to the particular item.

121

FORM 1   123

PETITION (Other Than In Small Tax Case)

(See Rules 30 through 34)

UNITED STATES TAX COURT

....
           Petitioner(s)
               v.
COMMISSIONER OF INTERNAL REVENUE,
              Respondent

} Docket No.

PETITION

The petitioner hereby petitions for a redetermination of the deficiency (or liability) set forth by the Commissioner of Internal Revenue in his notice of deficiency (or liability) [Service symbols] dated ...., 19 ..., and as the basis for his case alleges as follows:

1.   The petitioner is [set forth whether an individual, fiduciary, corporation, etc., as provided in Rule 60] with legal residence (or principal office) now at

....
       Street   City   State   Zip Code

Petitioner's taxpayer identification number (e.g., Social Security or employer identification number) is
The return for the period here involved was filed with the Office of the Internal Revenue Service at ....
           City   State

2.   The notice of deficiency (or liability) (a copy of which, including so much of the statement and schedules accompanying the notice as is material, is attached and marked Exhibit A) was mailed to the petitioner on ...., 19 ..., and was issued by the Office of the Internal Revenue Service at ....
           City   State

3.   The deficiencies (or liabilities) as determined by the Commissioner are in income (estate, gift, or certain excise) taxes for the calendar (or fiscal) year 19 ..., in the amount of $ ...., of which $ ...., is in dispute.

4.   The determination of tax set forth in the said notice of deficiency (or liability) is based upon the following errors: [Here set forth specifically in lettered subparagraphs the assignments of error in a concise manner and avoid pleading facts which properly belong in the succeeding paragraph.]

5.   The facts upon which the petitioner relies, as the basis of his case, are as follows: [Here set forth allegations of fact, but not the evidence, sufficient to inform the Court and the Commissioner of the positions taken and the bases therefor, in orderly and logical sequence, with subparagraphs lettered, so as to enable the Commissioner to admit or deny each allegation. See Rules 31(a) and 34(b)(5).]

WHEREFORE, petitioner prays that [here set forth the relief desired].

                    (Signed) ....
                                 Petitioner or Counsel

                          ....
                                 Post office address

Dated: ...., 19 ...   .
                               Telephone (include area code)

FORM 2

PETITION (Small Tax Case)

(Available—Ask for Form 2)

(See Rules 170 through 179)

UNITED STATES TAX COURT

....
                    Petitioner(s)

                         v.

COMMISSIONER OF INTERNAL REVENUE,
                         Respondent   } Docket No.

PETITION

1.   Petitioner(s) request(s) the Court to redetermine the tax deficiency(ies) for the year(s) ...., as set forth in the notice of deficiency dated ...., **A COPY OF WHICH IS ATTACHED.** The notice was issued by the Office of the Internal Revenue Service at ....

City   State

2.   Petitioner(s) taxpayer identification (e.g., Social Security) number(s) is(are) ....
....

3.   Petitioner(s) make(s) the following claims as to his tax liability:

Year	Amount of deficiency disputed	Addition to tax (penalty), if any, disputed	Amount of overpayment claimed
....	....	....	....
....	....	....	....

4.   Set forth those adjustments, i.e., changes, in the notice of deficiency with which you disagree and why you disagree.

....

....

....

....

....

Petitioner(s) request(s) that the proceedings in this case be conducted as a "Small Tax Case" under section 7463 of the Internal Revenue Code of 1954, as amended, and Rule 172 of the Rules of Practice and Procedure of the United States Tax Court.*(See page 8 of the enclosed booklet.) A decision in a "Small Tax Case" is final and cannot be appealed by either party.

....
     Signature of Petitioner   Present Address—Street, City, State, Zip Code,
                                  Telephone (include area code)

....
  Signature of Petitioner (Spouse)   Present Address—Street, City, State, Zip Code,
                                  Telephone (include area code)

....
        Signature and address of counsel, if retained by petitioner(s)

*If you do not want to make this request, you should place an "X" in the following box. ☐

FORM 3

ENTRY OF APPEARANCE
(Available—Ask for Form 3)

(See Rule 24)

UNITED STATES TAX COURT

....
Petitioner(s)
v.
Commissioner of Internal Revenue,
Respondent

} Docket No.

ENTRY OF APPEARANCE

The undersigned, being duly admitted to practice before the United States Tax Court, hereby enters his appearance for the petitioner in the above-entitled case.

Dated:

....
Signed

....
Type signature

....
Office address

....
City   State

....
Telephone (include area code)

A SEPARATE ENTRY OF APPEARANCE MUST BE FILED IN DUPLICATE FOR EACH DOCKET NUMBER.

FORM 4

DESIGNATION OF PLACE OF TRIAL
(Available—Ask for Form 4)

(See Rule 140)

UNITED STATES TAX COURT

....
Petitioner(s)
v.
Commissioner of Internal Revenue,
Respondent

} Docket No.

DESIGNATION OF PLACE OF TRIAL

Petitioner(s) hereby designate(s) .... as the place of trial of this case.
City and State

....
Signature of Petitioner or Counsel

Dated: ...., 19 ...

FORM 5   129

SUBPOENA

(Available—Ask for Form 5)

(See Rule 147)

UNITED STATES TAX COURT

....

Petitioner(s)

v.

COMMISSIONER OF INTERNAL REVENUE,

Respondent

} Docket No.

SUBPOENA

To ....

....

YOU ARE HEREBY COMMANDED to appear before the United States Tax Court

....
(or the name and official title of a person authorized to take deposition)

at .... on the .... day of ...., 19... at.............................

    Time   Date   Month   Year

....
Place

then and there to testify on behalf of ....

                                        Petitioner or Respondent

in the above-entitled case, and to bring with you ....

....

....
Use reverse if necessary

and not to depart without leave of the Court.

Date: ....

....

Attorney for (Petitioner) (Respondent)   Title

Return on Service

The above-named witness was summoned on the .... day of ...., 19 ...
at .... by delivering a copy of this subpoena to h ......, and, if a
witness for the petitioner, by tendering fees and mileage to h ...... pursuant to Rule
148 of the Rules of Practice and Procedure of the Tax Court.

Dated .... Signed ....

Subscribed and sworn to before me this .... day of ...., 19....

....[SEAL]

           Name   Title

FORM 6

APPLICATION FOR ORDER TO TAKE DEPOSITION[*]

(Available—Ask for Form 6)

(See Rules 81 through 84)

UNITED STATES TAX COURT

....
$$\left.\begin{array}{c}\text{Petitioner(s)}\\ \text{v.}\\ \text{COMMISSIONER OF INTERNAL REVENUE,}\\ \text{Respondent}\end{array}\right\}$$ Docket No.

APPLICATION FOR ORDER TO TAKE DEPOSITION[*]

To the United States Tax Court:

    1. Application is hereby made by the above-named ....
Petitioner or Respondent

for an order to take the deposition(s) of the following named person(s) who has (have) been served with a copy of this application, as evidenced by the attached certificate of service:

Name of witness	Post office address
(a)	....
(b)	....
(c)	....
(d)	....

    2. It is desired to take the deposition(s) of the above-named person(s) for the following reasons (With respect to each of the above-named persons, set forth the reasons for taking the depositions rather than waiting until trial to introduce the testimony or other evidence.):

(continued)

_____

[*]Applications must be filed at least 45 days prior to the date set for trial. When the applicant seeks to take depositions upon written questions, the title of the application shall so indicate and the application shall be accompanied by an original and five copies of the proposed questions. The taking of depositions upon written questions is not favored, except when the depositions are to be taken in foreign countries, in which case any depositions taken must be upon written questions, except as otherwise directed by the Court for cause shown. (See Rule 84(a).) If the parties so stipulate, depositions may be taken without application to the Court. (See Rule 81(d).)

132

3. The substance of the testimony, to be obtained through the deposition(s)—, is as follows (With respect to each of the above-named persons, set forth briefly the substance of the expected testimony or other evidence.):

4. The following books, papers, documents, or other tangible things to be produced at the deposition, are as follows (With respect to each of the above-named persons, describe briefly all things which the applicant desires to have produced at the deposition.):

5. The expected testimony or other evidence is material to one or more matters in controversy, in the following respects:

6. (a) This deposition (will) (will not) be taken on written questions (see Rule 84).

(b) All such written questions are annexed to this application (attach such questions pursuant to Rule 84).

7. The petition in this case was filed with the Court on ....
month, day, year

The pleadings in this case (are) (are not) closed. This case (has) (has not) been placed on a trial calendar.

8. An arrangement as to payment of fees and expenses of the deposition is desired which departs from Rules 81(g) and 103, as follows:

....

....

9. It is desired to take the testimony of .... on the .... day of ...., 19 ..., at the hour of ...... o'clock ...m., at

....
Room number, street number, street name, city and state

before ....
Name and official title

10. .... is a person who is authorized
Name of person before whom deposition is to be taken

to administer an oath, in his capacity as .... Such person is not a relative or employee or counsel of any party, or a relative or employee or associate of such counsel, nor is he financially interested in the action. (For possible waiver of this requirement, see Rule 81(e)(3).)

11. It is desired to record the testimony of ....
before .... by videotape. The name and address of the videotape operator and the name and address of his employer are ....

....

Dated .... 19 ...   (Signed) ....
Petitioner or Counsel

....
Post office address

FORM 7   133

CERTIFICATE ON RETURN

UNITED STATES TAX COURT

.... ⎫
             Petitioner(s)   ⎪
                  v.   ⎬   Docket No.
COMMISSIONER OF INTERNAL REVENUE,   ⎪
                  Respondent   ⎭

CERTIFICATE ON RETURN
OF DEPOSITION

To the United States Tax Court:

   I, ..., the person named in an order of this Court dated
...................., to take depositions in this case, hereby certify:

   1.   I proceeded, on the .... day of ...., A.D. 19 ..., at the office
of ...., in the city of ....,
State of ...., at .... o'clock .....m., under the said order
and in the presence of .... and .... the counsel
of the respective parties, to take the following depositions, viz:

   ...., a witness produced
on behalf of the ....
                            Petitioner or Respondent
   ...., a witness produced
on behalf of the ....
                            Petitioner or Respondent
   ...., a witness produced
on behalf of the ....
                            Petitioner or Respondent

   2.   Each witness was examined under oath at such times and places as conditions
of adjournment required, and the testimony of each witness (or his answers to the
questions filed) was taken stenographically or otherwise recorded and reduced to
typewriting by me or under my direction.

   3.   After the said testimony of each witness was reduced to writing, the transcript of
the testimony was read and signed by the witness and was acknowledged by him to be
his testimony, in all respects truly and correctly transcribed except as otherwise stated.

   4.   All exhibits introduced during the deposition are transmitted herewith, except
to the following extent agreed to by the parties or directed by the Court (state disposition of exhibits if not transmitted with the deposition):

   5.   This deposition (was) (was not) taken on written questions pursuant to Rule 84
of the Rules of Practice and Procedure of the United States Tax Court. All such written questions are annexed to the deposition.

   6.   After the signing of the deposition, no alterations or changes were made therein.

   7.   I am not a relative or employee or counsel of any party, or a relative or
employee or associate of such counsel, nor am I financially interested in the action.

                    ....
                    Signature of person taking deposition

                    ....
                    Official title

_____

NOTE.—This form, when properly executed, should be attached to and bound with the transcript
preceding the first page thereof. It should then be delivered to the party taking the deposition or his counsel.

FORM 8

NOTICE OF APPEAL TO COURT OF APPEALS

(See Rules 190 and 191)

UNITED STATES TAX COURT

....
Petitioner(s)
v.
COMMISSIONER OF INTERNAL REVENUE,
Respondent

} Docket No.

NOTICE OF APPEAL

Notice is hereby given that ....
hereby appeals to the United States Court of Appeals for the ....
Circuit from [that part of] the decision of this court entered in the above-captioned
proceeding on the .... day of ...., 19...
[relating to ....].

....
Party or Counsel

....
Post office address

FORM 9

APPEAL BOND, CORPORATE SURETY

(See Rule 191)

The following is a satisfactory form of bond for use in case bond with a corporate surety approved by the Treasury Department is to be furnished to stay the assessment and collection of tax involved in an appeal from a decision of the Tax Court. The original bond and one copy are required. There are no printed forms. Each petitioner must execute the bond, and the corporate seal or a designation of seal in the case of individuals must be affixed.

UNITED STATES TAX COURT

....

Petitioner(s)

v.

COMMISSIONER OF INTERNAL REVENUE,

Respondent

}

Docket No. ....

BOND

KNOW ALL MEN BY THESE PRESENTS that we .... as principal, and ...., as surety, are held and firmly bound unto the above-named COMMISSIONER OF INTERNAL REVENUE and/or the UNITED STATES OF AMERICA, in the sum of $............, (double the deficiency or such sum as the Tax Court has fixed upon petitioner's prior motion), to be paid to the said Commissioner of Internal Revenue and/or the United States of America for the payment of which well and truly to be made we bind ourselves and each of us and our successors and assigns jointly and severally firmly by these presents.

. Signed, sealed, and dated this .... day of ...., 19 ....

WHEREAS, the above-named .... is filing or is about to file with the United States Tax Court, an appeal from the said Court's decision in respect of the tax liability of the above petitioner for the taxable year or years ...., by the United States Court of Appeals for the .... Circuit to reverse the decision rendered in the above-entitled cause.

Now, THEREFORE, the condition of this Obligation is such that if the above-named .... shall file its appeal and shall prosecute said appeal to effect and shall pay the deficiency as finally determined, together with any interest, additional amounts or additions to the tax provided for by law, then this obligation shall be void, otherwise the same shall be and remain in full force and virtue.

.... [SEAL]
For an individual petitioner

....
For a corporate petitioner

By ....
Title

(Corporate seal)

....
Surety

Attest:

By ....
Title (surety corporate seal)

....
Secretary

FORM 10

APPEAL BOND, APPROVED COLLATERAL

(See Rule 191)

A satisfactory form of bond for use in case an appellant desires to furnish approved collateral (Treasury Department Circular No. 154, Revised), instead of furnishing a corporate surety bond, and also forms of powers of attorney covering the pledged collateral are shown below. The original and one copy are required in either case. There are no printed forms. Each petitioner must execute the bond, and the corporate seal or a designation of seal in the case of individuals must be affixed.

UNITED STATES TAX COURT

....

Petitioner(s)

v.

COMMISSIONER OF INTERNAL REVENUE,

Respondent

Docket No.

BOND

KNOW ALL MEN BY THESE PRESENTS that .... is held and firmly bound unto the above-named Commissioner of Internal Revenue and/or the United States of America in the sum of .... (\$ ....) Dollars, to be paid to the said COMMISSIONER OF INTERNAL REVENUE, and/or the UNITED STATES OF AMERICA, for the payment of which, well and truly to be made, the .... binds itself and its successors, firmly by these presents.

Signed, sealed, and dated this .... day of ...., 19 ....

WHEREAS, the above-named .... is filing or is about to file with the United States Tax Court, an appeal from the said Court's decision in respect of the tax liability of the above petitioner for the taxable year or years ...., by the United States Court of Appeals for the .... Circuit to reverse the decision rendered in the above-entitled cause.

Now, THEREFORE, the condition of this obligation is such that if the above-named .... shall file its appeal and shall prosecute said appeal to effect and shall pay the deficiency as finally determined, together with any interest, additional amounts or additions to the tax provided for by law, then this obligation shall be void, otherwise the same shall be and remain in full force and virtue.

(continued)

140

The above-bounded obligor, in order the more fully to secure the Commissioner of Internal Revenue and/or the United States in the payment of the aforementioned sum, hereby pledges as security therefor bonds/notes of the United States in a sum equal as their par value to the aforementioned sum, to wit: .... dollars ($ ....), which said bonds/notes are numbered serially and are in the denominations and amounts, and are otherwise more particularly described as follows:

....

....

which said bonds/notes have this day been deposited with the Clerk of the United States Tax Court and his receipt taken therefor.

Contemporaneously herewith the undersigned has also executed and delivered an irrevocable power of attorney and agreement in favor of the Clerk of the United States Tax Court, authorizing and empowering him, as such attorney to collect or sell or transfer or assign, the above-described bonds/notes so deposited, or any part thereof, in case of any default in the performance of any of the above-named conditions or stipulations.

[SEAL]

....
For an individual petitioner

(Corporate seal)

Attest: ....
                                                For a corporate petitioner

.... By ....
            Secretary   Title

FORM 11   141

POWER OF ATTORNEY AND AGREEMENT BY CORPORATION

(See Rule 191)

KNOW ALL MEN BY THESE PRESENTS: That ....,
a corporation duly incorporated under the laws of the State of ....
and having its principal office in the city of ...., State of ....,
in pursuance of a resolution of the Board of Directors of said corporation, passed on
the .... day of ...., 19 ..., a duly certified copy of which resolution
is hereto attached, does hereby constitute and appoint the Clerk of the United States
Tax Court as attorney for said corporation, for and in the name of said corporation to
collect or to sell, assign, and transfer certain United States Liberty bonds or other bonds
or notes of the United States, the property of said corporation, described as follows:

Title of bonds/notes	Total face amount	Denomination	Serial No.	Interest dates
....	....	....	....	....
....	....	....	....	....
....	....	....	....	....

such bonds/notes having been deposited by it, pursuant to the Act of July 30, 1947,
c. 390, 61 Stat. 646, as security for the faithful performance of any and all of the conditions or stipulations of a certain obligation entered into by it with (here enter "the Commissioner of Internal Revenue and/or the United States") under date of....................,
which is hereby made a part thereof, and the undersigned agrees that, in case of any
default in the performance of any of the conditions and stipulations of such undertaking,
its said attorney shall have full power to collect said bonds/notes or any part thereof, or
to sell, assign, and transfer said bonds/notes or any part thereof without notice, at public
or private sale, or to transfer or assign to another for the purpose of effecting either
public or private sale, free from any equity of redemption and without appraisement or
valuation, notice and right to redeem being waived, and the proceeds of such sale or collection, in whole or in part to be applied to the satisfaction of any damages, demands, or
deficiency arising by reason of such default, as may be deemed best, and the undersigned further agrees that the authority herein granted is irrevocable.

And said corporation hereby for itself, its successors and assigns, ratifies and con-
firms whatever its said attorney shall do by virtue of these presents.

In witness whereof, the ...., the corporation hereinabove named,
by .... (name and title of officer), duly authorized to act in
the premises, has executed this instrument and caused the seal of the corporation to be
hereto affixed this .... day of ...., 19 ...

....
(Corporate seal) Secretary   By ....
                                                                            Title

State of ....
                                                        } SS:
County of ....

Before me, the undersigned, a notary public within and for the said county and
State, personally appeared .... (name and title of officer),
and for and in behalf of said ...., corporation,
acknowledged the execution of the foregoing power of attorney.

Witness my hand and notarial seal this .... day of ...., 19 ...

[Notarial seal]   ....
                                                                    Notary Public

My commission expires ....

FORM 12

POWER OF ATTORNEY AND AGREEMENT BY INDIVIDUALS

(See Rule 191)

KNOW ALL MEN BY THESE PRESENTS: That I (we) ...., do hereby constitute and appoint the Clerk of the United States Tax Court as attorney for me (us), and in my (our) name to collect or to sell, assign, and transfer certain United States Liberty bonds, or other bonds or notes of the United States, being my (our) property described as follows:

Title of bonds/notes	Total face amount	Denomination	Serial No.	Interest dates
....	....	....	....	....
....	....	....	....	....
....	....	....	....	....

such bonds/notes having been deposited by me (us) pursuant to the Act of July 30, 1947, c. 390, 61 Stat. 646, as security for the faithful performance of any and all of the conditions or stipulations of a certain obligation entered into by me (us) with (here enter "the Commissioner of Internal Revenue and/or the United States") under date of ...., which is hereby made a part thereof, and I (we), agree that, in case of any default in the performance of any of the conditions and stipulations of such undertaking, my (our) attorney shall have full power to collect said bonds/notes or any part thereof, or to sell, assign, and transfer said bonds/notes or any part thereof without notice, at public or private sale, or to transfer or assign to another for the purpose of effecting either public or private sale, free from any equity of redemption and without appraisement or valuation, notice and right to redeem being waived, and the proceeds of such sale or collection, in whole or in part to be applied to the satisfaction of any damages, demands, or deficiency arising by reason of such default, as may be deemed best, and I (we) further agree that the authority herein granted is irrevocable.

(continued)

144

And for myself (ourselves), my (our several) administrators, executors, and assigns, I (we) hereby ratify and confirm whatever my (our) said attorney shall do by virtue of these presents.

In witness whereof, I (we) hereinabove named, have executed this instrument and affixed my (our) seal this .... day of ...., 19 ...

....[SEAL]

State of ....

County of .... } SS:

Before me, the undersigned, a notary public within and for the said county and State, personally appeared .... (name of obligor), and acknowledged the execution of the foregoing power of attorney.

Witness my hand and notarial seal this .... day of ...., 19 ...

[Notarial seal]

....
Notary Public

My commission expires ....

FORM 13

CERTIFICATE OF SERVICE

(See Rule 21)

This is to certify that a copy of the foregoing paper was served on ....
by (delivering the same to him at .... on ....) or
(mailing the same on .... in a postage-paid wrapper addressed to
him at ....).

Dated:

....
Party or Counsel

IRS Publication 908
(Bankruptcy)

Department of the Treasury
Internal Revenue Service

Publication 908
(Nov. 82)

Bankruptcy

Introduction

This publication covers the federal income tax rules relating to bankruptcy and discharge of debt. These rules were substantially affected by the Bankruptcy Tax Act of 1980, which reflected a recent general revision of the U.S. bankruptcy laws.

The discussions in this publication are limited to the tax aspects of individual and small business bankruptcies. The publication is not intended to cover bankruptcy law in general, or to provide detailed discussions of the tax rules for corporate bankruptcy reorganizations or other highly technical transactions. In these areas, you should seek competent professional advice.

The tax rules explained here generally apply to bankruptcy cases begun after 1980. Some of these rules also apply to bankruptcy cases begun after September, 1979, but before 1981, if the debtors in the cases chose to have them apply and the court gave its approval.

Cancellation of Indebtedness

If a debt you owe is cancelled or forgiven, other than as a gift to you, you generally must include the cancelled amount in your gross income for tax purposes. A debt includes any indebtedness for which you are liable or which attaches to property you hold.

Example. You obtained a mortgage loan on your personal residence several years ago at a relatively low rate of interest. This year, in return for your paying off the loan early, the lending institution cancels a part of the remaining principal. You must include the amount cancelled in your gross income.

Purchase-money debt reduction. If you owe a debt to the seller for the purchase of property, and the seller reduces the amount you owe, generally you do not have income from the reduction even though you are not bankrupt or insolvent. The reduction of the debt is treated as a purchase price adjustment, and reduces your basis in the property.

Exclusion from gross income. In spite of the general rule requiring inclusion of a cancelled debt in gross income, you do not include a cancelled debt in gross income if *any* of the following three situations apply:

1) The cancellation takes place in a bankruptcy case under title 11 of the United States Code.

2) The cancellation takes place when the debtor is insolvent (see *Insolvency*, later), and the amount excluded is not more than the amount by which the debtor is insolvent.

3) The cancelled indebtedness is qualified business indebtedness, that is, a debt of a corporation or debt that relates to business property and the debtor chooses to reduce the basis of the property by the cancelled amount.

Order of exclusions. If a debt cancellation is excluded from income because it takes place in a title 11 bankruptcy case, the insolvency exclusion and the business indebtedness exclusion ((2) and (3) above) do not apply. Also, the business indebtedness exclusion does not apply to the extent the debtor is insolvent.

Bankruptcy case exclusion. For this purpose, a bankruptcy case is a case under title 11 of the United States Code, provided that the debtor is

under the jurisdiction of the court and the discharge of the debt is granted by the court or is pursuant to a plan approved by the court.

None of the indebtedness cancelled in a bankruptcy case is included in the debtor's gross income in the year cancelled. Instead, the amount cancelled must be used to reduce certain tax attributes of the debtor. See *Reduction of Tax Attributes*, later. The debtor may choose to first reduce the basis of depreciable property by the amount of debt cancelled before reducing other tax attributes. This is also discussed later.

Insolvency. A debtor is insolvent when, and to the extent, liabilities exceed the fair market value of assets. For any discharge of indebtedness, liabilities and the fair market value of assets are determined immediately before the discharge.

Indebtedness cancelled when the debtor is insolvent is excluded from gross income up to the amount by which the debtor is insolvent. The amount excluded, however, must be used to reduce certain tax attributes, as explained later under *Reduction of Tax Attributes*. But in reducing tax attributes, the debtor may choose to first reduce the basis of depreciable property, as discussed later.

Example. $4,000 of the Simpson Corporation's liabilities are cancelled outside bankruptcy. Immediately before the cancellation, the Simpson Corporation's liabilities totalled $11,000 and the fair market value of its assets was $7,500. Since its liabilities were more than its assets, it was insolvent.

The corporation may exclude $3,500 of the debt cancellation from income. This is the amount by which it was insolvent; that is, the amount by which its liabilities exceeded the fair market value of its assets. The remaining $500 of cancelled debt may qualify for exclusion as qualified business indebtedness (see below).

Qualified business indebtedness exclusion. The debtor may exclude the discharge of qualified business indebtedness from gross income if he or she chooses to reduce the basis of depreciable property. Qualified business indebtedness is debt that was incurred or assumed by a corporation, or by an individual in connection with property used in the individual's trade or business.

The amount excluded cannot be more than the total adjusted basis of all depreciable property held by the taxpayer at the beginning of the tax year following the tax year in which the discharge takes place. This total adjusted basis is determined after any required reduction of tax attributes for a discharge in bankruptcy and/or insolvency, discussed later.

Example. After the cancellation of $4,000 of its liabilities, the Simpson Corporation in the previous example is now solvent. If the $500 of cancelled liabilities that could not be excluded from income under the insolvency exclusion is qualified business indebtedness, the Simpson Corporation may choose to exclude it from income provided it reduces the basis of its depreciable property by $500. However, if the remaining total adjusted basis of the corporation's depreciable property at the beginning of the tax year after the tax year in which the debt cancellation took place, after any required reduction in basis because of excluding the $3,500 of cancelled liabilities, is less than $500, the corporation may exclude only that lesser amount.

Inclusion in gross income. If an amount of cancelled debt is not excludable from income under these three provisions, it must be included in gross income. However, income is not realized from debt cancellation to the extent that payment of the debt would have given rise to a deduction.

Example. You use the cash method of accounting for your business. You obtain business accounting services on credit. Later, when you are having trouble paying your business debts, although you are not bankrupt or insolvent, your accountant forgives part of the amount you owe for the accounting services. You do not include the amount of the debt cancellation in income, because payment for the services would have been deductible as a business expense.

If you use the accrual method of accounting, however, your accountant's cancellation of your debt must be included in your income. This is so since, under the accrual method, the expense is deductible when the liability is incurred, not when the debt is paid. For information on the cash and accrual methods, see Publication 538, *Accounting Periods and Methods.*

Reduction of Tax Attributes

The indebtedness that is excluded from income because it is cancelled in a bankruptcy case or during insolvency must be used to reduce certain "tax attributes" of the debtor. By reducing these tax attributes, tax on the cancelled indebtedness is in part postponed instead of being entirely forgiven. This prevents an excessive tax benefit from the debt cancellation.

Tax attributes. Generally, the amount of cancelled indebtedness must be used to reduce the tax attributes in the following order. However, the debtor may choose to first reduce the basis of his or her depreciable property before reducing the other tax attributes. This choice is discussed later.

Net operating loss. First, reduce any net operating loss for the tax year in which the debt cancellation takes place, and any net operating loss carryover to that tax year.

Credit carryovers. Second, reduce any carryovers, to or from the tax year of the debt cancellation, of amounts used to determine the following credits:

1) The investment credit (except amounts attributable to the employee plan credit),

2) The work incentive program (WIN) credit,

3) The jobs credit, and

4) The alcohol fuel credit.

Capital losses. Third, reduce any net capital loss for the tax year of the debt cancellation, and any capital loss carryover to that year.

Basis. Fourth, reduce the basis of the debtor's property as described under *Basis Reduction,* later. This reduction applies to the basis of both depreciable and nondepreciable property. However, you may choose to reduce the basis of depreciable property first before reducing any other tax attributes. This reduction of the depreciable property basis cannot be more than the total basis of depreciable property held by the debtor at the beginning of the tax year following the tax year of the debt cancellation.

Foreign tax credit. Last, reduce any carryover, to or from the tax year of the debt cancellation, of an amount used to determine the foreign tax credit.

Effective date. The tax attribute reductions just described must generally be made for all excludable bankruptcy or insolvency debt cancellations that take place after 1981, unless the cancellations are in bankruptcy cases or similar judicial proceedings begun before 1982. For debt cancellations that take place in bankruptcy cases or similar proceedings begun before 1981, only reduction of the basis of the debtor's property is required. But the basis is not to be reduced below the fair market value of the property on the date of the debt cancellation. No attribute reduction is required for debt cancellations in bankruptcy cases or similar judicial proceedings begun before 1981.

Similar judicial proceeding. For purposes of this effective date, a "similar judicial proceeding" means a receivership, foreclosure, or similar proceeding in a federal or state court, including certain agency proceedings involving financial institutions.

Amount of reduction. Except for the credit carryovers, the tax attributes listed earlier are reduced one dollar for each dollar of cancelled indebtedness that is excluded from income. The credit carryovers are reduced 50¢ for each dollar of cancelled debt that is excluded from income. Any excluded cancelled debt that remains after the necessary attribute reductions have been made does not result in income to the debtor or have other tax consequences.

Making the reduction. The required reductions in tax attributes are made after figuring the tax for the tax year of the debt cancellation. In reducing net operating losses and capital losses, first reduce the loss for the tax year of the debt cancellation, and then any loss carryovers to that year in the order of the tax years from which the carryovers arose, starting with the earliest year. Reductions of credit carryovers are made in the order in which the carryovers are taken into account for the tax year of the debt cancellation.

Individuals' tax attributes. If the debtor is an individual filing for bankruptcy under chapter 7 (liquidation) or chapter 11 (reorganization) of title 11 of the United States Code, the required reduction of tax attributes must be made to the attributes acquired by the bankruptcy estate, a separate taxable entity resulting from the filing of the case. Also, the choice of whether to first reduce the basis of depreciable property before reducing other tax attributes must be made by the trustee of the bankruptcy estate. See the discussion of *Individuals' Bankruptcy Estates,* later.

Basis Reduction

The basis of the debtor's property must be reduced in the following three situations:

1) The debtor chooses to exclude from income the cancelled qualified business indebtedness and, accordingly, reduces the basis of depreciable property by the amount excluded.

2) The debtor excludes from income cancelled indebtedness in bankruptcy or in insolvency, and chooses to reduce the basis of depreciable property before reducing other tax attributes by the amount excluded.

3) The debtor excludes from income cancelled indebtedness in bankruptcy or in insolvency, and does not have enough net operating losses, credit carryovers, or capital losses to absorb the full amount of required tax attribute reduction.

When to make the reduction. The reduction in basis is made at the beginning of the tax year following the tax year of the debt cancellation, and applies to property held by the taxpayer at that time. A choice to reduce basis under situations (1) or (2), above, must generally be made on the tax return for the tax year of the debt cancellation. However, if reasonable cause is established for failure to file the choice with the original tax return, the choice may be filed with an amended return or claim for credit or refund. Such a choice may be revoked only with I.R.S. approval.

Limit on basis reduction. In situation (1), above, the basis of depreciable property cannot be reduced on account of cancelled qualified business indebtedness by more than the total adjusted basis (after any required reductions in situations (2) and (3), above) of all depreciable property held by the taxpayer at the beginning of the tax year following the tax year of the cancellation.

In situation (3), above, the reduction in basis because of cancelled indebtedness in bankruptcy or in insolvency cannot be more than the total basis of property held by the debtor immediately after the debt cancellation, minus the total liabilities of the debtor immediately after the cancellation.

Exempt property. If debt is cancelled in a bankruptcy case under title 11 of the United States Code, no reduction in basis is made for property that the debtor treats as exempt property under section 522 of title 11.

Depreciable property. In situations (1) and (2), above, the reduction in basis is made only to depreciable property held by the debtor. Depreciable property, for this purpose, means any property subject to depreciation, but only if a reduction of basis will reduce the amount of depreciation or amortization otherwise allowable for the period immediately following the basis reduction.

Real property inventory. You may choose to treat as depreciable property, for this purpose, any real property that is stock in trade or is held primarily for sale to customers in the ordinary course of trade or business. This choice must generally be made on the tax return for the tax year of the debt cancellation, and, once made, can only be revoked with I.R.S. approval. However, if reasonable cause is established, the choice may be made with an amended return or claim for refund or credit.

How to make choices in reducing basis. The choices to reduce the basis of depreciable property in situations (1) and (2) above, as well as the choice to treat real property inventory as depreciable property, are made on a statement that is part of, or attached to, Form 982, *Adjustment of Basis of Property Under Sections 1017 or 1082(a)(2) of the Internal Revenue Code.* The statement must contain the taxpayer's name, address, and taxpayer identification number, and must specify the choice that the taxpayer is making.

2

Recapture of basis reductions. If property, the basis of which is reduced under these provisions, is later sold or otherwise disposed of at a gain, the part of the gain that is attributable to this basis reduction is taxable as ordinary income. The ordinary income part is figured by treating the amount of this basis reduction as a depreciation deduction and by treating any such basis reduced property that is not already either section 1245 or section 1250 property as section 1245 property. In the case of section 1250 property, the determination of what would have been straight line depreciation is made as though there had been no basis reduction for debt cancellation. Sections 1245 and 1250 and the recapture of gain as ordinary income are explained under *Part IV—Gain on Dispositions of Depreciable Property* in Publication 544, *Sales and Other Dispositions of Assets.*

Individuals' Bankruptcy Estates

If an individual debtor files for bankruptcy under chapter 7 or 11 of the Bankruptcy Code, a separate "estate" is created consisting of property that belonged to the debtor before the filing date. This bankruptcy estate is a new taxable entity, completely separate from the individual debtor. The estate is managed by a trustee for the benefit of any creditors, and it may produce its own income as well as incur its own expenses. The creation of a separate bankruptcy estate also gives the individual debtor a "fresh start" — wages earned and property bought by the individual after the bankruptcy case has begun belong to him or her and do not become a part of the bankruptcy estate.

A separate entity is not created for a corporation, a partnership, or for an individual who files for bankruptcy under chapter 13. The bankruptcy estate can only be created for an individual who has begun bankruptcy proceedings based on liquidation (chapter 7) or reorganization (chapter 11). However, the partnership interest of an individual debtor is treated in the same way as any other property of the debtor.

If a bankruptcy case involving an individual debtor was begun but is later dismissed by the bankruptcy court, the estate is not treated as a separate entity. The individual debtor is treated as if the bankruptcy petition had never been filed in the first place.

Choice to End Tax Year

An individual debtor who has assets other than those that may be treated as exempt property may choose to end his or her tax year on the day before the filing of his or her bankruptcy case. This choice, once made, is irrevocable. If the choice is made, the debtor's tax year is divided into two "short" tax years of less than 12 months each. The first year ends on the day before the filing date, and the second year begins with the filing date.

Once the choice is made, the individual debtor's income tax liability for the first short tax year becomes an allowable claim (as a claim arising before bankruptcy) against the bankruptcy estate. Any tax liability for that year is collectible from the estate as long as enough assets are available to pay off the estate's debts. However, to the extent that assets of the bankruptcy estate are not enough to pay any tax due for that year, the remaining liability is not dischargeable in the bankruptcy case, and

can be collected from the individual debtor after the case. If no choice to end the tax year is made, then no part of the debtor's tax liability for the year in which bankruptcy proceedings begin can be collected from the estate.

Choice by debtor's spouse. If the debtor making the choice is married, his or her spouse may also join in the choice to end the tax year, but only if the debtor and the spouse file a joint return for the first short tax year. These choices must be made by the due date for filing the return for the first short tax year. Once the choice is made, it cannot be revoked for the first year; however, the choice does not mean that the debtor and spouse must file a joint return for the second short tax year.

Making the choice. An individual debtor who chooses to end his or her tax year does so by filing a return on Form 1040 for the first short tax year on or before the 15th day of the fourth full month after the end of that first tax year. To avoid delays in processing the return, the debtor should write "Section 1398 Election" at the top of the return. He or she may also make the choice by attaching a statement to that effect to an application for extension of time to file a tax return (Form 4868 or other). The application for extension must be filed by the due date of the return for the first short tax year. The statement must say that the individual debtor chooses under section 1398(d)(2) to close his or her tax year on the day before the filing of the bankruptcy case. If the debtor's spouse decides to also close his or her tax year, he or she must file a joint return with the debtor for the first short tax year, as well as join in any application for extension and attached statement.

Later bankruptcy of spouse. A debtor's spouse filing for bankruptcy later in the same year may also choose to end his or her tax year, regardless of whether the spouse joined in the choice to end the original bankrupt debtor's tax year. Because each has a separate bankruptcy, one or both of the spouses may have three short tax years in the same calendar year. If the spouse had joined in the original debtor's choice, or if the debtor had not made the choice to end the tax year, the original debtor can join in the spouse's choice. But if the debtor had made a choice and the spouse had decided not to join in the choice, the debtor cannot join in the spouse's later choice. This is because they, having different tax years, could not file a joint return for a year ending on the day before the spouse's filing of bankruptcy.

Example 1. Paul and Mary Harris are calendar-year taxpayers. A bankruptcy case involving only Paul begins on March 4.

If Paul does not make a choice, his tax year does not end on March 3. If he does make a choice, Paul's first tax year is January 1—March 3, and his second short tax year begins on March 4. Mary could join in Paul's choice as long as they file a joint return for the tax year January 1—March 3. They must make the choice on or before July 15, the due date for filing the joint return.

Example 2. Fred and Ethel Barnes are calendar-year taxpayers. A bankruptcy case involving only Fred begins on May 6, and a bankruptcy case involving only Ethel begins on November 1 of the same year.

Ethel could choose to end her tax year on October 31. If Fred had not chosen to end his tax year on May 5, or if he had chosen to do so

but Ethel had not joined in his choice, Ethel would have two tax years in the same calendar year if she decided to close her tax year. Her first tax year is January 1—October 31, and her second year is November 1—December 31.

If Fred had not decided to end his tax year as of May 5, he could join in Ethel's choice to close her tax year on October 31, but only if they file a joint return for the tax year January 1—October 31. If Fred had chosen to end his tax year on May 5, but Ethel had not joined in Fred's choice, Fred could not join in Ethel's choice to end her tax year on October 31, because they could not file a joint return for that short year.

Example 3. Jack and Karen Thomas are calendar-year taxpayers. A bankruptcy case involving only Jack begins on April 10, and a bankruptcy case involving only Karen begins on October 3 of the same year. Jack chooses to close his tax year on April 9 and Karen joins in Jack's choice.

Under these facts, Karen would have three tax years for the same calendar year if she makes the choice relating to her own bankruptcy case. The first tax year would be January 1—April 9; the second April 10—October 2; and the third October 3—December 31.

Jack may (but does not have to) join in Karen's choice if they file a joint return for the second short tax year (April 10—October 2). If Jack does join in, he would have the same three short tax years as Karen. Also, if Jack joins in Karen's choice, they may file a joint return for the third tax year (October 3—December 31), but they are not required to do so.

Annualizing taxable income. The individual debtor who chooses to close his or her tax year must annualize his or her taxable income for each short tax year in the same way that is done for a change in an annual accounting period. For information on this, see *Short Tax Year* in Publication 538, *Accounting Periods and Methods.*

Note. This special choice is available only to an individual debtor whose bankruptcy case begins after March 24, 1981.

Treatment of Income, Deductions, and Credits

The gross income of the bankruptcy estate of an individual debtor includes any of the debtor's gross income to which the estate is entitled under the bankruptcy law. It does not include amounts the debtor receives or accrues as income before the beginning of the bankruptcy case. However, the estate, and not the individual debtor, must include any gross income the estate receives or accrues after the beginning of the bankruptcy case.

The bankruptcy estate may deduct or take as a credit any expenses it pays or incurs, in the same way the debtor would have deducted or credited them had he or she continued in the same trade, business, or activity and actually paid or accrued the expenses. Allowable expenses include administrative expenses, such as attorney fees and court costs.

The taxable income of the bankruptcy estate is figured in the same way as for an individual. The estate is allowed one personal exemption, individual deductions, and the zero bracket amount for a married individual filing separately in arriving at its taxable income. The tax on the taxable income is figured by using the rates for a married individual filing separately.

3

Return Requirements and Payment of Tax

If the gross income of a bankruptcy estate is $2,700 or more, the trustee in bankruptcy must file a federal income tax return on Form 1041, *U.S. Fiduciary Income Tax Return,* for the year.

To avoid confusion with the individual debtor's short year return, the trustee should show the name, address, employer identification number, tax year, and tax liability of the bankruptcy estate on Form 1041. The trustee must sign it and attach a Form 1040, *U.S. Individual Income Tax Return,* to it as a supporting schedule showing the income, deductions, credits, etc., of the estate.

The trustee in bankruptcy is responsible for obtaining an employer identification number for the estate for use in filing any tax returns. This number is obtained by filing a Form SS–4, *Application for Employer Identification Number,* available from I.R.S. offices.

Caution: The trustee (or debtor in possession) must withhold income and social security taxes and file employment tax returns with respect to any wages paid by the trustee (or debtor), including wage claims paid as administrative expenses. Until these employment taxes are deposited as required by the Internal Revenue Code, they should be segregated in a separate bank account to ensure that funds are available to satisfy the liability. If the employment taxes are not paid as required, the trustee may be held personally liable for payment of the taxes.

The trustee has the duty to prepare and file Forms W–2, *Wage and Tax Statement,* in connection with wage claims paid by the trustee, regardless of whether the claims accrued before or during bankruptcy.

The individual debtor must generally also file a return for the tax year on Form 1040. If the choice to end the tax year on the day before filing the bankruptcy case is made, the return for the first short year must be filed as explained earlier. For short years ending during 1982 and requiring filing before the 1982 tax forms are available, filers should use a 1981 Form 1040 and change the date to 1982.

If the bankruptcy case is later dismissed or converted to a chapter 13 case, filers should inform the I.R.S. of that fact by notifying the Service Center where the short year Form 1040 was filed. In this situation, the tax must be recomputed because no separate bankruptcy estate is considered to have been created. The individual debtor must file an amended return to replace any return filed by the bankruptcy estate and any full or short year returns filed by the debtor.

A debtor choosing to end the tax year must also file a separate Form 1040 for the second short tax year by the regular due date. The debtor should note on the return that it is the "Second Short Year Return After Section 1398 Election."

Transfers between Debtor and Estate

A transfer (other than by sale or exchange) of an asset from the individual debtor to the bankruptcy estate is not treated as a "disposition" for income tax purposes. This means that the transfer does not result in gain or loss, recapture of deductions or credits, or acceleration of income or deductions. For example, the transfer of an installment obligation to the estate would

not accelerate gain under the rules for reporting installment sales. The estate is treated just as the debtor would be with respect to the transferred asset.

When the bankruptcy estate is terminated, that is, dissolved, any resulting transfer (other than by sale or exchange) of the estate's assets to the debtor is not treated as a disposition. Therefore, as with the transfer of an asset to the estate, discussed above, this transfer does not result in gain or loss, recapture of deductions or credits, or acceleration of income or deductions. The debtor is treated in the same way the estate would be regarding the transferred assets.

Attribute Carryovers

The bankruptcy estate must treat its tax attributes, discussed earlier, in the same way that they would be treated by the individual debtor. These items must be determined as of the first day of the debtor's tax year in which his or her bankruptcy case begins. The bankruptcy estate gets the following items from the individual debtor:

1) Net operating loss carryovers.
2) Carryovers of excess charitable contributions.
3) Recovery exclusion (relating to bad debts, prior taxes, and delinquency amounts).
4) Credit carryovers.
5) Capital loss carryovers.
6) Basis, holding period, and character of assets.
7) Method of accounting (the same one used by the debtor).
8) Other tax attributes to the extent provided in regulations.

Administration Expenses

The bankruptcy estate is allowed a deduction for administrative expenses and any fees or charges assessed against it under chapter 123 of title 28 of the United States Code. These expenses are deductible whether or not they are considered trade or business expenses or investment expenses. However, they are subject to disallowance under other provisions of the Internal Revenue Code, such as the provisions disallowing certain capital expenditures, taxes, or expenses relating to tax-exempt interest. Those expenses belonging to, or directly related to, the estate can only be deducted by the estate, and never by the debtor.

If the administrative expenses of the bankruptcy estate are more than its gross income for the tax year, the excess amount may be carried back three years or forward seven years. The amounts can only be carried back or forward to a tax year of the estate and never to a tax year of the individual debtor. The excess amount to be carried back or forward is treated like a net operating loss and must first be carried back to the earliest year possible. For a discussion of the net operating loss, see Publication 536, *Net Operating Losses and At-Risk Limits.*

Termination of the Estate

If the bankruptcy estate has any tax attributes (discussed earlier) at the time it is terminated, the individual debtor must assume the attributes and treat them in the same way the estate had treated them. The debtor must assume these attributes even if they first arose during the administration of the estate.

Other Special Rules

Change of accounting period. The bankruptcy estate is allowed to change its accounting period, that is, its tax year, one time without getting approval from the Internal Revenue Service. This rule allows the trustee of the estate to close the estate's tax year early; that is, before the expected termination of the estate. The trustee can then submit a return for the first short tax year to get a quick determination of the estate's tax liability.

Carrybacks from the estate. If the bankruptcy estate itself incurs a net operating loss, apart from any losses passing to the estate from the individual debtor, it can carry the loss back not only to its own earlier tax years, but also to those of the individual debtor before the year in which the bankruptcy case began. The estate may also carry back excess credits, such as the investment credit, to pre-bankruptcy years of the individual debtor.

Carrybacks from the debtor's activities. An individual debtor cannot carry back any net operating loss or credit carryback from a tax year ending after the bankruptcy case has begun to any tax year ending before the case began. The estate, however, can carry the loss back to offset the debtor's pre-bankruptcy income.

Disclosure of information. In cases of individuals filing for bankruptcy under chapter 7 or 11 of title 11, whether or not the bankruptcy case is later dismissed, the income tax returns of the individual debtor for the year the bankruptcy case begins and for earlier years are, upon written request, open to inspection by or disclosure to the trustee. If the bankruptcy case was not voluntary, disclosure cannot be made before the bankruptcy court has entered an order for relief, unless the court rules that the disclosure is needed for determining whether relief should be ordered.

In title 11 bankruptcy cases, other than those of individuals filing under chapter 7 or 11, and in receivership proceedings where substantially all the debtor's property is in the hands of the receiver, current and earlier returns of the debtor are also, upon written request, open to inspection by or disclosure to the trustee or receiver, but only if the Internal Revenue Service finds that the trustee or receiver has a material interest which will be affected by information contained in the returns.

The bankruptcy estate's income tax returns are open, upon written request, to inspection by or disclosure to the individual debtor. The disclosure is necessary so that the debtor can properly figure the amount and nature of the tax attributes, if any, that he or she must assume when the bankruptcy estate is terminated.

Partnerships

If a partnership's indebtedness is cancelled because of bankruptcy, insolvency, or discharge of qualified business indebtedness, the rules for exclusion of the cancelled amount from gross income and for tax attribute reduction are applied at the individual partner level. This means that all choices, such as the choices to exclude the cancellation of qualified business indebtedness, to reduce the basis of depreciable property before reducing other tax attributes, to treat real property inventory as depreciable property, and to end the tax year on the day before filing the bankruptcy case, must be made by the individual partners and not by the partnership.

4

Depreciable property. For purposes of reducing the basis of depreciable property in attribute reduction, a partnership interest of a partner is treated as depreciable property to the extent of the partner's proportionate interest in the partnership's depreciable property. This applies only if the partnership makes a corresponding reduction in the partnership's basis in its depreciable property with respect to the partner.

Partner's basis in partnership. The allocation of an amount of debt discharge income to a partner results in that partner's basis in the partnership being increased by that amount. At the same time, the reduction in the partner's share of partnership liabilities caused by the debt discharge results in a deemed distribution, in turn resulting in a reduction of the partner's basis in the partnership. These basis adjustments are separate from any basis reduction under the attribute-reduction rules described earlier.

Corporations

The following discussion covers only the highlights of the bankruptcy tax rules applying to corporations. Because the details of corporate bankruptcy reorganizations are beyond the scope of this publication, you may wish to refer such issues to a professional tax advisor.

Equity-for-Debt Rules

Generally, if a corporation issues its own stock to a creditor in exchange for the cancellation of its debt, there is no debt discharge amount included in gross income or subject to the attribute reduction rules. This is true even if the stock issued to the creditor is worth less than the face amount of the obligation cancelled.

De minimis exception. In spite of this general rule, a corporation will have a debt discharge amount that may be subject to inclusion in gross income or attribute reduction if it issues only nominal or token shares in exchange for the cancellation of its indebtedness. Also, the corporation will have a debt discharge amount that is subject to inclusion in gross income (or attribute reduction) with respect to an unsecured creditor in a workout, if the value of stock received by the creditor in exchange for cancellation of the debt is less than half the value of stock that the creditor would receive if all the corporation's unsecured creditors taking part in the workout received a pro-rata amount of the stock issued. A "workout" includes a title 11 bankruptcy case or other transaction or series of transactions involving a significant restructuring of the debt of a corporation in financial difficulty. These two debt discharge amounts are subject to the rules discussed earlier under *Cancellation of Indebtedness* relating to inclusion in gross income, attribute reduction, etc.

Example. Mr. Smith, a creditor, held $1,000 of unsecured debt against a debtor corporation. In a workout, the corporation fully satisfied $10,000 of its unsecured debt by the transfer of $6,000 of its stock to creditors. Mr. Smith must receive at least $300 of stock in satisfaction of his claim in order for the debtor corporation to rely on the general rule that it has no debt discharge income with respect to the cancellation of Mr. Smith's claim in exchange for stock. If Mr. Smith receives only $100 of stock for his $1,000 debt, then the debtor corporation will have a debt discharge amount of $900 with respect to Mr. Smith.

Recapture of gain on later sale. If a creditor receives stock of a debtor corporation in satisfaction of the corporation's debt, the stock, and any other property the basis of which is determined by reference to the adjusted basis of the stock, is treated as section 1245 property (discussed earlier, and fully explained in Publication 544). For purposes of section 1245, the total amount allowed to the creditor as a bad debt deduction or as an ordinary loss on the exchange, reduced by any amount included in the creditor's gross income on the exchange, is considered an amount allowed as a depreciation deduction. This means that a gain on the later sale of the stock by the creditor is ordinary income to the extent of the creditor's bad debt deduction or ordinary loss.

Indebtedness contributed to capital. If a debtor corporation's shareholder cancels a debt the corporation owes to the shareholder as a contribution to capital, the corporation realizes a debt discharge amount only to the extent that the amount of debt cancelled exceeds the shareholder's adjusted basis in the indebtedness.

Example. An accrual-basis corporation accrues and deducts, but does not actually pay, a $1,000 liability to a shareholder-employee as salary. The shareholder-employee is on the cash basis and so does not include the $1,000 in income. In a later year, the shareholder-employee forgives the debt. In this situation, the corporation has a debt discharge amount of $1,000, the amount of debt cancelled ($1,000) that exceeds the shareholder's adjusted basis in the debt (zero). If the corporation is insolvent or in bankruptcy, it must apply the $1,000 debt discharge amount to reduce tax attributes, as explained earlier. If the corporation is solvent and outside bankruptcy, it can choose to reduce its basis of depreciable assets by $1,000 instead of including $1,000 in income in the year of the debt cancellation.

On the other hand, if the shareholder-employee is on the accrual basis and includes the salary in income when accrued, the shareholder's basis in the debt is $1,000. At the time of the cancellation, the corporation has no debt discharge amount, and no tax attribute reduction is required.

Tax-Free Reorganizations

The tax-free reorganization provisions of the Internal Revenue Code apply to a transfer by a corporation of all or part of its assets to another corporation in a title 11 or similar case begun after 1980, but only if, under the reorganization plan, stock or securities of the corporation to which the assets are transferred are distributed in a transaction which qualifies under section 354, 355, or 356 of the Code.

A "title 11 or similar case," for this purpose, is a bankruptcy case under title 11 of the United States Code, or a receivership, foreclosure, or similar proceeding in a federal or state court, but only if the corporation is under the jurisdiction of the court in the case and the transfer of assets is under a plan of reorganization approved by the court. In a receivership, foreclosure, or similar proceeding before a federal or state agency involving certain financial institutions, the agency is treated as a court.

Generally, section 354 of the Internal Revenue Code provides that no gain or loss is recognized if a corporation's stock or securities are exchanged solely for stock or securities in the same or another corporation under a quali-

fying reorganization plan. Thus, under section 354, shareholders in the bankrupt corporation would recognize no gain or loss if they exchange their stock solely for stock or securities of the corporation acquiring the bankrupt's assets.

Section 355 generally provides that no gain or loss is recognized by a shareholder if a corporation distributes solely stock or securities of another corporation that the distributing corporation controls immediately before the distribution. Section 356 provides that in an exchange that would qualify under section 354 or 355 except that other property or money besides the permitted stock or securities is received by the shareholder, gain is recognized by the shareholder only to the extent of the money and the fair market value of the other property received. No loss is recognized in this situation.

12-Month Complete Liquidation

If a corporation distributes all its assets in complete liquidation within a 12-month period beginning on the date it adopts a plan of complete liquidation, no gain or loss is recognized by the corporation from the sale or exchange of certain property within that period. The corporation may retain assets needed to meet claims and still come under this rule.

The "property" that qualifies for nonrecognition of gain or loss includes all assets *except:*

1) Stock in trade and property held primarily for sale to customers in the ordinary course of trade or business, *unless* substantially all of this property is sold or exchanged to one person in one transaction,

2) Installment obligations resulting from the sale or exchange of stock in trade as described in (1),

3) Installment obligations resulting from the sale or exchange before the date of adoption of the liquidation plan of property *other* than stock in trade, and

4) Any item acquired on or after the date of adoption of a liquidation plan in a title 11 or similar case (defined earlier), unless the item is stock in trade substantially all of which is sold or exchanged to one person in one transaction.

In a title 11 or similar case, the nonrecognition of gain or loss in a 12-month complete liquidation applies to sales and exchanges by the corporation of property within the period beginning on the date the liquidation plan is adopted and ending on the date the case is terminated.

Earnings and Profits

The earnings and profits of a corporation do not include income from the discharge of indebtedness, to the extent of the amount applied to reduce the basis of the corporation's property as explained earlier in this publication. Otherwise, discharge of indebtedness income, including amounts excluded from gross income, increases the earnings and profits of the corporation (or reduces a deficit in earnings and profits).

If there is a deficit in the earnings and profits of a corporation and the interest of any shareholder of the corporation is terminated or extinguished in a title 11 or similar case (defined earlier), the deficit must be reduced by an amount equal to the paid-in capital allocable to the shareholder's terminated or extinguished interest.

5

Personal Holding Company Tax

A corporation that is subject to the jurisdiction of the court in a title 11 or similar case is exempt from the personal holding company tax, unless a major purpose of beginning or continuing the case is the avoidance of this tax. A "title 11 or similar case" is defined earlier under *Tax-Free Reorganizations.*

Subchapter S Corporations

A bankruptcy estate of an individual in a title 11 case may be a shareholder in a Subchapter S small business corporation without disqualifying the corporation from Subchapter S treatment. This rule applies to bankruptcy cases begun after September 1979. For more information on the requirements for Subchapter S treatment, see Publication 589, *Tax Information on Subchapter S Corporations.*

Related Parties

In determining the income of a debtor from the discharge of indebtedness, the acquisition of outstanding indebtedness of the debtor by a person related to the debtor from an unrelated person generally may be treated as the aquisition of the indebtedness by the debtor. This rule is intended to treat a debtor as having debt discharged if a party related to the debtor purchases the debt at a discount, for example, where a parent corporation purchases at a discount debt issued by its subsidiary.

Related persons. For this purpose, the following persons are considered related:

1) An individual and the individual's spouse, children, grandchildren, parents, or any spouse of the individual's children or grandchildren,

2) An individual and a corporation more than 50 percent in value of the outstanding stock of which is owned, directly or indirectly, by or for that individual,

3) Two corporations more than 50 percent in value of the outstanding stock of each of which is owned, directly or indirectly, by or for the same individual, if either corporation was a personal holding company for the tax year of the corporation preceding the date of the acquisition of indebtedness,

4) A grantor and a fiduciary of a trust,

5) A fiduciary and a beneficiary of a trust,

6) A fiduciary of a trust and a fiduciary of another trust, if the same person is a grantor of both trusts,

7) A fiduciary of a trust and a beneficiary of another trust, if the same person is a grantor of both trusts,

8) A fiduciary of a trust and a corporation more than 50 percent in value of the outstanding stock of which is owned, directly or indirectly, by or for the trust or by or for a grantor of the trust,

9) A person and a tax-exempt organization controlled directly or indirectly by that person or, if the person is an individual, by members of that person's family,

10) A partnership and a partner owning, directly or indirectly, more than 50 percent of the capital or profits interest in the partnership,

11) Two partnerships in which the same persons own, directly or indirectly, more than 50 percent of the capital or profits interests, and

12) Two corporations or other business entities that are under common control.

Tax Procedures

The following section discusses the procedures for determining the amount of tax due from a bankrupt debtor or estate, paying the tax claim, and obtaining a discharge of the tax liability. These procedures generally apply to bankruptcy cases begun after September 1979.

Determination of Tax

The first step in obtaining a determination of the tax due is filing a return. An individual bankrupt debtor files a Form 1040 for the tax year involved, and the trustee of the individual's estate files a Form 1041, as explained earlier under *Individuals' Bankruptcy Estates.* A bankrupt corporation, or a receiver, bankruptcy trustee, or assignee having possession of, or holding title to, substantially all the property or business of the corporation, files a Form 1120 for the tax year.

After the return is filed, the Internal Revenue Service may redetermine the tax liability shown on the return. When the administrative remedies within the Service have been exhausted, the tax issue may be litigated either in the bankruptcy court or in the U.S. Tax Court, as explained in the following discussion.

Bankruptcy court jurisdiction. Generally, the bankruptcy court has authority to determine the amount or legality of any tax imposed on the debtor or the estate, including any fine, penalty, or addition to tax, whether or not the tax was previously assessed or paid.

The bankruptcy court does not have authority to determine the amount or legality of a tax, fine, penalty, or addition to tax that was contested before and finally decided by a court or administrative tribunal of competent jurisdiction (that became *res judicata*) before the date of filing the bankruptcy petition.

Also, the bankruptcy court does not have authority to decide the right of the bankruptcy estate to a tax refund until the trustee of the estate properly requests the refund from the Internal Revenue Service and either the Service determines the refund or 120 days pass after the date of the request.

If the debtor has already claimed a refund or credit for an overpayment of tax on a properly filed return or claim for refund, the trustee may rely on that claim. Otherwise, if the credit or refund was not claimed by the debtor, the trustee may make the request by filing the appropriate original or amended return or form with the District Director for the district in which the bankruptcy case is pending. The return or claim for refund should be marked "For the personal attention of the special procedures function. Do not open in mailroom."

The appropriate form for the trustee to use in making the claim for refund is as follows:

1) For income taxes for which an individual debtor had filed a Form 1040 or Form 1040A, the trustee should use a Form 1040X, *Amended U.S. Individual Income Tax Return.*

2) For income taxes for which a corporate debtor had filed a Form 1120, the trustee should use a Form 1120X, *Amended U.S. Corporation Income Tax Return.*

3) For income taxes for which a debtor had filed a form other than Form 1040, Form 1040A, or Form 1120, the trustee should use the same type of form that the debtor had originally filed, marking the form "Amended Return" at the top.

4) For taxes other than income taxes for which the debtor had filed a return, the trustee should use a Form 843, *Claim,* attaching an exact copy of any return that is the subject of the claim along with a statement of the name and location of the office where the return was filed.

5) For overpayment of taxes of the bankruptcy estate incurred during the administration of the case, the trustee may choose to use a properly executed tax return (for income taxes, a Form 1041) as a claim for refund or credit.

The I.R.S. Examination Function will examine the appropriate amended return, claim, or original return filed by the trustee on an expedite basis, and will complete the examination and notify the trustee of its decision within 120 days from the date of filing of the claim.

Tax Court jurisdiction. The filing of a bankruptcy petition automatically results in a stay (suspension) of the commencement or continuation of any U.S. Tax Court proceeding to determine the tax liability of the debtor. This stay continues until the granting or denial of a discharge, or dismissal or closing of the bankruptcy case. The stay may be lifted by the bankruptcy court. Since the bankruptcy court has power to lift the stay and allow the debtor to begin or continue a Tax Court case involving the debtor's tax liability, the bankruptcy court has, in effect, during the pendency of the stay, the sole authority to determine whether the tax issue is decided in the bankruptcy court itself or in the Tax Court.

The bankruptcy court could lift the stay if the debtor seeks to litigate in the Tax Court and the trustee wishes to intervene in that proceeding. In that case, the merits of the tax controversy may be determined by the Tax Court.

Suspension of time for filing. In any title 11 bankruptcy case, the 90–day period for filing a Tax Court petition, after the issuance of the statutory notice of deficiency, is suspended for the time the debtor is prevented from filing the petition because of the bankruptcy case, and for 60 days thereafter.

Trustee may intervene. The trustee of the debtor's estate in any title 11 bankruptcy case may intervene, on behalf of the debtor's estate, in any proceeding in the U.S. Tax Court to which the debtor is a party.

Assessment of tax. After the determination of a tax by either the bankruptcy court or the U.S. Tax Court, the Internal Revenue Service may assess the tax against the estate, the debtor, or a successor to the debtor, subject to applicable law.

Immediate assessments. In bankruptcy situations, the Internal Revenue Service has limited authority to immediately assess tax deficiencies, without following the normal procedure under which a deficiency notice is issued and the taxpayer is able to challenge the asserted tax liability in the U.S. Tax Court without payment of tax. In a title 11 bankruptcy case, an immediate assessment of tax may be made for a tax liability incurred by the debtor's estate, or on the debtor provided the liability for the tax has been finally decided (has become *res judicata*) in the bankruptcy case. No purpose would be served by requiring issuance of a deficiency notice prior to assessment of taxes imposed on the

6

bankruptcy estate, or on the debtor when the liability has been finally determined in the bankruptcy court, because in neither case can the issue be litigated in the Tax Court.

Statute of limitations for assessment. In a title 11 bankruptcy case, the period of limitations for assessment of tax (generally, 3 years after the later of the date the return was due or was filed) is suspended for the period during which the Internal Revenue Service is prohibited from making the assessment, plus 60 days thereafter.

Payment of Tax Claim

After the filing of a bankruptcy petition and during the period the assets of the debtor or the bankruptcy estate are under the jurisdiction of the bankruptcy court, these assets are not subject to levy. To collect these taxes, the Internal Revenue Service must file a proof of claim in the bankruptcy court, in the same way as other creditors. This claim may be presented to the bankruptcy court even though the taxes have not yet been assessed or are subject to a Tax Court proceeding.

Prepetition taxes. The following federal taxes are prepetition unsecured priority taxes of the government:

1) Income taxes for tax years ending on or before the date of filing the bankruptcy petition, for which a return is last due (including extensions) after a date three years before the filing of the petition.

2) Income taxes assessed within 240 days before the date of filing the petition. This 240-day period is increased by any time, plus 30 days, during which an offer in compromise with respect to these taxes was pending, that was made within 240 days after the assessment.

3) Income taxes, other than those for which no return, a late return (filed within two years of the filing of the bankruptcy petition), or a fraudulent return was filed, that were not assessed before but were assessable after the filing of the petition.

4) Withholding taxes for which the debtor is liable in any capacity.

5) Employment taxes on the first $2,000 of wages, salaries, or commissions (including vacation, severance, and sick leave pay) earned by each individual employee from the debtor within the 90-day period before the earlier of the date of cessation of the debtor's business or the date of filing the bankruptcy petition (whether or not actually paid before that date), and employment taxes for which a return is last due (including extensions) after a date three years before the filing of the petition.

6) Excise taxes on transactions occurring before the date of filing the bankruptcy petition, for which a return, if required, is last due (including extensions) after a date three years before the filing of the petition. If a return is not required, these excise taxes include only those on transactions occurring during the three years immediately before the date of filing the petition.

7) Taxes arising in the ordinary course of the debtor's business or financial affairs in an *involuntary* bankruptcy case, after the filing of the bankruptcy petition but before the earlier of the appointment of a trustee or the order for relief

Priority of payment. Following the filing of a proof of claim by the Internal Revenue Service, the preceding prepetition taxes may be paid out of the assets of the debtor or the bankruptcy estate, to the extent that there are assets remaining after paying the claims of secured creditors and certain enumerated creditors having a higher priority.

Taxes assessed during administration of the bankruptcy estate are paid first, as administrative expenses. Taxes in an involuntary case specified in (7) above are included in the second priority of payment. The employee's portion of the employment taxes on the first $2,000 described in (5) above is included in the third priority. The rest of the taxes listed in (1) through (6) above are included in the sixth and last priority of payment.

Relief from penalties. A penalty for failure to pay tax, including failure to pay estimated tax, will not be imposed with respect to the period during which a title 11 bankruptcy case is pending, under the following conditions. If the tax was incurred by the bankruptcy estate, the penalty will not be imposed if the failure to pay resulted from an order of the court finding probable insufficiency of funds of the estate to pay administrative expenses. If the tax was incurred by the debtor, the penalty will not be imposed if: (1) the tax was incurred before the earlier of the order for relief or (in an involuntary case) the appointment of a trustee, and (2) the bankruptcy petition was filed before the due date for the tax return (including extensions) or the date for imposing the penalty occurs on or after the day the bankruptcy petition was filed.

This relief from the failure-to-pay penalty does not apply to any penalty for failure to pay or deposit tax withheld or collected from others and required to be paid over to the U.S. government. Nor does it apply to any penalty for failure to timely file a return.

Preservation of FUTA credit. An employer is generally allowed a credit against the federal unemployment tax (FUTA tax) for contributions made to a state unemployment fund, provided the contributions are paid by the last day for filing an unemployment tax return for the tax year. If the contributions to the state fund are paid after that date, generally only 90% of the otherwise allowable credit may be taken against the federal unemployment tax.

However, for unemployment tax on wages paid by the trustee of a title 11 bankruptcy estate, the full amount of the credit is allowed if the failure to pay the state unemployment contributions on time was without fault by the trustee.

Discharge of Unpaid Tax

As a general rule, there is *no discharge* for an individual debtor at the termination of a bankruptcy case for *prepetition taxes* (as defined earlier) or for taxes for which no return, a late return (filed after a date two years before the filing of the bankruptcy petition), or a fraudulent return was filed. Claims against an individual for other taxes predating the bankruptcy petition by more than 3 years may be discharged.

Exception for wage earner's plan. If the debtor fails to complete all payments under a chapter 13 wage earner's plan, these taxes are not discharged although the court may grant a discharge of other debts in limited circumstances.

Discharge of bankruptcy estate's tax liability. The trustee of the bankruptcy estate may request a determination of any unpaid liability of the estate for tax incurred *during the administration of the case* by the filing a tax return and a request for such a determination with the Internal Revenue Service. Unless the return is fraudulent or contains a material misrepresentation, the trustee, the debtor, and any successor to the debtor are discharged from liability for the tax upon payment of the tax:

1) As determined by the Internal Revenue Service,

2) As determined by the bankruptcy court, after the completion of the I.R.S. examination, or

3) As shown on the return, provided the I.R.S. does not: (a) notify the trustee within 60 days after the request for the determination that the return has been selected for examination, or (b) complete the examination and notify the trustee of any tax due within 180 days after the request (or any additional time permitted by the bankruptcy court).

Making the request for determination. To request a prompt determination of any unpaid tax liability of the estate, the trustee must file a written application for the determination with the I.R.S. District Director for the district in which the bankruptcy case is pending. The application must be submitted in duplicate and executed under the penalties of perjury. You must submit with the application an exact copy of the return (or returns) filed by the trustee with the I.R.S. for a completed tax period, and a statement of the name and location of the office where the return was filed. Mark the envelope "For the personal attention of the special procedures function. Do not open in mailroom."

The I.R.S. Examination Function will notify the trustee within 60 days from receipt of the application whether the return filed by the trustee has been selected for examination or has been accepted as filed. If the return is selected for examination, it will be examined on an expedite basis. The Examination Function will notify the trustee of any tax due within 180 days from receipt of the application or within any additional time permitted by the bankruptcy court.

Notice of qualification as bankruptcy trustee. Every bankruptcy trustee in a title 11 case, as well as every receiver, assignee for benefit of creditors, or similar fiduciary, must give notice of his or her qualification as such to the Internal Revenue Service within 10 days of appointment or authorization to act. The period of limitations for assessment of tax on the bankruptcy estate is extended by the time from the filing of the bankruptcy petition to a date 30 days after the notice of qualification is received by the I.R.S. However, this extension cannot be for more than 2 years.

The notice of qualification must be in writing and must be filed with the District Director for the district in which the debtor files tax returns. It should be marked for the attention of the special procedures staff. The notice must contain the following information:

1) The name, address, and date of appointment of the trustee or other fiduciary,

2) The name, address, and taxpayer identifying number of the bankrupt debtor,

3) The name and location of the bankruptcy court,

4) The date on which the bankruptcy proceedings were instituted, and the docket number, and

7

5) When possible, the date, time, and place of any hearing, meeting of creditors, or other scheduled action in the proceedings.

This notice is not required if any notice regarding the bankruptcy proceeding has been given to a proper officer of the Treasury Department under any provision of title 11 of the United States Code before or within 10 days after the date of the trustee's appointment or authorization to act.

Statute of limitations for collection. In a title 11 bankruptcy case, the period of limitations for collection of tax (generally, 6 years after assess-

ment) is suspended for the period during which the Internal Revenue Service is prohibited from collecting, plus 6 months thereafter.

Choice of Effective Date

The rules discussed in this publication generally apply to transactions in bankruptcy cases or similar judicial proceedings begun after 1980.

However, the debtor (or debtors) in a bankruptcy case or similar judicial proceeding begun before 1981 but after September 1979 may have chosen, with the approval of the bank-

ruptcy court, to have the rules described in this publication apply as though the case had begun after 1980. This choice, once made, applies to all parties and all transactions in the proceeding, and may be revoked only with the consent of the Internal Revenue Service.

A debtor must have made this choice by November 2, 1981, by filing a written statement and evidence of court approval with the I.R.S. District Director or Service Center Director with whom the debtor's tax returns would be filed. The debtor should attach a copy of the statement and evidence of court approval to the next income tax return filed after the choice was made.

How to Get IRS Forms and Publications

You can order tax forms and publications from the IRS Forms Distribution Center for your state at the address below. Or, if you prefer, you can photocopy tax forms from reproducible copies kept at many public libraries. In addition, many libraries have reference sets of IRS publications which you can read or copy—on the spot.

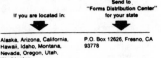

If you are located in:	Send to "Forms Distribution Center" for your state
Alaska, Arizona, California, Hawaii, Idaho, Montana, Nevada, Oregon, Utah, Washington	P.O. Box 12626, Fresno, CA 93778
Arkansas, Colorado, Kansas, Louisiana, New Mexico, Oklahoma, Texas, Wyoming	P.O. Box 2924, Austin, TX 78769
Illinois, Iowa, Minnesota, Missouri, Nebraska, North Dakota, South Dakota, Wisconsin	6000 Manchester Trafficway Terrace, Kansas City, MO 64130
Indiana, Kentucky, Michigan, Ohio, West Virginia	P.O. Box 636, Florence, KY 41042
Alabama, Florida, Georgia, Mississippi, North Carolina, South Carolina, Tennessee	Caller No. 848, Atlanta, GA 30370
Connecticut, Maine, Massachusetts, New Hampshire, Eastern New York (including New York City), Rhode Island, Vermont	P.O. Box 1040, Methuen, MA 01844
Western New York	P.O. Box 240, Buffalo, NY 14201
Delaware, District of Columbia, Maryland, New Jersey, Pennsylvania, Virginia	P.O. Box 25866, Richmond, VA 23260

Foreign Addresses—Taxpayers with mailing addresses in foreign countries should send their requests for forms and publications to: Director, Foreign Operations District, Internal Revenue Service, Washington, DC 20225.

Puerto Rico—Director's Representative, U.S. Internal Revenue Service, Federal Office Building, Chardon Street, Hato Rey, PR 00918

Virgin Islands—Department of Finance, Tax Division, Charlotte Amalie, St. Thomas, VI 00801

✶ U.S. GOVERNMENT PRINTING OFFICE: 1984 461-506 10,065 36-1004130

8

Index

Index

Other Bestsellers From TAB

☐ **BECOMING SELF-EMPLOYED: HOW TO CREATE AN INDEPENDENT LIVELIHOOD—Susan Elliott**

If you've ever felt the urge to leave the corporate world to become your own boss, you'll want this book. It reveals what it's like to become successful, and what mistakes to avoid. Includes case studies of twenty successful entrepreneurs—what they did right, what they did wrong, and what they plan for the future and why. 160 pp., 19 illus.
Paper $7.95   **Book No. 30149**

☐ **HOW TO WRITE YOUR OWN WILL—John C. Howell**

Written by a nationally respected trial lawyer and corporate attorney with over 25 years experience, this invaluable book defines all the necessary terms, offers precise explanations for each type of will, and even relates the circumstances under which consultation with a lawyer is advisable. The necessary forms are clearly illustrated and easy to follow. Also presented are the methods of completely avoiding or minimizing the effect of probate. The instructions and documents discussed are in accordance with the statutes of all 50 states. 192 pp.
Paper $9.95   **Book No. 30137**

☐ **THE ENTREPRENEUR'S GUIDE TO STARTING A SUCCESSFUL BUSINESS—James W. Halloran**

Here's a realistic approach to what it takes to start a small business, written by a successful entrepreneur and business owner. You'll learn step-by-step every phase of a business start-up from getting the initial idea to realizing a profit. Included is advice on: designing a store layout, pricing formulas and strategies, advertising and promotion, and more. 256 pp.
Paper $15.95   **Book No. 30049**

☐ **UNDERSTANDING WALL STREET—2nd Edition—Jeffrey B. Little and Lucien Rhodes**

This bestselling guide to understanding and investing on Wall Street has been completely updated to reflect the most current developments in the stock market. The substantial growth of mutual funds, the emergence of index options, the sweeping new tax bill, and how to keep making money even after the market reaches record highs and lows are a few of the things explained in this long-awaited revision. 240 pp., illustrated.
Paper $9.95   **Hard $19.95**
Book No. 30020

☐ **FORMING CORPORATIONS AND PARTNERSHIPS—John C. Howell**

If you're considering offering a service out of your home, buying a franchise, incorporating your present business, or starting a business venture of any type, you need this time- and money-saving guide. It explains the process of creating a corporation, gives information on franchising, the laws of partnership, and more. 192 pp., 5 1/2″ × 8″.
Paper $9.95   **Book No. 30143**

☐ **WINNING AT WORK: THE ROAD TO CAREER SUCCESS—Kenneth E. Norris**

The employee who knows the secret of "doing the little things well" gets ahead! Norris gives you important tips on: working with the boss toward making the company successful . . . mastering the art of making friends with other employees, especially those in important positions . . . developing a winning work philosophy . . . accomplishing work tasks without getting involved in administrative games . . . managing subordinates . . . and more. 126 pp.
Hard $14.95   **Book No. 30077**

☐ **THE SMALL BUSINESS TAX ADVISOR: UNDERSTANDING THE NEW TAX LAW—Cliff Roberson, LLM, Ph.D**

The passage of the Tax Reform Act presented business and corporations with the most dramatic changes in tax laws and liabilities ever. Now, this thorough, easy-to-follow sourcebook provides the information you need to reduce your tax liability—while staying within the recently tightened guidelines! Writing especially for the small business, corporation, and stockholder, business law and tax expert Cliff Roberson gives you a practical overview of: All the new income tax rates. 176 pp., 6″ × 9″.
Paper $12.95   **Book No. 30024**

☐ **EVERYDAY LAW FOR EVERYONE—John C. Howell**

Everyday Law for Everyone explains everything the average citizen needs to know to confidently handle a variety of common legal problems. By following this guide you will be able to: write your own will, change your name, win landlord/tenant disputes, set up partnerships, avoid a probate, adopt a child, form your own corporation, and draw up business contracts—without the expense of complications of hiring a lawyer! *Everyday Law for Everyone* presents the facts about our legal system. A number of legal forms and documents that you can use in specific situations, or refer to when writing your own are included. By doing some of the work yourself, you can save on costly legal fees. Knowledge is your greatest defense! With this laymen's guide, you can be in a controlling position when the unexpected happens. 238 pp.
Paper $9.95   **Book No. 30011**

Other Bestsellers From TAB